Grace Calls

GRACE

calls

ROBIN WEIDNER

WITH DAVID WEIDNER

Robin Weidner
Author of *Grace Calls, Eve's Song* and *Secure in Heart*
rwcopywriting@comcast.net

David Weidner
Author of *Grace Calls* and *Pure in Heart* (Audio Series)
purityrestored@gmail.com

David and Robin Weidner
Authors of *Pure the Journey: Forty Days of Seeing God*
(Daily Devotional Series)

ISBN: 978-1-941988-43-5

Illumination Publishers
www.ipibooks.com

*to our numerous friends in recovery who
have blessed us with their wisdom and insight*

RECOVERY

To gain back what has been stolen from us.

During the night Abram divided his men to attack them
and he routed them, pursuing them as far as Hobah, north
of Damascus. He *recovered* all the goods and brought back
his relative Lot and his possessions, together with the women
and the other people. Genesis 14:15-17 [emphasis mine]

SPIRITUAL RECOVERY

A beautiful process of re-creation by God.

Table of Contents

Grace Calls

INSPIRED BY PROVERBS 2

Friend, if you accept my call
If you store up all I teach
Set your heart on my value
Cry aloud for my lessons

Plant your feet on my stones
Step on them like holy ground
Then you'll be closer to Jesus
The only one who gives rest

For Jesus came full of grace
From his mouth comes truth
He shields our tender places
His hands hold the victory

Grace will free you so that
Prayer soothes your pain
Peace guides conversation
Tears flow without shame

Knowing the pain of the fall
He storms fortified walls
As his resurrection unveils
A journey of new creation

Grace will rescue you from
Women who throw their bodies
At men who clamor to console
Those who delight in deceit

Grace reveals a place of safety
A higher path trod by the Spirit
From deepest darkness to sanity
From chaos to God's embrace

Grace can save you from adultery
Center you after abandonment
Comfort you as you face abuse
Renew the beauty of covenant

Friend, if you accept my call
Trust me to invest your pain
Set your heart on my value
Cry aloud for my lessons

Grace will lead to wholeness
Treasures you're yet to know
A guard for all that's sacred
Redemption in letting go

For Jesus came full of grace
From his mouth comes truth
He shields our tender places
His hands hold the victory

Plant your feet on my stones
Accept hope as holy ground
Extend the healing of Jesus
Then watch as grace abounds

PREPARING THE GROUND
an unexpected journey

"Unless a kernel of wheat falls to the ground
and dies, it remains only a single seed.
But if it dies, it produces many seeds […]
Whoever serves me must follow me."

JOHN 12:24-26

THE PAPER SHOOK IN MY HANDS AND MY VOICE quivered. With each word I read, I felt both the weight of long-held hurts and the lifting of the enormous load I had carried for far too long. We were in a counseling session with a trusted mentor after twenty-two years of marriage. At his request, I had written two letters and brought them to the session. One was written to Dave. The other was written to my father. Although both letters escorted me into dark terrain inside my heart, my message to Dave flowed easier from my pen. The pain was closer to the surface and came pouring onto the paper. But the letter to my father was agonizing to compose. It required excavating memories hidden under layers of denial and repressed pain. Nestled into our mentor's small basement office, I read my letter to Dave first.

I remember very little of what it said. Afterwards, I remember Dave's expression of remorse and the anger that flashed across our mentor's eyes over my vivid description of the heartbreak resulting from Dave's twenty years of on and off sexual addiction within our marriage.

Then I read my letter to my father. Although only two pages long, it pointed to some poignant moments. My father taking me shopping for my first bra (since my mother was at home with an infant), and him trudging heavily into the women's department announcing in a loud, dramatic voice, "Do you have any bras that would fit this girl?" As a highly sensitive, I read the embarrassment of the sales clerk as disdain for my crazy family.

I reminded my father of our one and only driving lesson in our tiny import car with taped leather seats and a cranky clutch. Him screaming, "Good God, stupid girl! Brake after the clutch!" Finally, rolling towards our home, how I jerked the car to a stop, again with no clutch, and how he punched me hard in the right shoulder, leaving my arm throbbing and my soul bruised. I resolved at that moment, never to let him hurt me again.

But there was so much more represented in my words. The brown paper packages in the top of our cupboards that signaled the start of his alcoholism. The sheer terror of his wild addictive anger and rampant physical abuse of my two brothers. The Halloween night when he telephoned my Methodist church where I was an actress in a haunted house. My shame as my father cursed and called me names, because mom was in labor and he had to track me down. The times he chuckled as he put a little beer in my baby sister's bottle. All the mechanisms I had to develop in order to block and blunt my emotions so he couldn't shatter me. The way he never told me he loved me, until my late teens, after I initiated saying, "I love you." I ended the letter by saying, "Dad, you were never there for me when I needed you most. And now I wonder, will you ever be?"

After I read these words, I looked at our mentor and shrugged, still not convinced that my father was relevant. After all, I wasn't really in these sessions to examine my relationship with him. I was there to get help for Dave. Plus, at seventeen I had surrendered my life to God. Hadn't God used all my father's alcoholism, abandonment and abuse for my good? Hadn't I had a conversation with my father seeking to repair some of these wounds? It was then our mentor said the words that stunned me, "Robin, with the severe degree of your losses, I don't think you will ever fully recover." Looking at Dave, he said, "Dave, one day soon, your wife is going to reach a point where she can't bear another offense. She will collapse under the weight of so much loss."

It took another six months for me to reach this breaking point and ask Dave to leave indefinitely (more in Stone six: dignity). After he gathered a few things and stormed out, I drove directly to a nearby bookstore to find a book that could help explain my own wounds. I was finally opening up to the possibility that God was calling me to a journey of my own. A few months later, I signed up for a recovery program, including a group for wives of sexual addicts. Yet something in me knew that this wasn't just about our marriage. It was a call for me, like the legendary Phoenix, to rise out of the ashes of a broken past to a new way of seeing.[1]

You see being in the wake of Dave's addiction was part of my story, but far from the whole story. Long before I met Dave, I had suffered trauma wounds from my dad's addiction, abuse and abandonment. From this rocky soil sprang a love addiction, an eating disorder during college, and a codependent lens through which I saw life. It took a long time for me to understand that our mentor was likely right—the blows from my childhood would be impossible to perfectly repair. To help me recover, God would usher me deep into these injuries, even surfacing the repressed memory of being sexually abused as young child. Recovery would escort me to the foot of the cross of Jesus, where I would need to examine the very essence of spirituality. As I warred for Dave in prayer, he embraced a recovery process that has endured to this day. And by God's grace, our mutual growth would restore our marriage not just for us, but for the sake of others. We would be called on to help hundreds of couples and individuals find hope after complex and bewildering losses. Through this long saga to find healing and extend it to others, I found a needed journey of the soul—something I now call spiritual recovery.

What is spiritual recovery?

> *Jesus said to him, What is written in the Law? How do you read it?*
>
> *And he replied, You must love the Lord your God with all your heart and with all your soul and with all your strength and with all your mind; and your neighbor as yourself.*
>
> *And Jesus said to him, You have answered correctly; do this, and you will live [enjoy active, blessed, endless life in the kingdom of God].* LUKE 10:26-28, AMPC

Here, in what is called the greatest commandment, Jesus instructs us in what it really means to love God. And here, I believe we find the key to understanding the journey of recovery reflected in the pages of this book. Having a significant other fall hard (husband, fiancé, father, mother) in a way that directly impacts you (addiction, abandonment, abuse) is a mental, physical, emotional and spiritual blow to our love for God. Therefore, loving God in the wake of someone else's fall requires recovery, healing and growth in all of these areas. From my own journey, that looks something like this:

Type of recovery	Work needed
Strength	As we recover our dignity, God releases our bodies from the oppression of present and past trauma.
Heart	As we mourn losses, we begin to trust intimacy with others again. We learn to give our hearts in a new, healthier way.
Mind	Obsessive thoughts begin to lose their grip, gifting us with a whole new way of seeing and processing all that has happened.
Soul/Spirit	We engage spiritual warfare against the evil one. The new perspective that is born allows God to use our stories to impact others.

From the extensive recovery work I've undertaken, the part that seems most neglected to me is the soul/spirit. I've found direction from many wise writers who share from various backgrounds about pain, faith and growth. But, as those struggling to find our bearings in the wake of abandonment, abuse and addiction, we need specific spiritual application from people who've wrestled with similar hurts.

Looking at the chart once more, notice that I've got soul on the bottom of the chart. This isn't because it is the least important, but rather because it provides the support that holds up all the other areas of recovery. It is foundational.

After five years of leading groups—both groups for wives of addicts and purity groups for women—I started experimenting with having a part of our group format called *spiritual recovery.* To do this, we opened our Bibles and found the common ground between recovery concepts and spiritual growth. A spiritual foundation kept us from the dangers inherent in recovery— like getting so caught up in the emotional pain of it all that we neglect the soul and began to flounder spiritually. Spiritual recovery provided a safe place from which to venture into other types of recovery. It changed our perspective on God's grace and his sovereignty. In fact, group members told me that spiritual recovery was the most valuable part of our time together.

After my husband and I led a church for a season, I realized that nearly every woman has a need for spiritual recovery of some sort. We all have losses that are somehow related to abandonment, addiction or abuse.

> *Spiritual recovery is a beautiful*
> *process of re-creation.*

As you make your way through this book, I pray that you will find recovery in all of these areas: strength, heart, mind and soul. But the soul will be our foundation. How can your soul recover in light of your own individual losses? And how can spiritual recovery give you the courage and strength to embrace all the other needed parts of recovery? To find complete healing, we will need to form a whole new way of looking at spiritual growth and recovery.

The spiral of spiritual growth

We do not solve one problem and move on to the next. We do not graduate from one set of difficulties to another [...] progress is not measured by leaving behind old problems and working on new ones [...] The growth process is cyclic rather than linear. We come up against the same old difficulties repeatedly. We believe we have overcome something, and there is it again, only much more subtle.

At the same time, there is movement, represented by the upward flow of the spiral. The problems come up, but we are in a different place with respect to them each time they appear. We don't buy into them as much. We get over them faster (Ken Russell).[2]

I've seen many growth models in my years of recovery. Some charts graph spiritual growth like a lightning bolt going up and down, but yet always somehow headed up. For me, a line graph doesn't represent the complexity of recovery. The twelve-step plans contain much wisdom, yet it can appear like these steps are always forward—don't go to the next step until you've "completed" the last.

Just recently it struck me that recovery can be thought of as a spiral. But not just any spiral. I'm thinking of the spiral that our Creator embedded in all of creation. Jacob Bernoulli discovered this marvelous spiral, also called the growth spiral or the logarithmic spiral. He called this spiral miraculous because although the size of the spiral increases as it moves outwards, its shape is unaltered with each successive curve. The exact degree of the curve stays the same. This spiral performs many functions in nature, such as providing equal light to each seed on a sunflower, or helping birds keep in view the light source that guides them. In fact, you can find this curve in everything from the arms of spiral galaxies to the nerves in your eye's cornea.

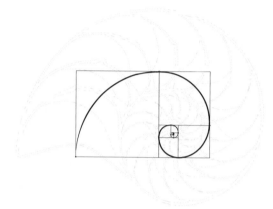

Growth Spiral

How does this relate to us on this journey? Think of trauma as a starting point. Like me, your trauma may have come from multiple places. Some trauma may have come from more current losses, some from your past. You may have suddenly discovered a loss that was playing out behind your back (like adultery or addictive behaviors). Or you may have suddenly remembered a loss long buried (like childhood abuse). As you begin to process these losses, the shock turns you inwards. You need to take care of yourself and find safety. Yet your Creator is there in the center, waiting for you to invite him into your hurts. As your heart opens up to see your own battles, the spiral widens a little, and then as time passes (and with further recovery) the spiral widens again and again. Wherever you are at in the process, it is the same exact curve. Whatever emotional, spiritual, mental or physical tasks you are focusing on, God stays nearby—even when he seems far away. Just when we find a level of comfort, there's another curve to go around. The further you spiral out, you gain perspective as your vision widens. With time and patience, you see God using the pain of your past and present losses for your good.

As you spiral upward and outward, your spiritual perspective is transformed.

Putting growth on a line (linear growth) feels neater, more predictable. But it also means there are only two directions you can go: forward or backwards, towards God or away from God. And having only two possible directions puts a lot of weight on repentance as a gatekeeper between the two extremes. *If you repent you'll go the "right" direction. Going the "wrong" direction means you haven't repented.* This turns repentance into an all-or-nothing event (either you've repented or you haven't) rather than a continual and progressive turning of focus and renewing of hope as God reveals, corrects, and shows his unconditional love. In contrast, viewing growth as a spiral gives security and safety by releasing us from the fear that it is wrong to go backwards! We enter the deep waters of our losses with Jesus, and he gifts us with long-term growth.

"But wait!" you might exclaim. "This spiral you are talking about is called miraculous and marvelous. How could the word marvelous be attached to the pain I've suffered? Don't you realize how rejected and despised I feel? Here's where Jesus can give us perspective:

> *Jesus asked them, Have you never read in the Scriptures: The very Stone which the builders rejected and threw away has become the*

Cornerstone; this is the Lord's doing, and it is marvelous in our eyes? MATTHEW 21:42 (AMP)

Rejecting Jesus, the very one sent to save the world, was the epitome of evil. Yet through God's redemptive nature, it became our salvation. Humanly thinking, there couldn't possibly be good in the rejection and humiliation that brought you to this book. Yet in God's marvelous plan of redemption, the hurts you've suffered can lead to amazing healing and growth.

I'd like to invite you to walk with me through the journey in these pages. Together, we will gently explore three different phases of healing: Darkness, Re-creation and Rest. Within these three phases, you find twelve Stones of spiritual recovery (more in just a moment). Based on my experience and the women I've mentored, this journey will be anything but straight forward. If you use the spiral analogy, sometimes in the middle of re-creation or rest, darkness will descend out of nowhere. But this doesn't make God farther away or take away from all you're learning. Each time you circle back onto an earlier Stone of recovery, you'll go there with new perspective, seeing that the journey is more about God and less about you. Let's return to Ken Russell's quotation ...

We come up against the same old difficulties repeatedly. We believe we have overcome something, and there is it again, only much more subtle. At the same time, there is movement, represented by the upward flow of the spiral. The problems come up, but we are in a different place with respect to them each time they appear. We don't buy into them as much. We get over them faster.

What this "upward flow" will look like will depend on your unique hurts and circumstances. If you are married, you will find fresh perspective on the covenant of marriage and what it means to reclaim your dignity. If you aren't married, you have a unique opportunity to throw yourself into recovery with an undivided focus. Spiritual recovery brings us all together, no matter how addiction, abandonment and/or abuse have been woven into our current and past situations.

Grace calls

Very truly I tell you, unless a kernel of wheat falls to the ground and dies, it remains only a single seed. But if it dies, it produces many seeds. JOHN 12:24

One thing you'll notice quickly is that there are no chapters in this book, only Stones, twelve to be exact. Since chapters have a sense of opening and closing, I've decided to frame this journey in Stones (the kind you can step on) instead. For clarity, whenever I refer to one of the Stones (serving as chapters), the first letter will be capitalized. Whenever I refer to a Biblical stone (like those in Bible altars) or the stones you will be collecting, I will leave the entire word lower case.

Here are the twelve Stones we will be exploring:

Phase of recovery	Stone	Recovery marker
Darkness	One	Trauma — Facing and processing our wounds
	Two	Thorns — Confronting the accuser's whispers
	Three	Triggers — Relating the past and present
Re-creation	Four	Tears — Learning true mourning
	Five	Warfare — Identifying the enemy
	Six	Dignity — Standing with God
	Seven	Acceptance — Finding freedom from shame
	Eight	Sanctuary — Understanding sexual healing
Rest	Nine	Pain Trading — Seeing our pain as investable
	Ten	Forgiveness — Letting go on a deeper level
	Eleven	Empathy — Finding a new tenderness
	Twelve	Hope — Becoming a wounded healer

What will this look like? Picture, if you will, God in the middle with twelve Stones spiraling outward to form a beautiful design. On the first pass, you'll see yourself to some degree in all the Stones. By the time you finish the book, you'll find a growing awareness of how each of these Stones of recovery are related to each other, and a growing comfort with resting your full weight on any given Stone at any given time. Of course, we all yearn for the Stones of rest. Please know that rest will come as you let God walk you through the darkness and his process of re-creation. On some days, this will seem a miraculous rest. More often than not, it will be a rest you'll have to battle for.

If we could personify grace, much like wisdom is personified in the book of Proverbs, I believe grace would have much to say. Grace would call us to let go of the hard outer shell of protection around ourselves (like that of a seed). We must let the old shell die, and trust God's empowering grace to bring a whole new creation. Grace calls us on this journey, promising us that after the darkness, re-creation will gift us with an outpouring of God's Spirit and love.* So near the end of each Stone, you'll find a section entitled, "Grace calls." Here, you'll find the Spirit gently urging you to trust his great work. I suggest that you find a blank journal to use just for this journey, taking notes and doing the exercise at the end of each Stone.

Why twelve Stones? Twelve has rich Bible significance,[3] but in particular I think of the altar of twelve stones that Joshua made after the Israelites crossed the Jordan River into the Promised Land. After they made the altar, God told them to call the place Gilgal because he had rolled away their reproach. Gilgal means circle of stones. What an amazing testimony to God's grace. I've come to see that women in the wake of addiction, abandonment and abuse need a personal Gilgal of their own—a rolling away of the reproach we fear. The good news is that Jesus, the Balm of Gilead,** is able to heal our wounds. Throughout this journey, I pray you hear him calling, offering to give you a circle of stones

---

* *For I will pour water upon him who is thirsty, and floods upon the dry ground. I will pour my Spirit upon your offspring, and My blessing upon your descendants.* ISAIAH 44:3 (AMPC)

** *Is there no balm in Gilead? Is there no physician there? Why then is not the health of the daughter of my people restored? [Because Zion no longer enjoyed the presence of the Great Physician!]* JEREMIAH 8:22 (AMP)

as a memorial of his work in your life. And as you step from Stone to Stone, I believe you'll discover that the reproach will begin to roll away. And that is worthy of worship!

After each Stone, I'll ask you to find a rock and write a word on it. By the end of the book, you'll have twelve stones that make up your own personal altar of worship: trauma, thorns, triggers, tears, warfare, dignity, acceptance, sanctuary, pain trading, forgiveness, empathy and hope.

Lastly, you'll find some "Words from Dave." My husband has been very involved in this journey. To make sure what I share about our story isn't one-sided, he'll share his perspective. You'll get a first-hand glimpse of how he's battled his way through addiction to the self-giving love he is known for. For those partners reading this book for insight, you'll find sage advice in his words. For all of us, listen for the perspective that we sometimes lack from those who hurt us.

Are you ready to get started? As you embark on this journey, please keep these guiding principles in mind:

Grace – This journey is an object illustration of grace—God's empowering presence. Watch for ways that he appears and shows you that he sees you and loves you.

Spiritual recovery – You will be learning about spiritual recovery and finding safety to do the work of emotional, physical and mental recovery as well.

Spiral of growth – Instead of viewing your growth as forward or backward, think of this process as more organic. You can always circle back to a previous step as needed.

Twelve stones – At the end of each Stone, you'll need your own stone to write words that signify each part of the journey. If you can't find literal stones, use something that symbolizes stones to you.

Group work – You will recover quicker if there is a relational component. Even if you read this on your own, I encourage you to find others you can share it with. Spiritual recovery groups are powerful mechanisms.

Note: We will visit my second book *Eve's Song* often as we move from Stone to Stone for its recovery messages. Reading the book isn't essential to understanding *Grace Calls*, but it may enrich your spiritual journey of recovery.

Treasures of darkness

As I mentioned earlier, although my journey came into focus as a result of my husband's fall, it gifted me with spiritual recovery from so much more. As God has unveiled this journey, I've mourned early sexual abuse, my father's alcoholism and verbal abuse, and his abandonment of me as a young adult. Of course, each of our stories is unique. My husband's sexual addiction spurred my journey into recovery; yours might be in the wake of alcoholism, drug abuse or a past abusive relationship. You may have never been married or have been divorced. I started my journey when I finally had the courage to ask Dave to leave. You might be in the wake of fresh pain, or looking to heal from hurts that took place years ago, with lingering after-effects. You might be seeking healing from something that happened in a past relationship. Since I have been married now for 35 years, I will return often to the idea of marriage, whether through a story from our journey or through insights I've gained. These stories aren't just offered for those of you who are married—they have relevance to all of us. I am convinced you will find insights that apply to your unique situation. In your stories and mine, God has embedded rich learning that is meant for us to share.

After all, our stories have a powerful link...our desire to discover God's grace in the midst of our hurts. Know that you aren't alone. God has beauty he wants to reveal in you... treasures of darkness that come as Jesus redeems all your losses and tenderly picks out the thorns that have pierced your heart. My heart thrills to think of all he will do!

We are hard pressed on every side, but not crushed;
perplexed, but not in despair; persecuted, but not
abandoned; struck down, but not destroyed. We always
carry around in our body the death of Jesus so that
the life of Jesus may also be revealed in our body.

2 Corinthians 4:8-10

PART ONE
Darkness Over the Deep

Now the earth was formless and empty,
darkness was over the surface of the deep,
and the Spirit of God was
hovering over the waters.
And God said, "Let there be
light," and there was light.[*]

* GENESIS 1:2

STONES ONE TO THREE:
Darkness Over the Deep

*Trust me, and don't be afraid. I want you to view
trials as exercises designed to develop your trust-
muscles. You live in the midst of fierce spiritual battles,
and fear is one of Satan's favorite weapons. When
you start to feel afraid, affirm your trust in me.*

— SARAH YOUNG, *JESUS CALLING*

FOR MOST FOLLOWERS OF JESUS, DARKNESS isn't one of our favorite words. *Didn't I leave that behind when I gave my life to Christ?* Personally, I have a slight case of night blindness. As the darkness deepens, my ability to see diminishes. Suddenly being thrust into total darkness (even with my glasses) can be disorienting, even downright scary. My fear is that I will fall, and fall hard. The first three Stones of this journey have to do with the pain that remains long after abandonment, abuse or addiction. These places feel dark. Trauma descends with blunt force and then leaves us with post-traumatic stress, causing nightmares, anxiety, heightened awareness, and adrenalin rushes. Thorns can feel like they are choking us. Triggers flood us with memories of pain we thought we'd left behind. It's easy to see why we would want to avoid this terrain. To understand the need to explore the darkness, let's go back to the beginning.

What ushered in spiritual darkness after the glorious light of God's creation? The answer is simple: the fall first took root in the Garden of Eden. From there the falls continued. In fact, the word "fall" appears 358 times in the NIV version of the Bible. In the Old Testament, we see that many types of people take a spiritual tumble: young people (Isaiah 40:30); the strong and swift (Jeremiah 46:6); leaders (Hosea 7:16); and even law keepers (Isaiah 28:13). In the New Testament, the theme of falling continues with the disciples (Matthew 26:31) and Peter in his denial of Christ (Matthew 26:69-74). The apostle Paul warns us that when we think we are standing firm we are susceptible to falling (1 Corinthians 10:12). What does this tell us? Spirituality doesn't necessarily insulate us from falling, failing or being devastated by someone else's fall. We won't escape by being strong, getting married, having good desires, or even being raised in a loving home.

For women, this is difficult to process. We are more susceptible to feeling the pain of the fall. Isn't falling kind of unfeminine? Our emotional complexity, larger limbic system (the emotional center of the brain) and our sophisticated relational abilities means we are more likely to retain hurts from other people in our psyche—the meeting place of mind, soul and spirit. In *Eve's Song*, an allegory told in the voice of the first woman, Eve understands this well. She says,

> *I know I am making my way around Jehovah's*
> *question. But forgiving myself will take time. It is*
> *as if every fiber within my body—muscle, tendons,*
> *skin and bones—holds the guilt of the fall.*[4]

4

For all of us, unless we are willing to process our pain from the falls of significant others and how they reveal our own shortcomings, we will struggle to extend forgiveness. This can make us susceptible to acting out our losses in ways that leave lasting damage, especially to our faith. We may be tempted to either turn inward or strike outward. Denying the possibility of falling, failing or going through extended times of weakness decreases our spiritual alertness,* needed more than ever when the darkness falls.

The Dark Night

A big part of my own journey has been figuring out what it means to walk through "the dark night of the soul," an idea first embraced by the 16ᵗʰ century writer John of the Cross. After being ordained for ministry in 1567, John joined a reform movement that challenged long-standing paradigms of religious practice. Eventually, he refused to obey an order that compromised his conscience and convictions, leading to his arrest. His nine months in a friar prison brought severe malnutrition, circular discipline (monks taking turns flogging him) and long periods of solitary confinement. Out of his great anguish, he penned three allegorical poems, including "Dark Night,"[5] a spiritual map of how suffering becomes a path to deeper trust in God. In John's legacy, the dark night of the soul refers to a period of time when it seems that God has abandoned us and cannot be clearly seen or heard in the midst of circumstances that threaten to undo us. This dark night feels like the spiritual lights have gone out. Using our illustration of the spiral of spiritual growth, it may seem that ominous storm clouds are hiding God from view. Yet this darkness can ultimately give birth to a cleansing grace, a new depth of surrender or a sense of being reborn spiritually, as it did for John of the Cross. As a type of spiritual discipline,

5

---

* *Be alert and of sober mind. Your enemy the devil prowls around like a roaring lion looking for someone to devour.* I PETER 5:8

this darkness drives us to a renewed need for God, unlocking spiritual treasures.

If we compare ourselves to the spiritual fathers like John, or others in the midst of deep suffering, we can end up feeling doubly bad when the dark night falls. *I don't have the right to feel this way. Obviously I'm just not spiritual enough.* From my experience, it isn't always easy to pinpoint why we suddenly feel so dark. Not too long ago, ten days of severe influenza, followed by another couple of weeks battling a bacterial infection, reminded me of the potency of having the lights suddenly go out spiritually. For the first ten days, my head wouldn't function. Although I had book deadlines, I couldn't write. Although I was on a 90-day schedule to read the New Testament, I couldn't read. Although I was supposed to attend a class on writing a memoire, I couldn't leave the house. Unrelenting fever, chills, severe headaches and pain meant most days I was in survival mode. Around the ninth day, I hit the end of my patience spiritually, and began cursing. Not the cussing variety, but the "I hate this!" variety. "I hate being sick," I said out loud to the empty house. "I hate being cooped up in this house. I hate being alone. (I should have been in Alaska on a speaking trip with my husband. My sickness meant he went by himself.) I hate not being able to think or write!" When I called my daughter, I tried to be spiritual but ended up voicing my complaints instead. The next morning, I felt deeply ashamed. Prayer felt awkward, while other people and even God seemed far away. Guilt stood by, ready to bring back old enemies of anxiety, hopelessness and regret. Talking with a friend, I realized I was nearing the anniversaries of the deaths of my mother, sister and father. The physical trial of influenza triggered the trauma of being a midlife orphan (with mom and dad gone). Old thorns popped up their piercing heads, ready to taunt me.

6

But even ten days of influenza and the twenty-some day struggle afterwards needed to fully recover pointed to grace. Not sure when or how I would heal, my heart turned to Jesus as the only answer. Psalm 23 came blazing out of the Bible like a beacon of light, particularly verse 2, "He makes me to lie down." Although the physical, emotional and spiritual vulnerability was hard to bear, I needed to remember that I don't just love God for the gifts he gives—writing a book, digging for Biblical treasure with a clear mind, keeping a tidy home (very much tied into me feeling peace), and driving up into the mountains that surround our town. Far above all this, my truest longing was for the Giver of the gifts. And, I could have God's presence whether I was victoriously moving forward (the way I typically measure progress) or whether I was flat on my back. When I started to slowly write again, I wrote differently, with a fresh infusion of grace. When I returned to my memoir class, barely well enough to go, I wrote an essay about my mother that my instructor called mesmerizing in its depiction of pain and beauty.

If you are currently in the midst of a dark night, do not fear. We have the perfect guide for the dark night. He came to his disciples around midnight, walking on the storm. He spent many nights alone on mountains, surrendering his will to God's through loud cries and tears. Yes, Jesus knows the dark night well, and he will guide you step-by-step to a renewed grace.

Our guide through the wake

The LORD MAKES FIRM THE STEPS *of the one who delights in him; though he may stumble, he will not fall, for the* LORD UPHOLDS HIM WITH HIS HAND. PSALM 37:23-24

Only Jesus can lead this journey of spiritual recovery described in *Preparing the Ground*. You see, my dear friends, being God's son didn't insulate Jesus from the pain of the fall. I think of him on a dusty road, with a heavy wooden beam on his shredded, bleeding back, while struggling to bear the emotional weight of all of our sins. Eventually he collapsed and fell to the ground, as shock waves of excruciating pain surged through every ligament of his suffering body. Jesus needed someone else to step in and carry this cross.* It was simply too much for him. As David Wilkerson says so beautifully:

> *The truth is, Jesus was too weak and frail to carry*
> *his cross. It was laid on another's shoulder. He*
> *had reached the end of his endurance. He was*
> *a physically broken and wounded man.*[6]

Although this thought brings remorse over my personal falls that Jesus carried with him, it also offers hope. First of all, I don't need to be strong enough to embark on this journey alone. Just as God brought Simon of Cyrene to Jesus in his moment of need, God has brought some amazing women into my life at just the right times. Secondly, I can trust Jesus that the pain isn't meaningless; in fact, it is his agent of re-creation. He told his followers he would be buried in the darkness of the ground, then be transformed from one seed into many.** The same is true for you. You will suffer, even lose parts of yourself you thought were essential, but as you surrender to this process, you will see amazing fruit.

8

---

* *As they were going out, they met a man from Cyrene, named Simon, and they forced him to carry the cross.* MATTHEW 27:32

** JOHN 12:23-26

This re-creation doesn't have to wait until heaven. Jesus walked through the dark nights to blaze a path into the deep places with God *in this life*—realms of healing, hope and true rest.

Although going on this journey doesn't guarantee pain-free relationships or perfect restoration (relationships are two-way streets that depend on both people involved), there's one thing you can be absolutely sure of: pain is a call into the deep places with God. Do remember that going deep with God doesn't mean being stuck in a pit. Rather it means sitting with Christ and gaining his higher perspective.*

In the second leg of this journey, *Re-Creation*, you'll explore this call and watch as it transforms the way you see your relationships, perhaps even with the very people who devastated you by their falls. By the time you reach the third stage of this journey, *Rest*, I hope you'll have already seen your pain bearing good fruit, gifts that have prepared you to become a wounded healer (Stone 12). What's more, you'll no longer see times of spiritual darkness as the enemy.

It's understandable to be a little afraid. If you are like me, the last place you want to be is in the wake of another person's fall. It feels like sitting on a remote beach when a tsunami alert starts sounding because a mountain fell into the sea. As much as I long for the ocean, a tsunami warning would keep me away. But a wake in God's hand is a miraculous element of re-creation. Did you catch that? A wake = awake.

a wake = awake

---

* *And He raised us up together with Him and made us sit down together [giving us joint seating with Him] in the heavenly sphere [by virtue of our being] in Christ Jesus (the Messiah, the Anointed One).* EPHESIANS 2:6 (AMPC)

Aha! In the wake of a fall, we get jolted out of places of apathy, false comfort and illusions of the fairy tale we so long for. The wake can rouse you from the brink of spiritual lethargy and cause you to reevaluate your walk with Jesus. Being in the wake of pain becomes redemptive in the hands of our loving Father.

It will take courage for us to dig up old wounds, especially if they feel far behind us. Do remember that the tasks of these first three Stones are needed no matter where you are in the process of healing.

Stone one: Trauma – On this Stone, we will process our most primal wounds. We'll see how trauma can leave us with a type of post-traumatic stress syndrome, but how it can also open us up to change. Do remember that your wounds may be similar to or different than mine. Resist the impulse to compare.

Stone two: Thorns – We'll confront the accuser's whispers, and the way he seeks to magnify our darkness through blaming us, getting us to blame others, or even to step away from God. Then we'll explore the redemptive qualities of thorns and how God confounds Satan by bringing good from what the evil one intends for our loss.

Stone three: Triggers – Here, we'll examine another pain magnifier, the way current losses circle us back to past pains. Understanding this connection will help us gain important skills and a new way of communicating in the heat of pain. Again, we'll find important keys to re-creation within triggers.

So welcome to the journey! Let's enter with a mustard seed of faith, trusting all that God will reveal in my life and yours as Christ shines on us.

For this reason He says, "Awake, sleeper, And arise from the dead, And Christ will shine [as dawn] upon you and give you light. EPHESIANS 5:14 (AMP)

Your spiritual journey: journaling

Where are you at as you prepare to step on the first Stone? Are you in the thick of trauma or will this part of the journey be revisiting past traumas? Are there any parts of your life that are still thorny?

Write a few paragraphs in your journal called "My Starting Place."

Friend, if you accept my call
If you store up all I teach
Set your heart on my value
Cry aloud for my lessons

STONE ONE
Spiritual Crisis: Trauma

Then they cried to the Lord in their trouble, and he saved them from their distress. He brought them out of darkness, the utter darkness, and broke away their chains.

PSALM 107:13-14

There are wounds that never show on the body that are deeper and more hurtful than anything that bleeds.
– LAURELL K. HAMILTON, *MISTRAL'S KISS*

I T WAS A TUESDAY AT NOON AND DAVE AND I were sitting in a restaurant on our way to an endocrinologist's office in Peoria, Illinois. It was before Dave realized his struggle represented a sexual addiction, before we started counseling. We were still in the years when his addiction would rise and fall, leave for a time and then reappear. Just a week earlier, I had been in my allergist's office getting an EKG as preparation to participate in an allergy study.[7] Even though the allergist repeated it twice, my EKG was abnormal. The doctor finally came in to examine me and exclaimed, "Oh my gosh Robin, your thyroid is huge!" After I explained that I had been to my doctor for a variety of complaints over the last five months, he called my primary physician's office demanding that I be seen that very hour. "You missed something big! This is

13

not acceptable!" An hour later, my primary physician examined my grossly enlarged thyroid and kept mumbling sadly, "How could I have missed this? I'm so sorry Robin." I was leaving the very next morning with Dave for a weekend event for pharmaceutical reps in Phoenix, so my doctor gave me a referral to an endocrinologist and a prescription. By the time we reached our hotel in Phoenix, I had an urgent message from the doctor's nurse, who tracked us down through family connections, saying I needed to call right away.

It turned out I needed to go on heart medication that very day. The nurse said that they suspected Grave's Disease. This explained so much. It shed light on nights where I would wake up and jerk into a sitting position—feeling like someone had reached into my chest and yanked me up by my heart. It explained the sudden weight loss, change of personality, racing heart and bouts of uncontrollable diarrhea. It gave credence to the gnawing fear during these episodes that I was close to death. My primary physician set an appointment for me with an endocrinologist for the day after we arrived home.

On the way to the appointment, we swung into a restaurant for lunch. Fear gnawed at my stomach. Would I need surgery? Could it be treated by medication? After being seated, Dave began to confess another trip to a strip club. As I peppered him with questions, his explanation of a lap dance put a knife in my chest and tore my fragile heart in two. The pain was worse than the heart palpitations. Afterwards, speechless and hardly able to take a bite, I watched Dave devour a big meal complete with dessert. He was relieved because his burden of secrecy had been lifted. In contrast, I was left reeling in disgust, fear and shock.[8] I now understand that this dynamic is common in the wake of disclosure.

From there we drove to the endocrinologist's office, where the doctor looked over my lab results from my family physician and confirmed the diagnosis of acute Grave's Disease. He explained I needed radiation to destroy my thyroid as soon as possible. In other less severe cases, surgery or medication might be possible, but if not treated immediately, my hugely overactive thyroid could cause my eyes to permanently bulge. Feeling like I had no choice, I opted for radiation. He explained that for five days after the radiation, I would need to keep away from pregnant women and small children. Dave would need to keep his distance as well. The doctor warned me that the majority of women with Grave's Disease become morbidly obese afterwards. He suggested a radical diet with him at the helm. I turned him down. Shaking his head, I saw in his eyes...*so you will become morbidly obese*. As I left, he emphasized how fortunate I was. We caught my sickness just in time. My eyes might still swell for years to come, but there would be no permanent damage.

The next day I was in the hospital, tossing a large radioactive iodine pill straight into my mouth from a lead jar so my fingers wouldn't touch it. This combination of disclosure, diagnosis and radiation mixed into a toxic brew. My instinct to repress the immensity of my fear from Dave's disclosure was supported by a physical reality—no one could come near me. I was also mortified. Couldn't I have seen my enlarged thyroid and the way it moved up and down when I swallowed? Shouldn't I have figured out about the strip club? Grave's disease gave me a place to focus, so that the disclosure could move into the background. Little did I realize that I was acting out a well-practiced coping mechanism from sexual abuse as a child, verbal abuse as a teen, and abandonment as a young adult.

What form has your trauma come in? The women I've sat with have described scenarios like this: Picking up my partner's phone and finding a series of sexual texts from a stranger. *Trauma.* On a honeymoon (anniversary, other special event), suddenly noticing him drinking in another person with his eyes. Gathering the courage to confront abuse, addiction or abandonment only to be further wounded by manipulation, guilt, or accusations. *Trauma.* Loss of a job. Loss of status. Loss of financial security. *Trauma.* Noticing my loved one is turning to alcohol more or abusing a prescription drug. *Trauma.* The police showing up with an arrest warrant for my husband, and then taking him and our computers away. *Trauma.* And trauma often gains power from past circumstances. Being sexually abused as a child or raped as a young adult. Your father abandoned you. Your mother had a drug addiction or a mental illness that caused her to abuse you. *Trauma upon trauma.* Whatever your unique experience, trauma just may bring along a subtle, unexpected and unprepared for companion—spiritual crisis.

Spiritual crisis

> *After I eat, I cocoon myself in blankets, like a caterpillar*
> *hoping for a transformation. I tuck the blanket beneath*
> *my knees, under my shoulders, up around my neck, so*
> *that nothing is exposed to the chilling air. I pull and*
> *tug and every part of my body feels sheltered. Then*
> *I allow myself to mourn. My sobs cause my cocoon*
> *of blankets to tremble, like life within is hungering*
> *to be unbound…to be free.* Eve's Song, *p. 36*

Crisis: An emotionally stressful event or traumatic change in a person's life. A point in the story when a conflict reaches its highest tension and must be resolved.[9]

Addiction, abandonment and abuse cover a spectrum of so many hurts. Yet in the pain there is commonality. All of these relational wounds, whether near or far, affect the way we view life and the way we interact in relationships. All of these impact our basic notions of safety and security. All of these inflict a type of trauma that impacts the way we interact with others now. But this also helps explain why a spiritual journey of recovery is so desperately needed in the wake of these types of pain. As spiritual people, every notion of ourselves is touched by our faith. God is a large part of our being complete, worthwhile and loveable. Without even thinking, we assume that faith gives a certain degree of insulation from danger. Now that same faith brings up so many questions. *Are all of my relationships based on lies? Why did this happen to me and not others? How did I attract this?* It also affects our view of ourselves spiritually. *Where were you God when this happened? Didn't I pray about this relationship? Will I always be the one who is abandoned? Do you show favoritism?*

In the introduction, we talked about the greatest command: to love God with all our mind, heart, soul and strength.* One reason spiritual recovery is needed in each of these areas is because trauma settles into mind, heart, soul and strength.

Trauma affects the **mind**. In the wake of trauma, we struggle to focus—like a type of Attention Deficit Disorder has descended. We are numbed, dazed, and unable to concentrate.

17

---

* *And he replied, "You must love the Lord your God with all your heart and with all your soul and with all your strength and with all your mind; and your neighbor as yourself."* LUKE 10:27 (AMP)

What is reality? We thought life was secure and then abruptly found out that we'd been at risk all along.

Trauma affects the **heart**. Emotion runs helter-skelter. Panic descends, putting us in an attack mode or causing us to shut down. One day we feel at peace, and then overwhelmed the next day as another wave of grief washes over. The security we placed in our primary roles—friend, spouse, parent, fiancé, follower of Christ—seems diminished.

Trauma wounds our **strength**. Our bodies absorb the blow. As time passes, we may find we are not as resilient to sickness. We may experience physical symptoms of depression, become sleep deprived or dependent on a medication. Phantom pains appear and then flee.

But most of all, trauma tears the fabric of our **souls**. Suddenly, we are questioning what we once thought were spiritual realities. *How could this have happened to me? Why did I remember this (and find out about this) now? You tell us to bear one another's burdens.* Who do I tell? Most of my family members don't know. On Sundays, I walk into a church where so many don't know. How much do I divulge?*

Well-meaning Christians urge us to be spiritual. "Trust God," they urge, "surrender to him." In their minds these answers seem clear. But what does Jesus' command to forgive mean when your partner hired someone for a sexual massage? What does the admonition to submit to one another mean in the wake of betrayal? How do friends' unsolicited advice fit with our own sense of what Jesus would have us do? *Can't I make my own decision?*

---

* *Bear (endure, carry) one another's burdens and troublesome moral faults, and in this way fulfill and observe perfectly the law of Christ…and complete what is lacking [in your obedience to it].* GALATIANS 6:2 (AMPC)

But take heart. Good can come out of trauma when it is placed in the loving hands of Jesus, the great physician.* Like the other eleven Stones in this journey, trauma needs to be faced boldly in order to process it. Trauma becomes more manageable as we understand it better.

Understanding trauma

The Lord is near to those who are discouraged; he saves those who have lost all hope. PSALM 34:18 (GNT)

Trauma. Even the word sounds like an assault. It comes to us from the Greek, *trau*, being an extended root of *tere*, to rub or turn, or a twisting or piercing. As a medical term, trauma is thought to come from the verb *diatitreno*, which means to penetrate. Not only does trauma pierce us, it also penetrates into our very core. Understanding trauma helps us better grasp why it is so painful to be in the wake of addiction, abandonment or abuse. In the aftermath of these hurts, many of us have found ourselves with a type of post traumatic stress disorder (PTSD). Now, you can look up many definitions online,[10] but I'd like to offer my own explanation for the purposes of this spiritual journey of recovery, by simply breaking down the phrase. See the chart on the following page (Understanding Post Traumatic Stress Disorder) for my definition.

* *Moreover we know that to those who love God, who are called according to his plan, everything that happens fits into a pattern for good.* ROMANS 8:28 (PHILLIPS)

Understanding Post Traumatic Stress Disorder	
Post	It sets in right after a trauma (or the memory or disclosure of a trauma) and symptoms continue over an extended period of time.
Traumatic	The pain of addiction, abandonment or abuse pierces us. Anything that reminds us of the trauma brings a fresh wave of pain.
Stress	The brain keeps the trauma nearby, so that we can detect further danger. We subconsciously set protections like control, throwing up emotional walls or self-medicating.
Disorder	Symptoms alternate being buried deep inside, and exploding in moments of fear. We find ourselves bewildered by our own responses.

Some of you may struggle with this. You only think of post traumatic stress disorder as resulting from really severe trauma, like a soldier who saw his close friend blown up by an IED. You may be hesitant to explore your own trauma (as I was about my relationship with my dad), because you don't think what happened to you is severe enough to really matter. Or you may fear that by facing what hurt you, that you are casting a black cloud on all the good that was in that relationship. But denying trauma is what makes it gain power. So let's consider the unique ways abandonment, addiction and abuse can cause us ongoing post traumatic stress.

Abandonment, whether physical or emotional, can leave a type of post traumatic stress disorder. Being neglected or deserted by someone we greatly value leaves a tear in our self-esteem—the sense whether we are acceptable and worth loving. We might even end up an "abandoholic," a term coined to describe the way those who have abandonment trauma go after relationships that are disconnected due to a fear of true connection, and with it the possibility of more abandonment.

Similarly, an "abandophobic" is so controlled by this fear, that they avoid relationships altogether.[11] We'll talk more about abandonment on Stone seven (acceptance).

Abuse is also a potent source of post traumatic stress. Verbal, physical and sexual abuse leave us torn emotionally, spiritually and even physically, causing long-term battles with trust. Perhaps this is because the brain is astute at collecting memories. The number of memories collected and the number of years they have existed multiplies the potential stress. This type of stress can emerge in an anxiety disorder. It could lie dormant with symptoms leaking out from time to time through avoidance, sensitivity to being startled (hyper-arousal), or even flashbacks or recurring bad thoughts.[12]

Adultery also causes PTSD, potentially leaving us with persistent flashbacks anytime we are reminded of the disclosure and the details of the betrayal.

But learning that your partner has been indulging in persistent pornography or masturbation, acts that supposedly "don't hurt anyone," has been slow to be identified as a type of trauma. It wasn't until 2006, that researchers set out to validate the hypothesis that weathering unexpected disclosure of sexual infidelity can cause a form of PTSD.[13] Barbara Steffens and Robyn Rennie's research study, "The Traumatic Nature of Disclosure for Wives of Sexual Addicts," explored the notion that wives of sexual addicts show the symptoms of trauma-related distress as a result of their husband's disclosure. They found that 70% of their participants met nearly all of the criteria to be diagnosed with PTSD. They also hypothesized that the severity of the trauma was related to the suddenness of surprise.[14]

Now we've come to understand that it isn't just the suddenness of a disclosure that causes trauma. There is also trauma embedded deeply within repeated disclosures that are spread out over a period of months, years or even decades. In my case, all the staggered confessions I'd weathered over the years had increased my trauma. Staggered disclosure is the way addicts progressively reveal bits of their addiction, making for multiple traumas for those who hear them.[15] These multiple traumas make for their own type of PTSD, the…"When is the bottom going to fall out from under me again?" variety. For me, this has been the toughest kind of trauma. After a confession, I would cycle through the stages of grief, and then finally relax into the new reality. Just when it seemed I had processed Dave's actions, he would reveal another dimension of it all, thrusting me into even deeper anger and grief, multiplied by the sense that I got duped. *I should have asked more questions.* This created a deep-seated anxiety that would flare up anytime I sensed something was wrong with our relationship.

I believe that sexual trauma is especially difficult to process because it holds shades of addiction, abandonment and abuse. Perhaps that's one reason why the Bible has such stern warnings about sexual sin:

> *"Haven't you read," he replied, "that at the beginning the Creator 'made them male and female,' and said, 'For this reason a man will leave his father and mother and be united to his wife, and the two will become one flesh'? So they are no longer two, but one flesh. Therefore what God has joined together, let no one separate."*
> MATTHEW 19:4-6

> *Do you not know that he who unites himself with a prostitute is one with her in body? For it is said, "The two will become one flesh." […] Flee from sexual immorality. All other sins a person commits are outside the body, but*

whoever sins sexually, sins against their own body.
2 CORINTHIANS 6:16, 18

To sum it up…When the two become one, they become one flesh. Whoever sins sexually sins against his/her own body. When someone in a covenant relationship falls sexually, they sin against their mate's body. Think of it this way. Marriage is a powerful attachment made by many hormones—primarily vasopressin and testosterone for men and oxytocin for women. When the bond with your mate is threatened by deception, pornography or marital infidelity, you suffer an attachment injury, a tearing in your very biology, a trauma.

This tear happens whether we fully realize it or not. Many of us can testify to living in a relationship for months, years, or even decades, with no clue of the multi-leveled falls of our partner. Yet something in our intuition sensed it long before the disclosure in the form of an unsettled feeling, the inability to connect, or even amping up of the impulse to control or constantly check on them. One woman I counseled described rolling up in a ball and crying after sexual intimacy with her husband. Before her mind and emotions could process the warning signs of infidelity, her body was already registering the fallout. Another woman told me about zoning mentally into a safe place far away while she fulfilled sexual demands from her husband that required her to compromise her convictions. She knew if she didn't fulfill them, she would pay a huge price through his disengagement, disinterest or even disdain. Her intuition told her that he was hooking up with other women. But she didn't dare ask. When she started having anxiety attacks, she managed them carefully, protecting him from the consequences of his actions. The power of her anxiety attacks frightened and bewildered her.

23

Some of us turn all that angst outward. Trauma explains why we can react in ways that seem so out of character in the heat of the moment. We may curse our partners, call them names, throw things, make threats and display other irrational behaviors that don't seem to fit with Christianity. We may pick up an old habit to seek comfort or push back against whoever hurt us—smoking, cursing, getting drunk or medicating with food or shopping. We may be tempted to dabble in the attention of someone else (and Satan specializes in sending "the perfect person" our way at just such a time) or get embroiled in an emotional affair. Instead of judging ourselves for these responses, I'd suggest that we ask Jesus to help us look below the surface. Why did I do or say that? What am I really feeling? Curiosity frees us to face our own shortcomings and humbly address them.

Whatever trauma you've faced, as we make our way through this journey of spiritual recovery, we'll do the work of facing our own responses and listening to what they would tell us about ourselves. To do this will require allowing Jesus, our Guide, to shine his light on the very places we fear.

The Stone of trauma

> Say this: "God, you're my refuge.
>   I trust in you and I'm safe!"
> That's right—he rescues you from hidden traps,
>   shields you from deadly hazards.
> His huge outstretched arms protect you—
>   under them you're perfectly safe;
>   his arms fend off all harm." PSALM 91:2-4 (MSG)

In Preparing the Ground, we talked about the twelve Stones of this journey being reminiscent of the altar of twelve stones that Joshua built. Let's picture that scene (Joshua 3-5) for a moment. Because of their unfaithfulness, the Israelites had wandered in the desert for 40 long years. And now the day had finally come for them to cross the Jordan into the land God promised them. According to God's command, Joshua had the priests carry the Ark of the Covenant ahead of the Israelites. Imagine watching as the priests step into the water, and suddenly a miracle begins to happen. The flood-season waters, which just moments earlier were overflowing the banks, are cut off. The water to their right roars and then disappears as it rushes away. Looking to their left, all you see is the riverbank stretching on for miles, dry and passable.* The priests take the Ark of the Covenant into the middle of the Jordan, and the whole Israelite nation slowly makes their way across, a process that takes many hours. When the last Israelite passes, Joshua instructs twelve men (one from each tribe) to go find a large rock from the riverbed, hoist it onto their shoulders and bring it up onto the other side. When that task is completed, the priests bring the Ark of Covenant up out of the Jordan to the other side. Joshua builds an altar with the twelve stones in Gilgal (which means rolled away), commemorating God rolling away the reproach of all their wanderings and literally rolling away the raging Jordan River.

I find so much rich symbolism here for our own journey of Stones. These Jordan River stones had been smoothed by the constant pressure and movement of the water above them— any rough edges had been removed. As we face our trauma, we

---

* JOSHUA 3:16 *says that the waters heaped up at the city of Adam. Bible Gateway footnotes that scripture with: "The city of Adam has been placed 16 miles up the river from Jericho, and it seems probable that a stretch of 20 or 30 miles of the riverbed was left dry."*

declare our faith in God, who is able to make the rough places smooth.

> *Every valley and ravine shall be filled up, and every mountain and hill shall be leveled; and the crooked places shall be made straight, and the rough roads shall be made smooth.* LUKE 3:5 (AMPC)

The altar stones of Gilgal had been long hidden under the water, but were only revealed because of God's moving. Once they were under a raging river, but now they became a declaration of God's sovereignty and his movement in their lives.

Isn't it the same for us? Our raging rivers of pain are more than we can bear. But our God finds a way to give us dry land to walk on, a path that leads straight through our pain. This is the hope of facing our trauma and owning our pain...abundant grace for our time of need.

Grace calls

> *I will give you hidden treasures, riches stored in secret places, so that you may know that I am the Lord, the God of Israel, who summons you by name.* ISAIAH 45:3

As much as none of us would ever ask for trauma, it offers gifts in the lives of those who experience it. The treasures I've gained through my pain are so precious; I now (*now* being the operative word) consider it worth all the suffering. With time, I discovered a God who mourned with me and then comforted me, teaching me to live boldly in all my imperfection. Grace calls...*I understand your vulnerability. I won't lead you anywhere that's more than you can bear.*

Are you ready for your own experience of grace? Grace calls…*My dear one, spirituality is one of God's greatest gifts to you. Let me guide you through your past trauma, so I can take you to the deep places with God.* As we embrace the spiritual discipline of hearing and then responding to the call of grace, Jesus can turn the pain of trauma into treasures of darkness. He alone can re-create us, giving us gifts that he will use to comfort and guide others.*

Your spiritual journey

You might be wondering…is this journey worth it? Do I really want help? Let me assure you, this is not a journey to take for someone else. And it is more than worth it, regardless of your current situation. Even if you primarily come to this journey of Stones seeking to help others, I'm convinced it will gift you with new perspectives, new eyes. Grace is the treasure hidden in a field (MATTHEW 13:44). To find it you may need to dig in the dirt, but its preciousness is beyond compare. It helps me to remember the promise of Jesus, our great physician…

> *Come to Me, all you who labor and are heavy-laden and overburdened, and I will cause you to rest. [I will ease and relieve and refresh your souls].* MATTHEW 11:28 (AMPC)

---

* *But to each one of us grace has been given as Christ apportioned it. This is why it says: 'When he ascended on high, he took many captives and gave gifts to his people.'* EPHESIANS 4:7-8

Circle of stones: trauma

Now it's time to find your first stone. It can be rough or smooth, small or big. Take a marker and write the word **trauma** on it. Hold it in your hand and feel its weight. What does your trauma want to say to you? What does God want you to know?

Put your stone in a safe place, preferably someplace where you see it from time to time. Remind yourself that you no longer have to be afraid of facing your trauma.

Journaling: Trauma

Open to a blank page in your journal and draw three columns across the top. Write the word abandonment at the top of the first column, addiction in the second and abuse in the third. Asking Jesus to lead you, start writing down any trauma from your life in the corresponding column. Some events may have shades of all three. If so, just draw an arrow to the second or even third column it goes in.

You may wonder, "How do I decide which events in my life have caused trauma?" If so, re-read the sections on trauma and post-traumatic stress syndrome. Ask yourself...*Is it possible that this left an unseen tear in my self-esteem, boundaries, or sense of safety?* Do include the faint whispers of trauma, i.e., "I've always had the sense I was sexually abused but have no clear memory."

This will be what I call a living list—in other words, you can amend it as you travel through this journey. And if you aren't ready to go there, simply leave the blank columns for when you feel the nudge to begin writing.

A word from Dave – Trauma

*They are darkened in their understanding
and separated from the life of God because
of the ignorance that is in them due to the
hardening of their hearts.* EPHESIANS 4:18

It is never pleasant to realize that you brought trauma into another person's life, especially when it is the person you love the most on this earth. It is even more unpleasant when the trauma you brought pierces the tender soul of one that has already been devastated by many previous injuries. It's kind of like poking a hot knife into someone's already painful wound.

Reading and reliving the story that Robin tells at the start of this stone, and the other stories that will be told in this book, will never be easy. But if you are to fully understand our recovery story, they must be told. In fact, I was the one who encouraged Robin to write a recovery book. And now, having watched God continually give her inspiration, I am very excited about how he will use it to bless many! My hope is that after hearing our story, you will find restored hope and renewed faith that God does indeed restore broken lives and marriages.

As Robin mentions, when the scene in the restaurant unfolded, I was very confused and perplexed by my sexual behaviors. Although I knew that my actions were sinful, it seemed at times like my desires were taking control of me, like the current of a river too strong to overcome was carrying me against my will. After every fall into pornography, masturbation or deeper sin, I would vow to "never do it again" and would recommit myself to more time in prayer and Bible study. (I know now that this type of vow actually strengthens the cycle of sexual addiction.) Years later, I would come to understand that real change must come from an ongoing process of recovery. I

29

had to replace my addiction to sexual pleasure with a passion for Godly pleasures that come from doing the work of recovery.

One of the most difficult things to think about on this Stone of trauma is how hard my heart had become. It is staggering to realize now how addiction stole my ability to empathize with my wife, causing me to inflict trauma upon trauma. I was stuck in my own world of contradictions. I wrestled endlessly with a severely accused conscience, and was desperately trying to do enough good to somehow make up for the bad.

EPHESIANS 4:18 explains that part of the consequence of sin is a darkened understanding and a hardened, desensitized heart. In spite of the fact that I never missed a church service, and would occasionally become emotional when inspired by worship or a good movie, my heart was hard and I was emotionally unavailable to Robin. As sin progressively desensitized my own heart, stealing my rightful brokenness before God, it also stole my sensitivity towards my wife. Denial toward the consequences of my falls turned into denial of how much my sin was tearing Robin and ripping the very fiber of our covenant relationship. So, I was unable to comfort her during her diagnosis of a life-threatening disease and unable to comprehend how my confession and subsequent actions further traumatized her. By the grace of God and a Spirit-led process of healing spanning a number of years, I can honestly say that our lives are in a dramatically different place today!

So, at Robin's invitation and insistence, I will be coming along with you on this journey of Stones. My hope is that what I share will help all who are reading, but I especially want to encourage those of you reading these words to find perspective on the ways your decisions have traumatized others. I pray you find courage to fully engage in your own battle of recovery, or to fully support your partner's journey to heal past wounds. I will also share some practical tools that may help you to avoid some of my mistakes. For those who've suffered in the wake of abandonment, addiction or abuse, I pray that "A Word from Dave" will broaden your understanding and bring you comfort that you are not alone.

Much like God did for his people in the days of Joshua, he can take away our reproach, even after we've wandered in the desert for decades. With God's power, seemingly impossible changes can and do happen. After listing a host of "impossible" heart hardening sins, Paul says…

> *And that is what some of you were. But you were washed, you were sanctified, you were justified in the name of the Lord Jesus Christ and by the Spirit of our God.* I CORINTHIANS 6:11

I will never enjoy retelling the stories of the darkest days of my life. I take comfort, however, from Paul's first letter to Timothy. Paul believed that the love and patience of God could be made known by the fact that God took him who was a violent persecutor of Christians, and turned him into a devoted follower of Jesus. In that he found comfort. Although I cannot undo the damage I did by my addiction, if God can be glorified through the telling of my story and if others can learn from my experiences, and find freedom, to him be honor and glory. Amen!

> *Here is a trustworthy saying that deserves full acceptance: Christ Jesus came into the world to save sinners—of whom I am the worst. But for that very reason I was shown mercy so that in me, the worst of sinners, Christ Jesus might display his immense patience as an example for those who would believe in*

31

him and receive eternal life. Now to the King eternal, immortal, invisible, the only God, be honor and glory for ever and ever. Amen. I TIMOTHY 1:15–17

Back to Your Journal:

Think back to a time when someone was unable to comfort you in a time you really needed it. Write down what comes to mind. What perspective does Dave offer?

Plant your feet on my stones
Step on them like holy ground
Then you'll be closer to Jesus
The only one who gives rest

The Accuser Enters: Thorns

What were the thorns really telling her? It's why she won't
let us see them, why she clings to them—or they cling to
her—as though she got herself buried in a bramble thicket
and she can't get out and we can't get in to free her.
– Patricia A. McKillip, *Alphabet of Thorn*

A COUPLE OF YEARS AFTER THE RELEASE OF my first book, *Secure in Heart*, I was invited to be a guest on a Christian talk show in Atlanta. Since I was also speaking at a church during my stay, one of their members volunteered to drive me. As we wove our way through heavy traffic to the television station, Andrea (I'll call her) and I chatted. As we neared our destination, she said abruptly, "Have you ever read *Redeeming Love* by Francine Rivers?" When I told her I hadn't, she gave my arm a squeeze, "I'm going to send it to you. Please let me know when you finish it." I was just a little surprised. Andrea wasn't asking me whether I'd like to read the book; she was telling me I would read it. "Sure," I said, amused at her boldness. Sure enough, a few weeks later *Redeeming Love* arrived. Since Dave was out of town, I dug right in that very night. As I quickly moved into the story, a desperate mother selling her young daughter Angel into sexual slavery deeply disturbed me. But I still wasn't so sure why Andrea sent it to me. Late at night and a third of the way in, I suddenly put the

35

book down, stunned as a flashback rolled over me. I had always had a vague sense that I was sexually abused as a little girl, but no clear memory. I looked up towards the ceiling...*No God. I'm not ready for this. Why now?* Tears began to run down my face. *I'm afraid it will be too much.* In reply, I felt a nudge in my heart, "Trust me. Please go there with me." *He is giving me a choice...*I thought.

I lay back and closed my eyes. Suddenly, it seemed like I was floating on the ceiling of the living room of the modest three-bedroom house I grew up in. Looking down I saw a little girl around five years old in a pretty dress with blond curls sitting on the lap of a dark-haired man in a suit. I recognized him as a relative in town from another city. I felt her confusion and fear as he reached under her dress with his hand, probing, searching... stealing something from her. *She is so confused. She doesn't understand.* Evil swelled, filling the room with its ugliness as he unzipped his pants to expose himself. *She's terrified.* My tears increased, wetting my cheeks and running onto my pillow. Then, the man faded from view. All I saw was the little girl and pure love swelled in my chest. I knew in that moment I would do anything to save her.

A chill of recognition ran down my back. The little girl in the pink-checkered dress her mother lovingly made...was me. *I love me.* Even more, I now understood that God was present at the time of my sexual abuse. While horrified by the abuse, his heart swelled with love for me. He yearned to intervene, yet was held back by his own gift of free will. Spurred by his own unconditional love and acceptance, he looked ahead to my redemption.* He was angered by my relative's lustful assault, but

---

* *But now, this is what the Lord says—he who created you, Jacob, he who formed you Israel: "Do not fear, l for I have redeemed you; I have summoned you by name; you are mine."* ISAIAH 43:1

in his great patience desired his repentance. My God mourned the loss when, as a small child, I couldn't yet comprehend the wound that had been inflicted. God would be standing by some forty years later to mourn with me as *Redeeming Love* finally nudged this injury into view. And now, ten years after that flashback, I can testify that my God, understanding how loss embeds itself into the most sensitive parts of the soul, has never tired of mourning with me. Until the day I pass from this life to the next, my flesh, spirit, mind and emotions will bear remnants of my relative's fall.

Sexual abuse stole my dignity by teaching me to sacrifice my intimate parts for love. This would bring even more abuse, heaping more pain and sexual confusion upon the already jumbled places inside. Although I had done nothing to deserve or attract my relative's acting out, sexual abuse would serve as a place where thorny accusations could take up residence in my soul—lies whispered by a terrible adversary, the evil one. The many thorns of my childhood, joined by the thorns of Dave's fall, formed a thicket that would engulf me.

The Stone of Thorns

> *To keep me from becoming conceited because of these surpassingly great revelations, there was given me a thorn in the flesh, a messenger of Satan, to torment me.*
> 2 CORINTHIANS 12:7, NIV 1984

God created thorns for an important purpose in his creation. But some thorns are easier to understand than others. We understand why a rose would have thorns, the beauty and pain both obvious. But what about those pesky goat heads that attach themselves to my legs as I hike up in the hills, and then stab me

37

as I pull them out? Some thorns seem more redemptive, like the thickets that protect tasty fruits. Others are a little harder to decipher, like the curved thorns that wriggle in under our skin bringing infection. I think it is much the same way spiritually. Some thorns pinch a little, but don't lodge in for the long haul. Others torment us. The apostle Paul understood the agony of an unrelenting thorn. Paul's ailment wasn't a literal thorn that he got by walking barefoot in the fields. Most scholars think he had a disabling physical ailment. But the torment went far beyond the flesh—the physical ailment came packed with a spiritual thorn, fueled by messages from the evil one himself. The Bible isn't specific on what these messages were, but some of Paul's hardships give us a clue…

You are less than the rest of the apostles
(2 CORINTHIANS 11:5).

Other people will never take you seriously
(1 CORINTHIANS 2:1).

Your past sin makes you difficult to trust
(ACTS 9:11-15).

These messages remind me of the thorns left in the wake of addiction, abandonment or abuse. Our thorns are similar to Paul's in that they are laden with messages from the evil one. But they have a different origin—coming in the wake of someone else's sin.

38 **Thorns in the flesh:** Painful challenges caused by a perplexing physical ailment. These affect the way we see ourselves, our standing with others and/or our spiritual security.

Thorns of the fall: Painful challenges in the wake of a loved one's choice to abuse us, abandon us, or break their promises to us through an addiction. These also affect the way we see ourselves, our standing with others and our spiritual security.

Picture the trauma you are facing—the anguish caused by someone you trusted falling hard. This trauma impacts your emotions, mind, spirit, and your body. As we discussed in the first Stone of trauma, when you love someone or have an intimate relationship with them, powerful hormones reinforce that bond. When the trauma came, you suffered an attachment injury, a ripping caused by the discrepancy between what you believed to be true and what turned out to be reality. You believed you were safe and then found you were at risk. Your body retains the memory of the trauma to protect you from suffering another trauma. This trauma is registered in the brain.

Trauma jolts and disorients us.

Trauma has a way of jolting and disorienting us. To understand the resulting thorns, think of your trauma as a walk in a forest. Someone you love is ahead of you. Although you've asked them repeatedly to please slow down and wait for you, they trip on a root, and grab hold of a large branch to keep from falling. When they release the branch, it swings back and whacks you in the head so hard you are almost knocked off your feet. "You okay?" they say, not even bothering to look back. You look up, stunned. To compound things, the branch was full of large thorns and it seems a few of them have lodged themselves into your skull, a few others into the back of your neck. You start to feel woozy and nauseous because these thorns injected a toxin into your system. You sit down on a log, holding your head in

39

your hands, having taken a terrible blow. A moment later you look up. Your loved one is making their way ahead, seemingly unaware you aren't following. You are left with trauma, thorns, and a panic bordering on terror.

This analogy helps us understand the lingering effects of being in the wake of someone else's fall. It's not just the jarring of the initial trauma (being hit in the head with a branch). It's not even just the sense that your partner (or father, mother or other loved one) doesn't understand how his or her actions wounded you. Now you have to fight other demons, determined to hijack your view of yourself and God. *Was I blind? How could they be so calloused? Does God see?* Even as the immediate effects of the trauma begin to subside, these thorns remain.

In the aftermath, we find ourselves fighting hard against the feelings of being unsafe, rejected, alone, unsure, misunderstood, judged. These thorns mount an attack against our most instinctive needs: the need for safety, for love, for acceptance, and for trust in God. They may create spiritual doubt and confusion. At times these thorns remain well hidden. In our determination to restore order, we shove them deep inside. We repress them. Other times they flare up, sending a rush of adrenalin and panic.

Going back to our analogy, getting hit by that branch and now having toxins in your system is even worse if you already have residue of toxins from past encounters with traumas and thorns (we'll talk more about this in Stone 3: *Triggers*). The more relational traumas you've suffered, the greater the accumulation of pain. As these inner thorns accumulate, new offenses (even if small) now seem unbearable. In fact, you may feel buried in a briar thicket.

These childhood traumas can take many forms. They might take the form of emotional or physical abandonment—a parent who wasn't available or who belittled you when you needed comfort. They could have come from a parent with an addiction or mental instability. Your trauma might include verbal or emotional abuse or a parent's alcoholism or drug abuse. Your father or mother might have been addicted to sex or love, exposing you to perversions children cannot process. You may have been marginalized or taught that the opposite sex gets more respect. Perhaps you were taught that your value depended on achievement. Perhaps your voice was stolen by harsh discipline or bullying.

In my case, Dave's addiction exposed many of these thorny places from my childhood, while adding new thorns. One of the most damaging from my childhood was the thorn of sexual abuse. My early sexual abuse seemed to put a target on me—she is vulnerable; she won't tell. And so even more sexual abuse came, including an incident with a maintenance worker on a school parking lot, and boys that took advantage of my lack of boundaries. In my adolescent years, I had the thorns of verbal abuse from a father descending into alcoholism. In my first job after high school, as a secretary at an institution for the mentally retarded, a doctor attempted to rape me. All this trauma caused my sexual self (one of the key parts of development) to grow up a little twisted, leaving thorny places inside. Emotionally and spiritually, I erected my own system of protection to keep me safe, either throwing myself at men (to stay in control), or erecting high walls that kept others out. Abandonment thorns came when my mother caught my father in an affair (more in Stone seven), and he left permanently.

41

How do addiction, abandonment or abuse from our childhoods turn into thorns? The natural world can bring some clarity. The thorns on a rose aren't actually considered by many botanists to be real thorns—they are prickles. Prickles are different from spiny thorns in that they can be peeled off the plant. But the worst thorns are those that are degenerative. These take the form of, "mutant leaves or parts of leaves that didn't unfold properly; leaf bases that have failed to grow into leaves or are left over when leaves fall; or failed branch development."[16] These spines can't be easily removed from a plant. They are degenerative because they came as a result of an injury or dysfunction of the plant.*

My experiences with abuse, abandonment and addiction did much the same to me. It caused me to unfold improperly. Parts of my spirit that needed development became stunted. Connections didn't develop properly, causing a lack of boundaries. With the deeply embedded shame present in my family, and the unfolding chaos, true spirituality was illusive. God's sovereignty became a threat rather than a gift. I wasn't given the tools to make the mental, spiritual and emotional connections needed for my healing. Seeing these places of pain, the accuser saw an opportunity—to convince me that I would never be enough.

The Accuser Enters

> *For the accuser of our brothers and sisters, who*
> *accuses them before our God day and night,*
> *has been hurled down.* REVELATION 12:10

---

* *Creationists think that* GENESIS 3:18 *isn't referring so much to prickles like those on a rose, but rather to these painful, spiny features. Ibid.*

It's easy to see why Satan sees thorns as a place to set up camp. He whispers that we deserve them because we are deficient and then seeks to convince us that these thorns make us less than others. He insinuates that thorns indicate a lack of approval, protection or concern from our Creator. *Hide your vulnerable places so that no one can hurt you like this again. Those thorns won't hurt as bad if you put up walls of protection.* The evil one incites questions in our hearts that pull us away from God and others. His underlying accusations press on our desire for acceptance, self-identity, and security.

Need for acceptance – Can I let others into the messiness of my fear and pain? Will they accept the parts of me that don't mesh with the way they expect me to be? If I share about the chaos in my marriage, will they accept us? If I'm divorced or unmarried, will they accept me? Or might they even blame me?

Sense of myself – Am I still the same person I was before this trauma? Am I damaged goods? Do I need to somehow make up for this? Is there a way to reconcile my beliefs and values with my day-to-day experience of life?

Security with God – Am I at risk with God? Will he come through for me like he does for others? How do I continue to rely on God's promises when they no longer seem to speak to me?

Cruel and malicious, Satan wants to attach personal, spiritual and relational shame to these questions. Remember how Paul called his thorn a messenger from Satan? Since Satan is at war with God's children, his messages are burning missiles hurled at the most vulnerable places in our souls.* To unmask Satan's messages, we need to face our thorns. Again, that requires walking straight into the places that hold so much fear and angst for us. In my own experience, God doesn't move into these tender places without our invitation. But how do we identify these?

In her groundbreaking book, *Daring Greatly*, shame researcher Brene Brown did extensive surveys with men and women to identify twelve (wouldn't you know it!) common areas of shame:

1) Appearance and body image
2) Motherhood/fatherhood
3) Money and work
4) Family
5) Parenting
6) Mental and physical health
7) Addiction
8) Sex
9) Aging
10) Religion
11) Surviving trauma
12) Being labeled[17]

These areas of shame are instructive in facing our thorns. On the following page you will see a chart that uses Brown's arenas of shame to identify where thorns have sprouted up in our hearts. My additions to her twelve areas are in brackets and "Satan's messages" comes from my own and other women's experiences.

---

* *Above all be sure you take faith as your shield, for it can quench every burning missile the enemy hurls at you.* EPHESIANS 6:16 (PHILLIPS)

Areas thorns sprout up (Brown's shame categories)	Satan's messages
Appearance and body image	If you were skinnier, sexier, stronger or smarter this wouldn't have happened.
Motherhood/fatherhood [or my parents]	What kind of mother would allow this to happen? If your parents didn't love you, how will anyone love you?
Money and work	Your finances are collapsing or your work life has been difficult because you simply aren't enough.
Family	Your family will never understand. If they find out what happened, they will abandon (or blame) you.
Parenting [or singlehood]	Your children [or you] will be forever marked by the unhealthy patterns in your [or your parent's] marriage.
Mental and physical health	You're just overreacting. If you don't control the person you love, he will abandon you.
Addiction	You are using all this as an excuse. Do you have convictions about sin?
Sex [or intimacy]	Intimacy will never be safe. Fully trusting another person is a huge mistake.
Aging [or life stage]	How many years did you lose to this pain? You'll never regain what you've lost.
Religion [spirituality]	God obviously wasn't listening to your prayers for deliverance. He responds more quickly to other people.
Surviving trauma	You'll never be as good as others.
Being labeled	Other people will always see you as the one who attracted sexual addiction, abandonment or abuse.

Satan's goal is to sneak in and steal the good gifts and spiritual growth that pain offers. But when we do take our stand against Satan's messages, we engage in spiritual warfare (more in Stone 5). There is redemptive power in calling out Satan's messages and identifying them as being from him. As we do this we tell our brain...*do not accept these messages because they are completely untrue!* And there is more good news! The very thorns that pierce can also heal. God allows thorns because they have a redemptive purpose in his creation.

The weapon that cures

> *No weapon forged against you will prevail, and you will refute every tongue that accuses you.* ISAIAH 54:17A

As I've been exploring thorns, I couldn't help but wonder what plants carry the most lethal thorns. One nasty thorn that I discovered in my research is aptly named the devil's club, also known as Alaskan ginseng. There are many websites that warn hikers about the dangers of this plant common to Alaska, the coastal Southeast and Pacific Northwest. It can take weeks to remove the sliver-sized needles that tend to embed deeply in the skin. One hiker had to extract them one by one with an X-Acto knife.[18] What's more, these thorns inject a mild, irritating toxin, gaining a myth-like status of being "poison." The plant's name, devil's club, is explained by its appearance. In the spring through fall, it has huge six- to fifteen-inch leaves, cane-sized stems and long yellow thorns. But in the winter it becomes even more lethal. If an unsuspected hiker steps on devil's club buried in the snow, the plant might just spring up, clubbing him with thorns.

Yet, as evidenced by the scientific name of devil's club, *Oplopanax horridum*, devil's club has a redemptive purpose. *Oplo* has to do with weapons, whereas *panax* signifies cure—a weapon that cures. Devil's club has been used by Native Americans for a variety of ailments, and is still being used as a cure to this day. In fact, the root is used "to help the body adapt to stressful situations or 'adrenal burnout' from mental, nervous, emotional and physical exhaustion," a healing property we could all use in the wake of abandonment, addiction or abuse. Some healing practitioners believe that the root of this plant lends "a sense of invigoration and strength on a physical or spiritual level."[19] The Tlingit and Haida people of Southeast Alaska hang a piece of devil's club over their doorway to ward off evil.[20]

This amazes me on many levels. A few years back, I was treated for adrenal exhaustion with a product that includes Korean ginseng, a thorny cousin of Alaskan ginseng that yields medicinal herbs from its root. Twice a day I ingested the weapon that cures. But the spiritual applications are what really wow me. Who wants to get clubbed by the devil? None of us! Yet, even in the worst of thorns, whether physical thorns or the spiritual thorns we are thinking about in this Stone, God has embedded the very nature of redemption, both physical and spiritual. Our father is so powerful that he can take Satan's weapons and use them in our healing! He uses thorns to gift us with adaptation, resiliency and perseverance, thus helping prevent the physical, mental and spiritual burnout spurred by our worst traumas. In the very root of thorns are these hidden healing treasures:

Adaptation: We acquire life skills that enable us to adjust more quickly as our life station and/or environment changes.

47

Resiliency: We learn to withstand stress and catastrophe. We develop an increased tolerance for troubles and stress.

Buoyancy: Our spirit becomes lighter and more resilient. Joy springs up and grows as we rise from troubles.

Perseverance: We persevere under misfortunes and trials, while holding fast to our faith in Christ.

I'm thinking Paul's thorn in the flesh allowed him a remarkable resilience. But it wasn't his angst about the thorn that gifted Paul... *Satan is making me mad, so I'll just be stronger.* Rather it was his surrender to the thorn...

> *Three times I pleaded with the Lord to take it away from me. But he said to me, "My grace is sufficient for you, for my power is made perfect in weakness." Therefore I will boast all the more gladly about my weaknesses, so that Christ's power may rest on me.*
>
> *That is why for Christ's sake, I delight in weaknesses, in insults, in hardships, in persecutions, in difficulties. For when I am weak, then I am strong.*
>
> 2 CORINTHIANS 12:8-10

As Paul prayed three times for God to remove the thorn, I picture him listening intently, hoping for God to say "yes." I can only guess how painful it was to admit that God's will was better than his own. Instead of removing it, God told him a whole new way to view his thorn, based on spiritual realities that only God could see. God taught him to claim the power outside of himself in order to wage the war inside of himself. *When you are weak, I am strong. When you aren't enough, I am enough.*

This is a lesson God has taught me as well. The power of the thorn of sexual abuse has been redeemed by the presence of God within the memory. By walking with me into the depths

48

of my trauma, God has gifted me with his perspective…that I am worth loving, worth fighting for, and perfectly equipped for the ways he would use me. As I have heard his voice, the thorns have lost their ability to undo me. In fact, Satan's weapon of sexual abuse has become a curing balm for a variety of other troubles I've faced. I now know when Satan is seeking to define a situation for me. Now I find myself asking Jesus to come with me into sensitive and/or painful situations.

How about you? Are you open to the possibility that God wants to use the thorns of the fall to bring you healing, resilience and even hope? Will you lift the messages Satan torments you with to Jesus, and then ask for his perspective? This will become easier as you listen for the call of grace.

Grace calls

> *But his answer was, my grace is all you need,*
> *for my power is greatest when you are weak.*
> *Therefore I will most gladly boast all the more*
> *about my weaknesses, so that Christ's power may*
> *reside in me.* 2 CORINTHIANS 12:9 (GNT)

At the beginning of this Stone, I shared about the full memory of my sexual abuse as a child. But I left out one important detail. The truth is that remembering my sexual abuse was an answered prayer. For years, I had the faintest whispers of the memory. But rather than let this cause me distress, I kept telling God, "When I am ready, and only if and when you know it is best for me, I trust you will give me the full memory of what happened in my childhood." I knew that God my vindicator would help me face down my abuse and all the thorns it contained. And sure enough, God answered that prayer at just the right time.

Through a woman I had never met (Andrea) insisting that I read a book I had never heard of (*Redeeming Love*), God exposed the very root of the thorn in order to use it as a healing salve for my pain.

Do you have losses buried so deeply that you're not sure when and if you'll remember them? Grace whispers…*Ask me for the memories you've lost. Then trust me with the timing of your remembering. I will help you stand.* In some ways, facing my thorns feels scarier than acknowledging trauma. Trauma comes and eventually goes, but thorns have a way of sticking around. As any gardeners can attest, thorns root deep and find a way to come back. Grace calls…*Let me provide you with empowering strength for your circumstances, perfectly measured to what you've suffered.*

Facing our thorns is part of the redemption process. If we don't face our buried thorns, they can pop up at us when triggered, throwing barbs into our psyche and clubbing our self-esteem. Intentionally facing our thorns allows us to do it on our terms, with Jesus our Guide telling us what our thorns mean. Grace beckons…*The accuser seeks to incorporate his taunts in your self-esteem without you noticing that he is simply pressing on old wounds. Let me teach you how to protect your vulnerable parts.*

As I've engaged this journey over time, my thorns have lost much of their sting. Their poison has been drained as I've continued to embrace recovery. Although my thorns can still taunt me from time to time, I've been able to dig deep into the roots of my pain and find amazing healing and comfort from my Great Physician, Jesus.

Your spiritual journey

> *While he lived on earth, anticipating death, Jesus cried*
> *out in pain and wept in sorrow [...] Though he was*
> *God's Son, he learned trusting-obedience by what he*
> *suffered, just as we do [...].* HEBREWS 5:7-10 (MSG)

Congratulations! You've taken a step onto the second Stone of this journey: thorns. Still, you may have concerns and fears. You might have even been tempted to shut the book and hide it away.

This is a good time to remember that you have a guide who is well versed in pain: Jesus, our brother in the flesh and Lord of Lords. Jesus understands thorns well. In fact, he wore a crown of thorns. Certainly, those who twisted the thick spiny thorns into a crown were incited by the evil one. And some speculate that these thorns were full of toxins that were injected into Jesus' system. Yet because Jesus wore thorns, openly, willingly (no one could have kept them on his head against his will), he redeemed our thorns once and for all.

Now it is time to start digging a little in the fertile earth of your soul, and let the thorns show themselves, trusting that Jesus will minister to you. With Jesus leading, you can trust that this journey of twelve Stones will lead you into a spacious place...a place you can safely stand.

Circle of stones: thorns

Now it's time to find your second stone and write the word **thorns** on it. As you hold the stone in your hand, say a pray over your own thorns, asking God for healing and redemption.

Put stone two, *thorns*, with the first stone of *trauma*, again somewhere where you will see them from time to time. Remind yourself that you no longer have to be ashamed of any of these losses. God is in the process of redeeming them for you.

Journaling: Thorns

Find a quiet place. Take a few moments to breathe deeply, offering this time to God.

Picture Jesus gently working a strand of thorns out of your heart, along with the full root. Now watch as he opens the root to harvest a healing balm, specifically formulated for your wounds.

Now journal about these questions:

- How does it feel to know Jesus can help with thorns?
- What thorns is Jesus finding in your heart?
- What thorny pains in your life most need a healing balm?

A word from Dave — Thorns

To love one another means to fully
understand his or her suffering.
– THICH NHAT HANH, ZEN BUDDHIST TEACHER

I grew up on a one and a half acre piece of land carved out of a cornfield in central Illinois. As soon as I was old enough, it became my job to mow the grass. On one occasion I worked especially hard to do it perfectly, mowing in straight lines with the riding mower, trimming it with a hand mower, then getting on my knees to chop down every last blade of grass with the shears. I eagerly awaited my dad coming home from work, expecting him to heap praise on me for my great achievement. For some reason, he was distracted and he barely said a word. It was many years later before I understood that a thorn had been implanted that day, part of a group of thorns that would lead to my unhealthy craving for affirmation wherever I could find it. Understanding those thorns would be key to my recovery and to supporting my wife.

Understanding Robin's thorns has filled me with compassion for her and helped me understand why my sexual wrongdoing was so devastating to her. I had no idea when we got married how many hits to her soul Robin had already endured. I wanted to be her hero and rescuer, but I ended up pushing her existing thorns deeper, while inflicting new wounds as well. The illustration about the hiker in this Stone hits me hard. I was running ahead of Robin trying to convince myself that if I ran fast enough and accomplished enough, the consequences of my actions wouldn't filter down to her.* I was oblivious to the pain I was causing her

53

---

* *Anyone who runs ahead and does not continue in the teaching of Christ does not have God.* 2 JOHN 1:9

and how each new disclosure was hitting her in the face like a thorny branch. To find self-esteem, I would mentally rehearse all the ways that I was a good husband, a good father, and a good Christian. I wanted this whole dark area of sexual sin in my life to go away and be forgotten just like it never happened.

Ironically, I eventually learned that one of the drivers of my thorn-filled sexual addiction was a desire to medicate the wounds caused by thorns. Satan's messages to me through these early thorns pierced my young soul with messages it would take years to unwind:

> *You will never be good enough.*

> *No one will ever desire you for who you are.*

> *Others won't notice the good you do unless you bring it to their attention.*

> *You are disgusting and hypocritical.*

My first counselor helped me understand the abandonment I felt when my father was too busy to spend time with me as a boy, and how that created in me a longing for connection and self worth. This left me vulnerable to the world of false intimacy, lust and pornography. While this wound seems minor, when coupled with early exposure to pornography and inappropriate nudity, rejection of my peers (especially girls), and a lack of sexual teaching and boundaries, one can begin to understand how a young boy with a sensitive heart could end up where I did. How sad but common it is for the wounded to become the inflictors of wounds.

54

Facing my own wounds, allowed me to break the grip of the narcissism inherent in addiction. Eventually, my calloused heart began to soften. Ironically, a new pain took the place of old wounds, one I call *the pain of having caused pain*. You see, when I first embraced recovery, my "addict" was desperately trying to survive and barraging me with so many mind tricks that it was difficult to expand my vision beyond my immediate reality.[21] Once I survived the initial weeks of withdrawal and my sanity was reawakened, my ability to empathize started to re-develop. It was then that regret came flooding in. Regret that I had…

- Pushed Robin's thorns even deeper into her sensitive soul.
- Withdrawn emotionally for years.
- Missed milestones and hurts that I should have picked up on in my children's spiritual and social development.

Knowing that I inflicted these wounds made them no less painful. My heartbreak was multiplied by the embarrassment and shame from so many bad choices. Yes, I had willfully chosen lies, secrets and betrayal. The decisions were mine and mine alone.

Robin has told me that she finally came to see that I had a sort of thorn in the flesh, an unwanted sexual vulnerability to temptation due to my own wounds. I'm finding that understanding thorns, like Paul's painful thorn in the flesh, can be of great value. In his case and in mine, they remind me of God's love that he has lavished on me through Christ (1 JOHN 3:1). Thorns are also messengers of humility. If ever I am tempted to take pride in the way God has used me, the prick of an embedded thorn quickly snaps me back into the reality that anything good that has come from my life is only through his grace.

While thorns pricked me with emotional pain that contributed to decades of self-medicating addictive behaviors, thorns now serve to keep me grounded. They remind me of the reality of emotional pain and allow me to be empathetic with Robin, my friends, and those I am seeking to help. Thorns also keep me humble and remind me that without God I would have done even more damage and ultimately shipwrecked my marriage and my soul. So I will embrace the pain of thorns and look forward to the next life where God will remove them because in the presence of God's perfect love, they will serve no purpose.

> *He will wipe every tear from their eyes. There will be no more death or mourning or crying or pain, for the old order of things has passed away.* REVELATION 21:4

Back to Your Journal:

Dave distinguishes between thorns than came from his own childhood and thorns that he inflicted.

Choose one or two of the people who have hurt you most. What thorns do you know of that were in their childhood? How might that help give you some insight into their struggles?

For Jesus came full of grace
From his mouth comes truth
He shields our tender places
His hands hold the victory

STONE THREE
Unturned Soil: Triggers

Sorrow oftentimes is God's plough. We dread
pain and shrink from it [...] the plough tears
its way with its keen, sharp blade, through our
hearts—and we say we are being destroyed!
— J.R. MILLER[22]

Riding in the car to our first couple's counseling appointment with our church mentor, I asked Dave if I could read out loud from *False Intimacy* by Harry Schaumburg. Flipping through the table of contents, I carefully searched for just the right thing. These opportunities didn't come often. Finding one called "The Recovering Marriage," I flipped there and began to read. The chapter started with a story about a couple named Ron and Judy. Dave and I were both intrigued by some uncanny similarities. They had met in Bible college. Dave and I met at Harding University where Dave was studying Hebrew and Greek and I was studying Social Work and Bible. Like us, they had given their lives to full-time ministry...in fact, they had served for twenty years. Like me, Judy's life had been shaken when she discovered a history of sexual immorality (in Ron's case, an extensive background of sex with prostitutes). Ron had fallen hard and often, and he had hidden his falls from Judy over a twenty-year time period.[23]

Pausing for a moment to take a deep breath, I silently reminded myself that Dave's falls were different. After all, he sought help again and again from friends and spiritual advisors to no avail. The time in between Dave's struggles spanned from two days to two years. Yet, the story of Ron and Judy was quickly surfacing pain. I urged myself to be thankful that Dave wanted to engage recovery together. I asked Dave if he was still able to follow me reading, and he assured me that he was.

Picking back up where I left off, I was relieved to read that Schaumburg had confronted Ron boldly about his adulterous lifestyle and the devastation he had inflicted on his wife. Ron was angry at first, but then considered Schaumburg's words and came back to the second session, "humbled and ready to face any consequence."

My relief fled, as I sighed a little. I wasn't so sure that any man with so many falls could be contrite that quickly. Although Schaumburg trusted Ron's repentance, I wasn't so sure. So, when Schaumburg tuned his attention to Judy, I felt my blood pressure go up a little. I kept reading...

> *For Judy, a battle raged in her soul between the desire for real intimacy and the resentment that came from betrayal, agony, and all the uncertainty real intimacy presented. She was sorely tempted to [...] try to control, survive or salvage the situation. But no one is prepared to handle such massive fallout. It is like dealing with a nuclear reactor meltdown (p. 137).*

Schaumburg then explained how Judy would need to honestly face the devastation of her husband who had "lived a lie and [had] a heart that felt justified in doing so." But she would also need to face her own battles, as he says:

60

*Judy needed to take a long hard look at the perversity of
her husband's heart—not just a glimpse followed by the
natural desire to run and hide…but even that was not
enough. Judy also had to look deeply at her own heart in
order to resist denial and avoid self-pity (p. 137).*

I shifted in my seat, uncomfortable. Was Schaumburg
insinuating, through Judy, that I had a role in all of this? A
couple of pages later he answered my question. Schaumburg
explained that the reason we choose false intimacy is because
we long for simplification. False intimacy is an illusion woven
by the father of lies, Satan. This illusion holds that certain
actions or thoughts, explicitly forbidden by God, hold great
power to give us satisfaction and relief from emotional pain.
False intimacy gives an illusion of predictability and control—
an illusion that we can make life work outside of God. And this
"simplification is the intention of the human heart unbroken by
sorrow, gratitude, and the admission of utter weakness before
God (p. 142)." But what Schaumburg said next shocked me.

*The same spiritual battle rages in the heart of a spouse
crushed by unfaithfulness. It is much simpler for the
spouse to withdraw from the marital relationship once
the masturbation, pornography, or affair is discovered
than to enter the tumultuous waters of godly sorrow,
gratitude and brokenness […] Who is more miserable
than the woman or man betrayed by a friend or spouse?
But the misery that cloaks a betrayed spouse's justified
self-protection is not that different from the offending
spouse's sin of self-protection. Neither spouse's self-
centered behavior will lead to a more intimate marriage
(pp. 142-143).*

61

Suddenly, I closed the book and flung it into the backseat (it took everything within me not to throw it out the window). Pure rage washed over me. "I don't agree with that!" I said angrily. Dave raised his eyebrows, but, wisely, didn't say a word. Not yet understanding myself, or where my reactions came from, I wasn't only tempted to be mad at the author of the book, but also at Dave, who might dare to think that I was just as guilty as him of sabotaging our relationship. I longed for Dave to reassure me that it wasn't my fault, but was scared to step out into such vulnerable conversation when my emotions were heightened.

What I didn't yet understand was that the intensity of the moment sprang from a thorny tangle of pain, both past and present. First of all, I had made a kind of transfer from Schaumburg's seemingly quick acceptance of Ron's repentance to my own situation. In the moment, it was hard to separate them from us. I had also been triggered into a childhood where, as the firstborn daughter, I was always the responsible one. In the painful years, I was the one who worked hard to maintain the façade of a happy family, taking the chores no one else would take. But, you see, through taking responsibility for the impression our family made (something a daughter cannot control), I also took on the shame of the dysfunction. In the light of these losses, accepting Schaumburg's version of recovery seemed threatening. Dave was in an impossible situation where anything he said or didn't say could come across as defensiveness.

Finding a new way to communicate would require both of us allowing God to till the soil of our hearts, revealing the self-protection we used to insulate ourselves from further pain. Only then could we begin to see triggers at work. Now, I'm able to understand that triggers serve a powerful purpose in my life, revealing unplowed ground in my heart—long neglected places from my past where Jesus wants to plant a new harvest of righteousness.

Breaking up the unplowed ground

Sow righteousness for yourselves, reap the fruit of unfailing love, and break up your unplowed ground; for it is time to seek the Lord, until he comes and showers his righteousness on you. Hosea 10:12

It doesn't take much gardening savvy to understand that planting seeds in unturned ground is very unlikely to produce a harvest. Almost impossible. First of all, the seed needs water and warmth in order to release the hard exterior. Well-tilled soil allows moisture and nutrients to enter the seed. Turning the soil also allows room for the tiny growth coming out of a seed to send out roots that draw in additional nourishment.

This helps me understand Hosea 10:12 a little better. God instructed the Israelites to break up the unplowed ground in their hearts in order to be ready for the work he wanted to do in them. The Hebrew word for unplowed is *nir*, meaning land that is unusable because it has not been tilled. God was urging his wandering people to look deeper, face the ways they'd shut him out in their pain and become hardened, unusable and unable to dig deep to find his righteousness.

Untilled ground is also an apt description of where we are at risk in the wake of abandonment, addiction and abuse. I've seen this within the marriages Dave and I have counseled. In the light of mutual promises made at the marriage altar, betrayal is utterly devastating. Pretty much every partner has described all-consuming thoughts of a different life without this pain.

63

How could he or she be living with me (and with our children), making like everything is fine, when they are decimating our relationship by impurity?

I've also seen it with unmarried women who've come to me for perspective. As we've gone deep together, I've helped them identify mechanisms they've developed to avoid pain. Many fear that whatever rejection they have suffered is an indictment on them—that they are not worthy of faithfulness, sacrifice or true love. Secretly they sometimes wonder whether God blesses other women relationally while withholding from them.

For all of us, after traumatic relational losses, it is tempting to find ways to avoid anything that reminds us of these wounds. So we choose not to expose them by "stirring the soil." These unplowed plots of unhealed losses hurt us relationally. They become a nesting place for thorns, as the evil one whispers that we should distrust others. Satan's goal? To keep us from the deeper work that God does through our relationships.

So it's easy to see how bewildering triggers can be when they drive us to the very places of our past pain, places we had hoped to never again return. Rather than face this hurt, we use human devices to keep the ground from being turned…

Let me numb myself.

Let me run far away.

Let me yell at the pain and call it names.

Let me distance myself from you, until you prove you are perfectly safe.

Let me strike out—if I inflict pain on you, perhaps you will understand how much you've hurt me.

The parable of the sower resonates with me here. I've begun to see that this parable speaks volumes to me about how I address my pain:

> *Listen then to what the parable of the sower means:*
> *When anyone hears the message about the kingdom and*
> *does not understand it, the evil one comes and snatches*
> *away what was sown in their heart. This is the seed sown*
> *along the path. The seed falling on rocky ground refers*
> *to someone who hears the word and at once receives it*
> *with joy. But since they have no root, they last only a*
> *short time. When trouble or persecution comes because of*
> *the word, they quickly fall away. The seed falling among*
> *the thorns refers to someone who hears the word, but the*
> *worries of this life and the deceitfulness of wealth choke*
> *the word, making it unfruitful. But the seed falling*
> *on good soil refers to someone who hears the word and*
> *understands it. This is the one who produces a crop,*
> *yielding a hundred, sixty or thirty times what was sown.*
> MATTHEW 13:18-23

In one of Charles Spurgeon's essays, he talks about the first soil that Jesus addresses, the path, as being those who don't have room for the word of God. But Spurgeon believes the path also applies to believers, those who no longer hear the Spirit's nudging due to a hard shell of protection around their hearts. Spurgeon describes those who listen but can't let the words in because "a secret armor blunts every dart, and no wound is felt."[24] I relate. Oh, yes…like when I got so mad at Harry Schaumburg that I wanted to throw *False Intimacy* out of the window. Even the insinuation that I might have had some soul-examining to do was disorienting. I already had protections in place.

Yet through Schaumburg's words, I sensed that God was gently nudging me to take a look inward. *Robin, let me turn the unplowed soil of past hurts and pains, so I can heal you.* God knew that unturned, unplowed ground in my heart could create spiritual trigger points—deeply painful, constricted places in my heart/soul/spirit that send out warnings whenever something brushes up against them.

Physical trigger point: A predictable response to some chronic stress or vulnerability in the body.

Spiritual trigger point: A predictable response to a chronic pain or vulnerability in the soul, mind or heart.

How does this work? To gain some clarity let's look to the very way God knit us together in our mother's womb…our physiology.

Triggers: a pathway to healing

> *"Eve, you are precious in my sight. I've called you by name and created you for my glory. Follow me to the places you are afraid to go." His call resonates through my entire being. It is a call of love. Jehovah is fighting for me, not warring against me.* Eve's Song, *p. 107*

I'm convinced that God embedded triggers into our very makeup as a doorway to healing. For insight, let's take at look at our physical bodies—another place where triggers exist.

There are two types of pain in our bodies—muscle pain and skin pain. Muscle pain is more complex than pain arising in the skin. When something cuts your skin, you immediately know the cause, location and severity of the wound. Muscle pain isn't so easy to track down. Most muscle pain is referred from a different site in the body, whereas virtually no skin pain is referred.[25] Skin pain takes place right at the site of injury. Muscle pain usually originates someplace different than where it shows up. This is where trigger points come in.

Trigger points have been called "the great mimics," since the pain doesn't originate in the place that's screaming out. It's been conjectured that *seventy to eighty-five percent of our muscle pain actually comes from triggers.*[26]

Where do triggers come from? Picture a muscle as a combination of long strands, with tiny microscopic pumps called sarcomeres moving blood and oxygen through them. Every muscle has a belly. In the belly there are nerve receptors that protect the muscle by alerting the brain of anything that could cause damage. When a muscle contracts too heavily (an injury) or over an extended period of time (stress), the strands compress, and then stay closed, preventing the nerve receptors and sarcomeres from doing their work. This point of contraction is called a trigger point. Oxygen-starved tissues and accumulating waste products cause the trigger point to refer pain somewhere able to express it.[27] The constricted nerves send the pain to a place where it can be expressed.

That's why body workers specializing in trigger point therapy have huge charts in their offices tracking muscles and nerves. Their specialty is finding those compressed muscles and releasing them, so they can speak for themselves.

How does this apply to spiritual recovery? Triggers also appear in our mental and emotional centers as one of the after effects of trauma. In fact, what we've learned about physical triggers can teach us much about spiritual triggers (see the chart on the following page for insight).

Physical Trigger	Spiritual Trigger
Constriction in a muscle refers pain to other places in the body.	Current pain presses on past pain buried within the soul, memories or emotions.
Pain sends us chasing down symptoms, when the real problem lies elsewhere.	Past pain amplifies the pain of current situations, causing us to over-react or over-simplify.
We unconsciously compensate, losing flexibility and circulation.	We compensate spiritually, by closing off sensitive memories, becoming more rigid or controlling.
The irritated muscle cuts off its own blood supply, complicating healing.	Panic muddies our thinking and makes it more difficult to hear God's spirit, complicating our response.
We unconsciously begin to guard against more pain.	We unconsciously guard against more pain or medicate with addictive behaviors. We create "unplowed ground" in our hearts.
Triggers help explain mysterious aches and pains.	Triggers help explain "unspiritual" and out-of-character responses.
Healing the trigger point requires releasing constricted muscles through pressure.	The trigger loses its power as Jesus releases the injury, as we mourn with him.

The roadmap of healing embedded in triggers is part of the marvelous way God created us. Let's take trauma (our first Stone). The remnants of post-traumatic stress can remain for decades. Why? Not because God delights in our suffering.* Rather, I'm convinced that Jesus, the great physician, cares about his children's lingering wounds. Triggers lead me to those buried wounds, allow me to mourn them, and release them.

68

* *Though he brings grief, he will show compassion, so great is his unfailing love. For he does not willingly bring affliction or grief to anyone.*
LAMENTATIONS 3:33

One of my common childhood experiences was falling asleep in our tiny three-bedroom house to the noise of the television on the opposite side of the wall. I've always had sensitive hearing, so the television shows playing made it difficult to sleep. Unfortunately, from my bed I could also hear word-for-word the expletive-loaded arguments between my parents. As they fought, my two younger sisters wept in their beds.

But here's where understanding the nature of a trigger can be helpful. Decades later, the noise of a television at night still made me feel slightly agitated, helpless or even a little testy. These feelings of helplessness caused tension between Dave and me. When Dave would turn on the sports to check on his team, I would sigh a little, and ask if we could turn it down or even off. After we had a few tense words, he might just go to the family room where he could watch it in peace. I knew he meant well. But to my triggered brain, it seemed like he didn't care about me. I felt lost and abandoned. To drain the trigger, I needed to make the connection between my feelings about the television in my marriage and my distress as a young girl. Much of the helplessness I felt as an adult was referred pain from my childhood. As I talked about it with Dave, it gave us a chance to deepen our trust and intimacy. As a result, Dave and I agreed that late night television in the bedroom wasn't best for us. (And if for some reason, we want to take exception, we'll talk before either of us turns on the television.)

So how does this apply in the wake of another person's fall? Being triggered means that your reaction is influenced not just by the event that brings it forth, but also by repressed pain from your past and pain from other present circumstances (referred pain). These triggers might include:

1) Past pain from someone who hurt you. For instance, your partner's current boundary break could trigger old fear from a larger, deeper fall in the past.

2) The pain of past hurts from other significant people, like your immediate family members. Or painful present situations trigger unresolved past abandonment, addiction or abuse.

3) Referred pain from other hurtful, unresolved present circumstances *unrelated* to whoever hurt you.

For me, wrestling through the pain of current situations has brought up many painful past memories: early sexual abuse, the performance mentality I used for security, early insecurities about my worth, verbal abuse from my father, finding myself in compromising situations with men, and more.

What we learned about the body and triggers is quite instructive here. Just as there are predictable ways that the body refers pain, there are predictable trigger responses that can alert us our current pain is being magnified by other related losses (see the chart below).

Trigger response	Might come out as...
Guard and freeze	I either throw shame at the one who hurt me (guard) or totally disengage (freeze).
Magnify the results	I use what they did to me to define *everything* about them and about our relationship, and always will.
Act out	I'll do anything to feel connected, putting myself in situations that lead to temptation or sexual sin.
Jump and shout	I overreact to small offenses. Adrenalin courses through my body when I'm touched or confronted.

Trigger response	Might come out as...
Revert to childhood	I act like a child: throwing a tantrum or hiding away. I put up walls to keep others out.
Judge the fall	I see their actions as equivalent to murder. *As a murderer, you deserve whatever I do or don't do.*

These responses may be completely out of character (a sure sign that a trigger is involved). Triggers bring panic as the body, mind or soul registers a threat. This anxiety decreases the oxygen going to our brain, clouding our thinking and decision making ability. This explains some of my reactions when I'm triggered: blaming, demanding, withholding, controlling, or even just being really grumpy.

But triggers are not valid excuses to justify pouring abuse on others, for instance thinking... *I can say anything I want in the wake of your behavior.* Triggers do not justify picking up our weapons to hurt the one who hurt us...*I am triggered so I can pull the trigger...hit you, throw things or slander you to others.* Rather, triggers help us understand ourselves. By graciously being curious about our own behavior, we can then find grace for the person and circumstances that are triggering us. This prepares us to apologize when we've caused damage and humbly listen to the other person's perspective.

With Jesus as our guide, triggers serve as a lighted pathway to long-buried wounds that are ready to be healed. As in Stone one (trauma) and Stone two (thorns), triggers have a beautiful redemptive side.

The Stone of triggers

*Family relationships trigger childhood wounds, and
those wounds often trump our rational thinking.
We can't "rationally" transcend the kind of primal
pain that such relationships can arouse.*
— MARIANNE WILLIAMSON

Triggers require effort to expose and explain to others. But yet, in the processing of triggers comes great knowledge. Triggers provide a light in the darkness guiding us towards true intimacy rather than away from it. So how does this work practically speaking? We need to develop communication tools that allow others to understand when triggers are in play. Since that early first counseling session, Dave and I have worked hard to implement the language of triggers into our relationship. When I want to explain my pain to Dave, he is better able to hear me when I admit that it doesn't all come from him.

The beginning of our conversation might go something like this. (I've added my feelings and thoughts in parentheses, so you can see how tricky these conversations can feel.)

Me: *(Feeling anxious and heavy about needing to talk. I remember the tool I use of admitting my fear, and how that opens Dave up to hearing me.)* Honey, I need to talk to you for a moment. I'm a little scared to talk about it, but it would help me if you could just hear me out.

Dave: I hear you. *(He glances up from his computer and smiles to reassure me.)* What's up?

Me: *(A wave of emotion rushes over me. I take a deep breath, not wanting to start crying.)* You remember earlier when we were having that kind of painful conversation, and suddenly you got up and walked out of the room? That triggered me back to when I was a little girl.

Dave: Really? Help me understand, Honey.

Me: *(When I pause, Dave's eyes go to his computer. I wait for a minute until Dave notices I'm waiting and closes his computer. My hands are shaking a little.)* My parents didn't allow painful emotions. When we were sad, we might even get punished because we weren't doing what my dad wanted. I felt like the unseen child, who learned not to talk about my feelings. Instead I went somewhere alone to protect myself.

Dave: *(Giving his full attention. In his eyes I see empathy.)* I'm so sorry they treated you that way.

Me: *(Still I'm not convinced Dave can understand how much pain this caused me and how much it relates to us. I press on, even though it is hard.)* So I just wanted you to understand that, although you don't mean it, when you walk out like that, it triggers me back to this feeling of emotional abandonment. And I'm tempted to shut down and hide my feelings from you.

Dave: *(In a reassuring voice.)* I'm sorry honey. Really, I just thought of something that needed to be done and I was anxious to finish it. It didn't have anything to do with you. I want you to feel safe with me.

73

Me: *(This is where it gets really hard for me. Part of me doesn't want to let go, because it seems like I'm letting go of something much bigger. But I push out the words, knowing they will help both of us.)* I forgive you.

Dave: *(Notices that I am still sitting there, now wiping away a fear tears. He glances as his computer and I read his action as his wanting this conversation over. Still I do see he is fighting to stay with me.)* Was there anything more you wanted to say? Did we cover it all?

Me: *(I want to be righteous, but I also know this is bigger than Dave realizes. This is a pattern for us, and one that hurts me. I try to think of a way to say it that doesn't back Dave into a corner.)* I think this is a pattern for us. How would you like me to handle it if it happens again?

Dave: *(Pauses for a second and thinks. I sense he wants me to know that he is hearing me. He smiles and I notice that his eyes are smiling too.)* Just gently remind me. I do want to give you my full attention.

Me: *(I still feel like there is more to say, but I can't figure out what in the moment. I decide to let it rest for now and accept Dave's humble response. We hug.)*

Of course, there are times when Dave is the one trying to explain a trigger, and I'm the one struggling to stay with him. My tendency is to get impatient instead of giving Dave the time and space he needs to figure it out. To be sure, this kind of talk feels awkward at first, like you are learning a brand new language. And as you can see from my internal wrestling, it is difficult to communicate when a trigger is in play. Go gently with other people as you try out talking about triggers. You might need to reassure them that you aren't attacking, but rather seeking to understand yourself better. When conversations get messy, do remember that Jesus is by your side. Ask him to use your triggers to teach you about yourself and about him. You see, Jesus is the only one who can shield your tender places. His insight, love and redemption are where you'll find victory.

Grace calls

> *I'll go ahead of you, clearing and paving the road.*
> *I'll break down bronze city gates, smash padlocks,*
> *kick down barred entrances. I'll lead you to buried*
> *treasures, secret caches of valuables—confirmations*
> *that it is, in fact, I, God, the God of Israel who*
> *calls you by name.* ISAIAH 45:2-3 (MSG)

This vivid illustration comforts me when the darkness seems just too great. I love the thought of my God clearing roads and kicking down barred doors in order to give me secret treasure. Take a moment right now to visualize God going to battle with you. At your invitation, picture God removing padlocks from your repressed emotions and disarming heavily barred entrances to old memories. Imagine your surprise as you easily open the bronze gates of performance and perfectionism that kept your vulnerabilities hidden. Grace whispers…*I see you and know you inside and out, including every trigger. I won't hurt you. Trust me and I'll bring pure gold out of your trials.*

In a mysterious way that isn't always readily apparent, Jesus understands your triggers. Remember when his disciples kept falling asleep in the Garden of Gethsemane at his moment of need, when he was overwhelmed to the point of death? Did

75

memories come flashing back of his mother and brothers, standing at the door of a home he was ministering in, demanding that he leave with them, thinking he was out of his mind? Did he remember all the people who were near him but never really saw him? Listened to him speak but never really understood him? Accepted healing from him but weren't willing to stand up for him? I truly believe that Jesus knows all about our troubles *and* triggers! And if you listen closely, you'll hear his grace serenading you with the very love song you yearn for.

> *My child, I see you. I know your pain. And oh, if*
> *you could only glimpse the treasures I have for you—*
> *treasures I've chosen specifically for you that speak*
> *to the pain of your battles and your heart's needs.*

Your spiritual journey

Congratulations! You have now walked with Jesus through the first three Stones of recovery: trauma, thorns and triggers. I'm hoping you see that the darkness isn't quite so dark with God beside you. Regardless, I'd encourage you to stay engaged. You see, after darkness comes the second leg of this journey: re-creation. Re-creation holds more pain, but all that you've learned as you've stepped from trauma to thorns to triggers will be there to help you. Re-creation also holds a generous helping of hope!

Circle of stones: triggers

By now, you have two stones: trauma and thorns. It's time to find a third stone to join them and write the word **triggers** on it.

Now look at your three stones. Have you ever heard the saying that troubles come in threes? Are your stones similar or different? Which of the three stones feels weightiest to you? Now hold the stone of triggers by itself. What triggers come to mind?

As you accumulate stones, you might want a special place to put them. You might find a jar for them, or even a special box. Or perhaps you want to line them up on a bookshelf. Remember, these stones of darkness don't need to be hidden away. They are stepping stones to glory.

Journaling: Triggers

What have you learned about triggers in this Stone? Skim back through the Stone searching for what most stood out.

Open your journal and make a list of the primary lessons you've learned about triggers. Then make a second list: things you've learned about yourself. You might even want to put these into two columns so that you can easily see the connection between intellectual learning and how you are applying these lessons to your spiritual journey.

A word from Dave — Triggers

My dear brothers and sisters, take note of this: Everyone should be quick to listen, slow to speak and slow to become angry, because human anger does not produce the righteousness that God desires. JAMES 1:19-20

Understanding triggers is an essential piece of successfully navigating the treacherous waters of recovery within relationships. The most common sign of a trigger is when a person's response to a situation seems to be stronger than would be expected. When Robin is triggered because of something I have said or done, my ingrained core belief (fear about being good enough to be loved) makes me want to run and hide, throw up walls of defensiveness, or possibly strike back in anger or sarcasm. If I give in to this impulse and get defensive, or if I am resistant to sharing my feelings about what might have caused my amplified response, it strengthens her trigger. And yes, I too am now experiencing my own trigger, leaving us in a situation that could turn very ugly! Staying emotionally present with Robin when she is triggered is my biggest challenge. Although I may be the clear offender in a situation, my own losses might make me vulnerable to being triggered into a place of extreme shame accompanied by self-pity. Obviously, our responses to triggers have the potential to become barriers that block us from deep and healthy interactions. Oh, how I wish that all our conversations could go like the one Robin shared in this chapter!

There are two sides to the trigger dilemma. First, I need to identify when my wife is being triggered and to respond in a compassionate way. Secondly, I have to reach for the humility and insight I need to see and communicate about my own triggers. Personally, it's easier for me to see the trigger in someone else than in myself.

Identifying when Robin is being triggered allows me to carry only my part of her pain. This also allows me to be empathetic with her, exploring her pain, rather than retreating into my own pain. These are sacred moments when I need to take a deep breath, and say a silent prayer, and become curious instead of reactionary. I've learned to move forward with a gentle question. "Honey, it seems like you may be having some strong feelings. Is this just my imagination?" Blurting out in an accusatory tone, "Are you being triggered?" may not go so well. The evil one loves to turn triggers into further pain and disconnection through defensive responses.

A trigger is an opportunity to learn something important about my partner. Underneath her reaction may be the memory of pain from her growing up, or a memory of some way that I hurt her in the past. My gentleness might allow her to access this memory and find insight and healing. Sometimes, Robin's triggers come from external stimuli, like driving past a strip club and being reminded of my infidelity. Since we live in a sexually charged world, these triggers can be particularly difficult to avoid. Conversations we have after counseling others can also be triggering as Robin may unintentionally relive her own wounds as she listens to the wounds of another. If she is triggered back to a pain I caused, the best thing I can do is to say, "Honey, I'm so sorry my sin still causes you this pain."

Perhaps even more difficult is facing my own triggers. When Robin senses my response is out of proportion to the situation, she commonly asks, "Have you ever felt this way before?" This gives me a gentle nudge to look underneath my own responses. It is an opportunity for her to understand me better, if I can go there with her. Sometimes, the part of me that is still sensitive wants to say, "No, you are wrong this time. This is one-hundred percent about this current situation." I've learned instead to ask

79

for time. I might say, "Honey, please let me think about this. I'm not convinced there is more here, but I'll think about it." After I've given it consideration and prayer, I can circle back to her, ready to talk on a deeper level.

As Robin noted, our understanding of triggers was slow to come on both sides. After we understood triggers, it took even more effort to learn how to communicate about them. One of our missions in helping others is to help them gain this skill much earlier in the recovery process. Like Robin, I'm convinced that triggers serve a redemptive purpose in our lives. Surely God embedded them in our nature as signposts to lead us to unresolved pain. He alerts us to these pockets of pain in order to bring us a deeper level of healing.

As for me, I've needed to accept that I have wounded Robin in traumatic ways, and that in this life, she may never be fully "over it," even though she has undoubtedly forgiven me. I take comfort that I serve the God of all comfort who is able to use our story to comfort others and bring glory to him.

Back to Your Journal:

Write a few practical applications you've learned from Dave's words. How did you see yourself or your relationships?

PART TWO
Re-Creation

"Though the heartfelt mercies of our God,
God's Sunrise will break in upon us,
shining on those in the darkness,
though sitting in the shadow of death,
Then showing us the way, one foot at a time,
down the path of peace.[*]

[*] LUKE 1:78-79 (MSG)

STONES FOUR TO EIGHT
Re-Creation

Healing is impossible in loneliness; it is the opposite
of loneliness…to be healed we must come with all
the other creatures to the feast of Creation.
— WENDELL BERRY, *THE ART OF THE*
COMMONPLACE: THE AGRARIAN ESSAYS

Welcome to Stones Four to Eight: the stones of new creation.
To prepare for re-creation, let's take a moment to honor the
foundations we've laid. Stones one to three—trauma, thorns
and triggers—helped us to look inwards and take stock of all
we bring into this journey. After all, if we are asking God for
healing, it makes sense that we'd *especially* want to bring our
losses to his loving light.* Part one called us to examine the soil
of our hearts, excavate the rocks and turn the hard soil we've
packed down lest we be hurt again. We reflected on the wisdom
of Jesus, who said that he must fall to the ground and die, so
that fruit could come.** I hope that you, like me, find comfort
in knowing we are going somewhere Jesus went first: "Whoever
serves me must follow me; and where I am, my servant also will

83

* *But the light makes all things easy to see, and everything that is made easy to*
see can become light. This is why it is said: "Wake up, sleeper! Rise from death,
and Christ will shine on you." EPHESIANS 5:13–14 (NCV)
** *Very truly I tell you, unless a kernel of wheat falls to the ground and dies, it*
remains only a single seed. But if it dies, it produces many seeds. JOHN 12:24

be. My Father will honor the one who serves me."* Hopefully, you now view your pain with more tenderness and curiosity. Are you sensing that your Father honors your courage in embracing this journey?

This middle stage, *Re-Creation*, builds on this knowledge. With Jesus out in front, you can be confident that this journey won't lead on a path too steep to climb. It may, however, be tempting at points to shift back to old familiar habits rather than risk changing. If you get overwhelmed, simply turn your eyes back to Jesus, steady yourself on the Stone where you stand, and keep putting one foot in front of the other. Jesus knows your yearning for something new, the redemption of your losses. But if you are honest with yourself, the repair needed is beyond your human capability. If none of us can fully redeem ourselves, how can we expect to redeem someone we love?**

You'll find that the Stones ahead not only relate to the consequences of other people's decisions, but also to choices you've made. God can simultaneously drain the pain of offences committed against us, while gently bringing our own self-centered responses into view. Although this stirring of the soil of our hearts can be painful, I've learned to see it as a benefit of this journey of recovery. Be assured that re-creation doesn't require losing the essence of you. As a master restorer, he brings out the true individual beauty he created in us. In my case, recovery has brought new perspective, greater patience, deeper convictions, deeper mourning, more vulnerable relationships, as well as more laughter and relational gifts. Ultimately, re-creation is an act of God's grace. And that grace has been present since the beginning of creation.

84

---

* JOHN 12:26
** *No one can redeem the life of another or give to God a ransom for them.*
PSALM 49:7

Why re-creation?

*See, I will create new heavens and a new earth. The
former things will not be remembered, nor will they
come to mind.* ISAIAH 65:17

God began opening my heart to the idea of re-creation in
May 2008, when I spoke at the Pepperdine Bible Lectureships in
Malibu, California. I had just started writing a book exploring
the losses of the first woman, Eve. I was intrigued to find a class
taught by Dr. Charles Rix titled "Loss, Grief and Re-Creation."
When I entered the small classroom, it quickly became obvious
that the twenty or so people who chose this class had all been
touched deeply by sorrow. Many were literally hunched over
with grief. There was no chatter, just complete quiet, as we
waited for Dr. Rix to begin. It felt like everyone in the room was
collectively holding their breath. *Will I find answers here?*

He began with a story. Ten or so years earlier at this very
lectureship, Dr. Rix's wife had found a suspicious spot on her
skin that turned out to be melanoma. After successful treatment
and years of remission, another spot appeared. Several short
months later...she was gone. Suddenly Dr. Rix felt the bottom
fall from under him. Long months passed and he still struggled
to put one foot in front of the other. As a scholar in Biblical
Hebrew, his shame was multiplied. It seemed the very spiritual
light that others had long sought from him had disappeared. All
was darkness. His friends and family were worried he may not
pull out of the depression that settled in. Finally, he remembered
that the book of Genesis was written for the Jews, as a book
of hope in their time of despair, division and disillusionment.
Turning to Genesis he began to read anew:

In the beginning God created the heavens and the earth. Now the earth was formless and empty, darkness was over the surface of the deep, and the Spirit of God was hovering over the waters. GENESIS 1:1–2

Dr. Rix explained that the words "formless and empty" come from a Hebrew phrase that is just used once in the Bible—*Tohu va bohu*, representing a darkness so deep, a chaos so complete, that a phrase had to be created to describe it. Yet the Spirit of God was hovering nearby, ready to work. Dr. Rix's heart began to lift as he started to envision God in a new way, as a sort of chaos slayer. As he read on and on in Genesis, he began to see that the same God who created the world could also re-create him in the face of his loss, grief and despair. Chaos isn't an obstacle to God—rather its substance is his raw materials.

After the lesson, I waited until every other person in the room had a chance to talk to Dr. Rix. Finally, it was my turn. Thanking him for his profound insights, I began explaining to him my theory about Adam and Eve—biblically that their story was one of redemption. I'll never forget his words, "Robin, you're really on to something important. You've got to write that book!"

Tohu va bohu has come to be a beacon of hope for me over the years as loss after loss has rolled over my head. Although Dave and I had turned the corner well before that lectureship, there would still be years where chaos would seem to hover nearby, sometimes flooding into our relationship at the most unexpected moments. There would be crushing setbacks and heart-numbing losses. Times when I would cry out to God while literally bowed over with grief, "God you must think I can handle a lot! How could any one person make it through so much pain?" Now God has redeemed our individual battles and brought purity out of a marriage scarred by sexual infidelity. Light out of darkness. Peace out of chaos. And that gives me hope for the unanswered questions that still lie ahead.

Now when I read GENESIS 1 and 2, I see a God whose creative materials aren't necessarily the materials I would have chosen. How about you? Would you have chosen darkness as the raw materials of light? I wouldn't have. As I shared earlier, darkness and I don't agree. Dirt as a building block for creating man and woman? I don't even like to get dirt on my hands! Would you have created great sea creatures that could awe but at the same time terrorize us? Having been stung by a jellyfish and having had a too-close encounter with a large but unaggressive shark, my answer would again be...*no thank you.*

In the phrase "God created" we see a Hebrew word only used of God...*bara. Bara* represents the creation/re-creation of life that only God can do. Creating from nothing. Starting from scratch. Even if it means getting his hands dirty. You see, God's creation is not hindered by darkness or chaos. And, just as God's creation of the great sea monsters reflected his wisdom, we can rest assured that God knows our feared monsters of the deep, the kind of relational falls that terrorize us.* In his perfect providence, he has a purpose for them.

What does this mean to you? The thought of re-creation can be scary, even intimidating, yet it streams with hope. Remember our vision in the introduction of spiritual growth as a spiral? Picture re-creation as a process with God at its very center. Each of the steps ahead can help keep you close to God, with your eyes on him. You may need to step back and forth between the Stones, or even find yourself circling back to an earlier Stone, but each time you circle back, you'll do so with new knowledge.

---

* *Praise the Lord from the earth, you great sea creatures and all ocean depths.* PSALM 148:7

Through the heartfelt mercies of our God,
God's Sunrise will break in upon us,
Shining on those in the darkness,
those sitting in the shadow of death,
Then showing us the way, one foot at a time,
down the path of peace. LUKE 1:78–79, (MSG)

Within part two of this journey, you will find five Stones: tears, spiritual warfare, dignity, acceptance and sanctuary. Let's take a moment to glance ahead and consider…why these particular stones? And why step on them in this order?

<u>Stone Four – Tears:</u> Weeping as the outgrowth of a tender, engaged, spiritually aware heart is a powerful weapon. And when we allow the full extent of our pain, we also widen the spectrum of our joy. As you step on this Stone, you'll begin to see tears less as a sign of weakness, and more as a purposeful creation of God aimed to cleanse you from losses. As you trust the redemptive power of tears, you'll begin to see vulnerability as one of your most sacred callings.

<u>Stone Five – Warfare:</u> To find this new creation will take engaging in spiritual warfare. Pain is a call to prayer that reminds us of the battle raging around us and helps us put on the armor of God.* Although none of us are exempt from his attack, we keep our eyes firmly fixed on Jesus, knowing, "greater is He who is in you than he who is in the world." (1 JOHN 4:4 NASB).

* EPHESIANS 6:10–17

Stone Six – Dignity: To protect the tender places exposed as we leave a trail of tears and engage in warfare, we'll need to set boundaries. Boundaries then help us reclaim our dignity—a dignity that doesn't depend on anyone else. It is a tender dignity that can all at once be fierce against the attacks of Satan and yet fragile, like a new shoot of a plant emerging out of the broken shell of a seed. This dignity is strongest when it flows out of your relationship with Jesus your guide, rather than springing from your own resources.

Stone Seven – Acceptance: On Stone seven, we will explore one of the accuser's most pervasive tools: shame. As someone who has experienced abandonment, you've developed some sensitive spots that could cause you to move away from others instead of towards them. On this Stone, we'll explore how the acceptance of Jesus helps us drain our well of abandonment. We will explore what it means to scorn the shame as Jesus did by choosing a higher perspective.

Stone Eight – Sanctuary: At the end of *Re-Creation*, we will enter a very sacred place, God's sanctuary. According to the Scriptures, our bodies are that very sanctuary.* This is holy ground, a place where we come to Jesus and accept wholeheartedly his plan of progressive redemption brought one step at a time. This healing will throw us on our knees before the cross, but will also transform our minds as we confidently entrust our pain to God.**

---

* *Do you not know that your bodies are temples of the Holy Spirit, who is in you, whom you have received from God? You are not your own.*
I CORINTHIANS 6:19

** *That is why I am suffering as I am. Yet this is no cause for shame, because I know whom I have believed, and am convinced that he is able to guard what I have entrusted to him until that day.* 2 TIMOTHY 1:12

Our guide to the wake

Christ gave each one of us the special gift of grace, showing how generous he is. That is why it says in the Scriptures, "When he went up to the heights, he led a parade of captives, and he gave gifts to people." EPHESIANS 4:7–9 (NCV)

Just as Jesus walked us through the first part of our journey, he will pilot us through this second part. Jesus is not only our navigator, but also the very agent of our re-creation. Yes, there will still be pain in this part of the journey—the pain of emerging into the light and suddenly recognizing ways we've maladapted to the pain. Yet pain is purposeful in God's hands. Just as a mother eagle has to often help her eaglets out of the nest by stripping the nest of all the comfortable feathers, leaves and moss, re-creation often comes only when we become so uncomfortable that we are willing to trust our fledgling wings to lift us into the air. *Are you a little unsure about what re-creation will mean and what pain it might require? Are you afraid you might lose yourself in the process?* Know that you aren't alone.

Although Jesus was one with God and was equal with God, he was willing to be re-created. Challenging thought isn't it? Re-creation for Jesus meant leaving heaven to begin again in Mary's womb as an embryo that progressively divided, multiplied and even specialized, becoming a heart that beat, blood that surged through veins, eyes able to see, ears that began to hear, synapses that fired and allowed pain. Just when he was most comfortable in this watery womb, he had to be violently pushed into a world that would eventually misunderstand, reject and crucify him. As an infant he would nurse at the breast of Mary, and then be raised in submission to loving parents who taught him to read, and to crave the very scriptures that he inspired from heaven. Truly the most stunning re-creation to ever take place was God pouring himself into the form of a human. What did that require? Humbling himself. Changing his form. Embracing weakness. Loud cries and tears. Spiritual warfare. Long nights of intercession on lonely mountains. Defining himself through God's acceptance. These foretell what we ourselves will need to walk on this path. The path of re-creation is safe because Jesus, our trusted companion, is the one who leads us there. It is safe because the Holy Spirit is hovering over the chaos left in the wake of the fall, ready to do his work of creation.

Are you ready to get started? Even as I write these words I am praying for God to give you the strength to persevere…

> *Look to yourselves (take care) that you may not lose*
> *(throw away or destroy) all that we* and *you have*
> *labored for, but that you may [persevere until you]*
> *win* and *receive back a perfect reward [in full].*
> 2 JOHN 1:8 (AMPC)

Grace will free you so that
Prayer soothes your pain
Peace guides conversation
Tears flow without shame

STONE FOUR
Trusting Pain: Tears

Heaven knows we need never be ashamed of
our tears, for they are rain upon the blinding
dust of earth, overlying our hard hearts.
I was better after I had cried, than before—more sorry,
more aware of my own ingratitude, more gentle.
— CHARLES DICKENS, *GREAT EXPECTATIONS*

SEVEN MONTHS PREGNANT, I WAS PADDING around the house making dinner, grateful that the nausea was finally behind me. The phone rang and I answered to hear, "Robin, it is Dave. I'm so embarrassed. I don't know how to tell you this, but our car has been towed. I'm going to have to pay $60 to get it out." I took a deep breath. This was money we didn't have. "So where are you, honey?" I asked. The phone went quiet. Finally, Dave spoke up, "Well, that's just it. I was towed from the parking lot of an adult bookstore." Shock shot through me. Dave continued, "I'm so sorry, honey. I don't know what to say, but I promise this won't happen again." I wrestled to think spiritually. "Well, it sounds like God is disciplining you for your sin." Thinking of Hebrews 12, I added, "And, if God is disciplining you that means that you are his son."* Dave said a friend was taking him to the towing company lot to retrieve the car. What I felt or did next is a blur. Even if I shed a few tears, by the time Dave came home I had resolved to move on.

Looking back, I had to ask myself, *Robin, why didn't you let Dave into the pain?* Perhaps, it was a survival instinct developed from the highs and lows of two years of ministry—from the joys of a quickly growing ministry (year one) to being ousted by a church eldership concerned that we were bringing in alcoholics and introducing prayer partners (year two). Afterward, God miraculously raised up a job for Dave managing a grocery store, yet the seedy location by "adult" establishments left him open to temptation. Wrestling to make ends meet financially, we shared whatever we had with others. Yes, Dave and I were faithful, but deep inside I feared that acknowledging pain gave it power—ground I wouldn't concede.

The adult bookstore incident triggered my childhood mechanisms for dealing with pain. As an extra-sensitive child, I learned quickly that too many tears were an embarrassment. Instead of comforting me, my parents would chide me, "Don't be so sensitive, Robin!" Another blow came in first grade when my teacher wouldn't let me go to the bathroom despite repeated requests. I still remember the warm liquid gathering on my chair and then dripping to the floor as the children pointed and shrieked around me. When my mother brought me clothing, I read the look on her face as irritation at the interruption to her day. As I changed clothes in the bathroom, I wiped away my tears and the realization that no one cared. I marched back into class re-clothed but emotionally guarded. A connection had been

* *My son, do not make light of the Lord's discipline, and do not lose heart when he rebukes you, because the Lord disciplines the one he loves, and he chastens everyone he accepts as his son.* HEBREWS 12:5-6

made…*if I don't let anyone in, they can't hurt me.* That and an undiagnosed case of Attention Deficit Disorder helps to explain why now, as an adult, I have almost no memories of elementary school—teachers, other students or even school experiences.

My ability to block out painful experiences was aided by my start into dance and baton around age 9, where I quickly became a prodigy. I was learning to file happy memories near the front of my memory, and stuff painful losses in a hidden compartment. My dad drifting into alcoholism starting in my preteen years went in the unsafe compartment. My world of performance became the safe side. If I brought home trophies from baton competitions, surely I was worthy of love. If I was partially tuned out at school (an unsafe place), no one could hurt me. If I buried myself in a book at home (a safe place), I wouldn't be harassed. Since my family didn't talk emotions, tears had no place except when no one was near. One night, as my mother and father screamed at each other in the next room, my two sisters wept in their beds. I put my hands over my ears and chanted softly, "I will not cry. I will not cry."

Two months after Dave's fall at that adult bookstore, we welcomed our first child with joy and moved to New Mexico to work in youth ministry. Another child came quickly after the first, and my tolerance for Dave's usage of pornography grew thin. When Dave confessed purity breeches, my angry reactions shamed him. Eventually, Dave decided to only let other men help him. I was holding my breath lest the bottom fall out. I still had a hard belly towards suffering.

What is a hard belly? In the body, a hard belly is more dangerous than a soft one. A hard belly is caused by visceral fat located in the spaces between your organs. It is tightly packed and can't move. A soft belly signals subcutaneous fat that is closer to the surface. It has room to jiggle and flex. And fat that can move has a better chance of dissolving. According to researchers a hard belly can be a ticking bomb, pointing towards serious diseases like heart disease, diabetes and high cholesterol.[28]

So my hard belly towards suffering meant that my pain was tightly packed, where it didn't breathe, didn't move. It wasn't that I never cried. There were many tears of hurt, frustration, confusion, self-hatred and self-pity. Yet true mourning evaded me. It would take twenty years of marriage before I exchanged the hard belly for a softer one—letting my emotions rise up towards the surface where they could move, jiggle and begin to diffuse.

This shift hasn't come easy. Along the journey I have accumulated shelves full of books on suffering. I have wept my way through journals and spilled trails of tears on bike paths. As I invited God to mourn with me, he became my safest place. Instead of suppressing my pain or medicating it through soft addictions,[29] I have learned to walk straight into the suffering in order to find my way out.

Rest assured, moving into the pain isn't the same as asking for suffering. Moving into the pain allows us to acknowledge the parts of our being that have been neglected. We release them as we mourn—deeming them worthy of special attention, curiosity and even honor.* But this kind of mourning will only come, as we trust the pain enough to allow it to speak to us.

97

*On the contrary, those parts of the body that seem to be weaker are indispensable, and the parts that we think are less honorable we treat with special honor. And the parts that are unpresentable are treated with special modesty, while our presentable parts need no special treatment.
1 CORINTHIANS 12:22–24

Making peace with pain

With a shiver, I realize what Jehovah sought to
teach me, that my vulnerability is my beauty. And
gratitude protects my vulnerable parts. It is my guard.
Gratitude allows the past to be a gentle teacher
instead of a harsh judge. Eve's Song, *p. 155*

Making friends with pain is kind of like praying to be humble. We're scared that if we invite suffering to pass through, that it will move in and never leave. And if we accept Satan's messages embedded in these thorns, we'll end up convinced we are bad, unworthy or unspiritual. To fight off these messages, we develop a quiver full of self-protective mechanisms. The problem is that these unhealthy habits keep us from integration, a key part of spiritual recovery. Here's my definition...

Integration is the process of accepting and
learning from all the parts of my experience,
both happy and painful. It helps me become
emotionally, relationally and spiritually whole.

You can see why a hard belly wouldn't lend itself towards integration! Where does integration start? To move from stuffing pain to integrating it, we've got to face the ways we've packed pain away by stuffing it in hidden crevices. On the body, we'd simply reach down and feel our gut. (Remember that a hard belly doesn't refer to six-pack abs! It is belly fat that is hard.) With our souls, we also require an honest look at how we respond to pain. Here's my simplified version of how spiritual and emotional pain gets turned into a hard belly:

1) **We avoid our pain.** Since messy emotions cause conflict, we devise ways to move past them or hide them. We stay on the surface with God and others, repressing our pain, pressing it down again and again.

2) **We squeeze pain into compartments.** To help us do this, we divide our day-to-day experiences into categories, for instance *good, bad, and unthinkably bad.*

3) **We compensate for pain.** When pain signals that it is still there, we turn to a variety of defense mechanisms that promise relief, from medicating to performing our way past it.

Where does all this lead? Avoiding, compartmentalizing and compensating lead to a coping mechanism called **dissociation**. Dissociation is the opposite of integration. With the advent of social media, we can all understand dissociation. Have you ever had someone (or what they posted) offend you so badly that you blocked them from seeing your social media? Dissociation is like that. *Pain, you are no longer on my friend list. I don't want to see what you think. I don't care what you have to say.* But this isn't always intentional or even within our awareness. We can *unconsciously* unfriend pain.

A phenomenon that might explain this is called Hebb's law, or "nerve cells that fire together, wire together." As Dr. Joe Dispenza explains: "If you repeatedly activate the same nerve cells, then each time they turn on, it will be easier for them to fire in unison again. Eventually, these neurons will develop a long-term relationship." These neuron clusters help form repetitive habits.[30] In other words, every time we divorce unwanted pain, the body learns and even rewires itself to accommodate our ongoing emotional repression.

99

A similar dynamic happens in the wake of abandonment, addiction or abuse. Whenever the memory of a loss washes through, we have emotional, mental and physical reactions to those hurts. If you use a coping mechanism to push away from the pain, neurons fire. The more they fire, the more they wire. With time, our brain forms a habit of pushing down pain. Dispenza says that the very repetition of our thoughts, behaviors and feelings become "automatic, unconscious habits."[31] In my thinking, this is why dissociation is so deceptive. It has a way of sneaking up on us a little bit at a time.

From the time I was a child I taught myself not to cry in the presence of others by developing well-rehearsed ways of thinking. These included… *I need to be strong. Other people will abandon me if I show weakness.* And there were more coping mechanisms that I developed in response to my father's alcoholism and my sexual abuse as a child. *No one can judge me if I don't tell. It will go away if I make up for it. One day I will wake up and it will all be gone. If I pretend to be asleep, my dad will take his belt and go away.* This created a kind of emotional fragmentation in my spirit, as well as a borderline anxiety disorder. My hard belly towards suffering was becoming an emotional time bomb.

By this point, you are probably wondering…how do I know if I also have used dissociation to cope? This list of symptoms helped me identify my own patterns:[32]

1) Feeling emotionally checked out within stressful situations.
2) Feeling separate from your body or emotions.
3) Experiencing extended periods of spacing out.
4) Extreme sensitivity to intense feelings or feeling numbed out.
5) Compulsive tendencies or excesses.

6) Extreme or excessive behaviors accompanied by self-blame.
7) Black and white thinking.
8) Inappropriate attachments to others.
9) Chronic anxiety, possibly even panic disorders.
10) Self-harm including eating disorders.
11) Intense fears.

When I first read these symptoms, I was a little stunned. I already knew that during sexual abuse, it is common for a child to separate themself from their body in order to cope with the pain. But I didn't realize that many of my relational bad habits sprang out of dissociation. Since Dave and I both brought dissociation into our marriage, it was even more complex to unravel. This double-dip of dissociation took many forms:

- **Abandonment** – leaving during intense arguments.
- **Body separation** – not being emotionally present during intimacy.
- **Self-comfort** – from addictive behaviors instead of God and each other.
- **Black and white thinking** – pegging my spouse as safe or unsafe.
- **Competitiveness** – arguments where there was one winner and one loser.
- **Emotional neglect** – when my partner was in need.

Facing the ways you've dissociated from pain can be overwhelming. But trust me here. As you dare to examine more closely how you deal with pain, you make a step forward. Once you are aware, you can make new habits through the spiritual discipline of choosing risk over self-protection. This discipline is at the heart of spiritual recovery.

Spiritual recovery: letting our wounds speak

*Sometimes in order to let the Divine enter, I must
cut myself open, find my wounds and let them
speak. (Anne Brener,* Mourning & Mitzvah*)*

Remember, in Preparing the Ground (at the beginning of the book), we talked about Jesus' teaching on what it means to be spiritual. When asked to identify the greatest commandment, Jesus told them to love God with all their heart, soul, strength and mind, and to love others as their own selves (Luke 10:26-28). Boiled down to its essence, spirituality is a process of coming into the presence of God and the presence of others. This ability to be present is one of our greatest gifts from God. Perfect intimacy would mean having every part of our being available in an interaction. Past and present would be perfectly integrated. Feelings would flow without obstruction.

None of us will ever experience perfect intimacy on this earth. Yet we can reach for true intimacy. This intimacy allows for imperfection. It grows as our guards go down and our presence goes up.[33] It is born of vulnerability. Spiritually, it helps us walk in redemptive relationships with God and others. To find this true intimacy, we've got to take down strongholds made up of neural connections that have wired together. We do this as we refuse to repress our pain. Instead, we mourn our losses and drain their power over us. And then, we ask our guide Jesus to show us the pockets of dissociation in our souls, knowing he will comfort us as the pain comes.

Personally, I've found great insight into how dissociation affects my relationship with God by applying these principles to my spiritual walk (see the chart on the following page).

Body Dissociation	Spiritual Dissociation
Emotionally checked out	I am too strong for "feelings." I only allow tears to be fleeting and then move on.
Feeling separate from your body	Being spiritual means my body (rest, health, spiritual wholeness) is a low priority.
Extended periods of spacing out	I hide my pain from others lest they judge me. I cry alone.
Deep sensitivity to intense feelings	When significant others disappoint me, I stay separate from them to avoid the hurt.
Addictive or compulsive behaviors	When pressure rises, I return to old "friends" for comfort like food, social media or shopping.
Self-criticism and self-blame	Shame and self-doubt about my spiritual life plague me, even when I seem confident.
All or nothing thinking	I'm either all in or all out, loved or unloved. Meanwhile, I fear falling off the edge.
Inappropriate attachment to others	I either cling when someone hurts me; or push away when true intimacy is offered.
Chronic anxiety and intense fears	I shift into a performance or control mode when anxiety threatens.

Are you feeling a bit overwhelmed? Wondering how to change? I have some really good news for you. The answer is simple, yet so profound. Please read this aloud. *Wounds, I am ready for you to speak to me.*

Wounds, I am ready for you to speak to me.

The only way I had the courage to begin doing this was by asking my guide Jesus to take me there. At my invitation, the master surgeon Jesus cut open my wounds, freeing them to speak.* As they spoke I mourned. And as I mourned, God comforted me. As God comforted me I began surrendering the hurt to him. You see, by giving my buried pain a voice, I reclaimed the gift of being present. The little girl Robin who was wounded in her first grade class could now safely bring her pain to the adult Robin who has Jesus by her side, and find comfort and perspective, musing...*maybe mom was irritated at the teacher, not me.* My tears (to this day) cleanse me from the buried stress that added to my fear...*you are enough for someone to care.* My tears matter to God; in fact, the Psalmist tells me that he cares enough to write them in a book, collect them in a bottle.** Our wise God embedded the path to redemption in the most unlikely place...within our pain. Our trauma, triggers and thorns help us overcome when they are surrendered to him:

<u>Trauma</u> – Forces us into a time of chaos. Chaos shifts our vision and opens up new possibilities, teaches us the value of self-care and self-love, and motivates us to seek help from others. I no longer need to stay on the surface.

<u>Thorns</u> – Take the punch away from Satan's whispers, as I allow my wounds to be drained, cleansed and redeemed. As I go deep with Jesus, I become re-associated with the truest parts of myself, including the value of my tears.

* *What God has said isn't only alive and active! It is sharper than any double-edged sword. His word can cut through our spirits and souls and through our joints and marrow, until it discovers the desires and thoughts of our hearts.* HEBREWS 4:12 (CEV)

** *You have kept count of my tossings; put my tears in your bottle. Are they not in your book?* PSALM 56:8 (ESV)

<u>**Triggers**</u> – Allow the past and present to become friends. Teach us to associate current troubles with past pains. Take the knowledge of the present and apply it to the past. As we stop putting our pain into compartments, we become whole.

To all this, I say, "Hallelujah." Only our God could take something as simple as tears to provide a way out of these complex losses. I praise God for his wisdom in giving us the most tender of Stones to step on...the Stone of Tears.

Standing on the Stone of Tears

Those who sow with tears will reap with songs of joy.
Those who go out weeping, carrying seed to sow will
return with songs of joy, carrying sheaves with them.
PSALM 126:5–6

These are precious seed, such as the husbandman sows
when corn is dear and he has but little for his family, and
therefore weeps to part with it, yet buries it under the
ground in expectation of receiving it again with advantage
(Matthew Henry's Commentary).[34]

I can't think of a more beautiful illustration of the redemptive power of tears than in Psalm 126. The psalmist's visual of someone sowing seed into the ground, but weeping as they go, refers to the Jews' tears while in captivity in Babylon. But redemption was only sweeter because of their many years of tears, as Matthew Henry says, "...at length they were brought forth with joy, and then they reaped the benefit of their patient suffering, and brought their sheaves with them to their own land, in their experiences of the goodness of God to them."[35]

To understand Psalm 126:5–6 better, let's picture a woman who has no way to feed her family except for a small amount of seed, her most valuable possession. For the seed to be usable, she has to bury it in the dark ground that she carefully prepared. She will watch daily to make sure it has moisture and pull weeds that threaten. But most of all, she will wait in the darkness of faith until the plant bursts forth as a seedling. So as she plants, she weeps. She weeps because it is so painful to let go of what is so precious. She weeps because her seed must disappear for a season. She weeps because she hopes. Yet the hope must be deferred and that makes her heart ache.* Although she weeps, she keeps sowing, showing her hope in action. I relate to her on so many levels.

In order to heal myself and bring hope to others who would follow, God asks me to sow in tears. But sowing my pain through tears isn't my first inclination. Sometimes I have to let anger wash through first so my spiritual calluses wear down enough to allow true mourning.

It takes faith to let the tears come as they may, trusting that by the miraculous working of God they have the power to heal my body, emotions and spirit.

Through Standing on the Stone of Tears again and again, I've seen God bring a harvest. Now my reactions are much more in proportion to my pain. My thinking isn't so black and white. Although I'll always be sensitive, I'm not so hypersensitive. Just as Dave hears my pain, I can hear his. But it isn't my own efforts that have brought these graces. God guards the investments each of us make in pain. He will bring a harvest as we continue to sow, especially in the darkness of our faith.

---

* *Hope postponed grieves the heart; but when a dream comes true, life is full and sweet.* PROVERBS 13:12 (VOICE)

Tears and intimacy

Before I can rest, I have one last task. I reach up,
and ignoring the nasty pricks, pull off a branch
bursting with thorns. I walk back to the white skin,
ease myself onto its creamy softness and lay the thorns
*on my chest...*Father I see now that pain is part of
your goodness. I thank you. Eve's Song, *p. 168*

Hopefully you are beginning to see tears as friends instead of enemies. But how does this relate to crying in front of someone who has hurt you? Does this give them a wrong kind of power over you? Or does it help them and you? Certainly, to cry when your partner can't show a shred of emotion puts us in a very vulnerable position. My deepest cries of mourning have been when Dave was nowhere nearby. This was mostly healthy. I worked out enormous amounts of anxiety through prayer or weeping with friends instead of heaping shame on Dave. After these times, I could tell Dave the truth without being carried away by unfiltered feelings. But at other times, crying away from Dave wasn't so healthy. Like when I would wait until Dave fell asleep and then pad quietly into a room where I could weep alone. These times reinforced barriers that would need to be taken down for us to find true intimacy.

Dave needs my tears. During our many sensitive conversations over impurity, I've shed boatloads of tears in Dave's presence, sometimes weeping into his chest. Dave says that my tears helped him in many ways. He needed my sorrow to understand how much God hurt over his sin. This is something that other men simply couldn't give him. But it also gifted him with a deeper empathy for me.

The results of a 2011 research study suggested that the emotional tears of a woman contain a chemically encoded message that causes a man's testosterone to lessen. Even though tears are odorless, sniffing tears while watching videos of women's faces or sad movies impacted participants' responses. Tears didn't increase a man's empathy (so don't be surprised if your tears don't always trigger an empathy response), but they did cause men to rate their sexual arousal as lower. Scientists confirmed this by redoing the same exact double-blind test, this time using an fMRI machine. Sure enough, the scans revealed a significant decrease in activity in the sections of a man's brain related to sexual arousal when he sniffed tears.[36]

Just the other night, Dave and I counseled a couple via Skype. When our time started they were on opposite sides of the room. As they spoke, their antagonism was obvious. Neither was hearing the other. As we gently explored each of his issues, her heart softened. When I began to speak to her about the lost little girl I saw under her shell of strength, she began to sob loudly. She had been cracked open. Seeing that her tears came from a place of deep vulnerability, her husband got up, went across the room and started rubbing her shoulders tenderly. He stayed by her for the rest of our time. It seemed that her tears allowed him to broaden his perspective, as testosterone receded.

Tears are friends, not enemies.

You see, our tears offer so much in our relationship with God, but also in our relationship with primary others (see the chart on the next page).

Our emotional tears...	Tears help to...
Signal our helplessness.[37]	Awaken the protective instinct of others.
Contain stress hormones.	Allow our body to release stress.
Excrete toxins that accumulate during stress.	Detoxify our body from the negative effects of stress.
Stimulate the production of endorphins.	Release the body's natural painkillers.
Help us process loss.	Emotionally clear sadness and other negative emotions.[38]

God created our tears to bring light to our eyes and open our hearts to the grace contained within our losses.

Grace calls

You number and record my wanderings; put my tears into Your bottle—are they not in Your book?
PSALM 56:8 (AMPC)

Stone four allows a new perspective on how God has embedded grace in your suffering. Your tears are precious to God—valuable enough to collect in a bottle. There is also a sense, as Charles Dickens postulated in *Great Expectations* (see the quote at the beginning of this Stone), that we are better after we cry. After the cleansing of tears, I am, "more sorry, more aware of my own ingratitude, more gentle." Grace calls. *I know how much you've suffered in the wake of abandonment, addiction or abuse. I've heard your cries. Your tears allow me to pour God's* *love into your heart though his Spirit.*[*] If crying just isn't your natural reaction, don't panic. The tears will come as you keep entrusting your pain to God.[**] Are your tears cloaked by anger? Grace calls. *Trust me for the strength to dig into the mourning that lies underneath. Remember that your tears are seeds in my hands— painful to sow, but able to reap a harvest of righteousness.*

Is it possible that addiction, abandonment or abuse has gifted you with a special outpouring of grace to give others? Grace calls. *Share your tears with others and you'll each learn to scorn the shame of the hurts you carry.* The promise of Psalm 126 is powerful—that if we will lift our eyes above, there will be a day when we shout for joy, carrying a harvest as God reveals the ways our sufferings have multiplied his grace to us and others.

Your spiritual journey

> *Blessed* and *enviably happy [with a happiness produced by the experience of God's favor and especially conditioned by the revelation of His matchless grace] are those who mourn, for they shall be comforted!"* MATTHEW 5:4 (AMPC)

Congratulations for stepping onto Stone four: tears. With this Stone, you step into the second part of the journey—re-creation! On the Stone of tears you are embracing the mourning that comes in the wake of the fall, trusting that your mourning will bring a revelation of God's grace. Most likely, you have shed many tears before you even came to this journey. But now it's time to claim their beauty. Remember that your guide, Jesus,

[*] *...suffering produces perseverance; perseverance, character; and character, hope. And hope does not put us to shame, because God's love has been poured out into our hearts through the Holy Spirit, who has been given to us.* ROMANS 5:3–5

[**] *For this reason I also suffer these things; nevertheless I am not ashamed, for I know whom I have believed and am persuaded that He is able to keep what I have committed to Him until that Day.* 2 TIMOTHY 1:12 (NKJV)

was a man well acquainted with sorrow, a man of loud cries and tears. He will stand beside you on this Stone. The strength you feel wash over you after a time of mourning is his arm around you. With Jesus by your side, hope appears. And even if it is a deferred hope, "Such hope never disappoints or deludes or shames us, for God's love has been poured out in our hearts through the Holy Spirit Who has been given to us."*

Here are a few practicals to help you shift your full weight onto this Stone:

1) **Work on being present.** Catch yourself when you go on autopilot. Instead, engage all your senses. Smell the air. Absorb the colors. Listen to the sounds around you. Feel the air on your clothing or skin. Be curious about any anxiety and ask it what it wants to tell you.

2) **Catch yourself when you are holding your breath.** Breathing is a powerful tool to re-establish presence. Take a deep breath before you respond in difficult conversations. When you let the breath out, release control.

3) **Work on appropriate self-comfort.** Notice if you are using social media, food, television, work, children or other pursuits to push out pain. Ask your body and spirit what they need instead.

4) **Learn how to mourn.** Ask God to teach you how to mourn and accompany you when you mourn. When mourning comes, let it wash through, knowing you will still stand with your guide Jesus.

III

* ROMANS 5:5 (AMPC)

5) **Invite others in.** Going back to painful memories can be traumatic. You might want to elicit support from other people in recovery, a trusted friend or a counselor.

Circle of stones: tears

Hopefully, you are now in the habit of gathering stones. If not, it is never too late to collect your stones. On this fourth stone you will write the word **tears**. This is a particularly sacred stone, one that you might want to find and hold the next time tears come. You might even anoint the stone with your tears.

Your stone of tears will join your other stones: trauma, thorns and triggers. Put all four stones on a table in front of you. How do they speak to each other? What does tears have to say to trauma? To thorns? To triggers?

As your stones begin to interact, you are experiencing the beginning fruits of the second part of the journey—re-creation.

Journaling: Tears

Picture Jesus sitting with you as you weep over the pain of the fall. Picture him taking your stone of tears and lifting it to his lips to kiss it, and then placing it back in your hand. Now think of Matthew 5:4: "Blessed are they that mourn for they will be comforted."

Take some time to journal about your relationship with tears…

- Are you someone who cries easily? Someone who hardly ever sheds a tear?
- What false truths have you told yourself about tears?
- What mourning do you sense you still have ahead of you?

- What does Jesus want you to know as you stand on this Stone?

A word from Dave — Tears

Tears have been a longstanding mystery to me, a source of confusion and embarrassment. Growing up, I never saw my dad or any of my male relatives cry. Even my favorite male television characters didn't whimper or bawl. I can't remember Andy Griffith, Matt Dillon of *Gunsmoke*, or Ben Cartwright of *Bonanza* ever wiping away a tear. Thus, I entered marriage unprepared for the tears that were ahead. During our first year together, when Robin would sit on our back steps and cry, it left me feeling uncomfortable and powerless. When she told me that her tears were caused by my insensitivity, I had a strong urge to leave the room. And sometimes I did!

But it wasn't always this way. As a child, I was in touch with my feelings. In my teens, I remember wiping away tears in response to powerful sermons. When my battles with lust were just beginning, I remember weeping on my knees as I called out to God to forgive me of my lust and masturbation. Tears flowed freely when I confessed my sexual offenses to others. But as the battle continued, my tenderness diminished.

Being stripped of my emotional sensitivity would become one of the greatest losses brought on by my addiction. Paul speaks about this connection between impurity and hardness of heart:

> *Having lost all sensitivity, they have given themselves over to sensuality so as to indulge in every kind of impurity, and they are full of greed."* EPHESIANS 4:19

As the years of exposure to pornography piled up, the hardness set in. As I greedily gave myself over to increasingly deeper and riskier levels of sexual indulgence, my empathy dried up. This felt like solid proof that I as an individual was unacceptable and possibly even unredeemable. Now, I know this isn't true. It was just the natural consequence of repeated exposure to harmful media. It was impossible to have a diet of dehumanizing videos and not be dehumanized. Certainly this was exactly what Satan intended—to steal the vulnerability of my sensitive heart.

By the time I was hitting bottom in 2001, my heart was covered in a hardened callus that numbed me to the pain I caused Robin. Intellectually, I knew that I should be crying, but tears of compassion for my hurting spouse were unavailable. I longed for tears, but feared them at the same time. I wanted the tenderness to return, but I couldn't force emotional healing. The tears would have to come in their own time.

How then was the tender heart that Robin refers to in this Stone restored? Much like a thumb that has been hammered into numbness by a clumsy carpenter, the first step to healing my heart was to stop hitting it with the hammer! In order for God to restore my sensitivity, breaking the cycle of addictive behavior became paramount. The hammering had to stop! Then, with time and consistent recovery work, the healing began to happen. Going to meetings every week and doing daily renewals allowed me to hear other men's stories. As my connections deepened, my ability to empathize began to return. Regular walks with my dog Mojo (our recovery dog) surrounded by the beauty of God's creation also helped. These times took me back to a season in my life when my heart was tender.

Being vulnerable with Robin was one of the last areas to heal. All of the shame I felt about the many wounds my actions had brought her formed a barrier. Why could I cry with others and not be able to cry with her? This perplexed both of us. When we learned that the root meaning of vulnerability is the idea of making yourself available to be wounded, it suddenly made more sense. I couldn't cry with Robin, because no one had more power to wound me than my closest friend.

Yet as trust and true intimacy grew, those barriers began to crumble. Year by year, our moments of tearful openness increased, sometimes as we watched a movie together, sometimes as we prayed together. As we learned to take the shame off of our conversations, it became easier to let tears come.

In 2008, an emotional dam inside me cracked when a gunman on the Northern Illinois University campus killed Gayle Dubowski. We had been friends with her parents since before we were married. The night before she was senselessly murdered, Gayle asked Robin to be her campus mom. We loved Gayle like a daughter. Waves of grief and tears hit me as we walked with her parents Joe and Laurel in the wake of this tragedy. Then in 2009, when our son Caleb's girlfriend died a sudden tragic death, the dam finally burst. I sobbed uncontrollably and without shame for the first time since I was a child.

Releasing shame and living daily in a relationship where there is complete acceptance means that tears now come more often, sometimes at unexpected moments. Once while walking and praying with Robin in the foothills near our home in Eagle Idaho, a wave of gratitude rolled over me like an avalanche. In that moment God gave me a clear view of how Robin had fought for me during my darkest days. I put my arms around her and sobbed out loud in her presence, and then her tears mixed with mine as we rejoiced together as what God had done to heal our marriage. No doubt this was a result of the ongoing work of God's Holy Spirit over time as Robin and I both consistently pursued a life of recovery.

Even though the unpredictability of tears still perplexes me as times, and I am still tempted to hold them back, tears are now one of my most treasured gifts!

Back to Your Journal:

In this vulnerable response, Dave shares his journey to being a man of mourning. He talks about how a few tragic events finally broke the dam inside his heart.

Write in your journal about your own journey to mourning. How has God used the pain of abandonment, addiction or abuse to soften your heart?

Knowing the pain of the fall
He storms fortified walls
As his resurrection unveils
A journey of new creation

STONE FIVE
Identifying the Enemy: Spiritual Warfare

Though we live in the world, we do not wage war
as the world does. The weapons we fight with are
not the weapons of the world. On the contrary, they
have divine power to demolish strongholds.

2 CORINTHIANS 10:3–4

Late April in Chicago meant unpredictable weather—one day would be cold, windy or rainy and then a summer-like day would arrive, only to disappear the next. Always having been a sunshine girl, I longed for the April showers to finally dissipate for good. I was trudging towards the park on one of those chilly days in 2003, wishing the sun just might peek out. Instead of being hopeful, my heart was weighed down like someone had filled it with concrete. The evening before, Dave and I had been sitting on our front porch playing a game that I had come to hate—battleship. No, it wasn't the one with the fold-up cases and little gray ships that you try to locate and then sink. Rather, we were playing a game I call purity battleship, where the only way I learned the full extent of Dave's purity lapses was to ask questions until I sunk his ship.

He would initiate with a vague confession. Then I would start in with questions like, "Did you watch a video?" *No, miss.* Did you go to multiple sites? *No, miss.* Did you masturbate?" *Yes, hit.* We would continue until I was out of guesses.

119

He left those sessions relieved. *Whew, it's out.* I was left devastated, unsure if I had the whole story. *Did I miss a ship?* It wasn't just his impurity that weighed me down. It was the high walls Dave had built around himself surrounded by a moat filled with self-loathing. Instead of taking down the walls himself, it seemed that he could only let me into his struggles if I was the one to uncover them. Every time Dave used this coping mechanism, it strengthened its hold.

When I arrived at the park, I found a lonely park bench. Since the air was chilly and heavy with moisture, no one else was around. Struck by sorrow, I threw myself face down on the bench weeping, no longer caring if anyone walked up. Then I began to pray. Nudged by the Spirit, I warred against the stronghold in my husband's heart, standing with Jesus against the demons undoubtedly involved in pornography. Summoning my courage, I asked for God to do whatever it took to remove Satan's strongholds.

These desperate pleas to God not only forced me to dig deep to find faith, but also called me to face the reality of our situation. My counselor had told me that my own abuse and abandonment was severe. I was ready to listen and emerge from denial in order to be re-created by God.

Afterwards, noticing that the clouds had separated, I sat on the bench seeking the sun's comfort. Finally, I whispered, "God how much longer will this last? Please, I need some reassurance. I don't know how much longer I can do this! When will he change?"

I closed my eyes and breathed deeply, surrendering as the warmth radiated through my skin to my very spirit. *Thanksgiving.* The holiday came to mind and I accepted it as being from God. "Okay, then. Thanksgiving," I said. "I can hang on until Thanksgiving."

Just a few months later our marriage hit the breaking point, and I asked Dave to leave (more later). And sure enough, somewhere around Thanksgiving, Dave started his bumpy journey into true recovery. Looking back, I now understand Thanksgiving wasn't the turning point. The day everything changed was when on a lonely park bench, I stood up to Satan and his evil minions and said, "No more." Finally, I embraced one of my most profound roles in life—fully engaging spiritual warfare.

Again, this warfare wasn't just for Dave. I would be warring for my own spiritual wholeness. And strangely enough, with that engagement came a tender joy, the recognition that I wasn't too helpless, lost or broken to engage in combat.* As God's precious daughter, I could boldly walk with him into the sanctuary of his war room.[39]

Did Satan immediately back down? Of course not!

In the years to come, warfare would only accelerate. It would extend to every bike path I traversed, leaving a trail of tears behind. When we moved to another city, I left more tears around our new neighborhood. Some days, being so full of grief that I couldn't pray, spiritual warfare would mean walking around our neighborhood singing or speaking the words of old hymns. Other days, as I prayed out loud on my elliptical trainer, I would suddenly hunch over the handlebars sobbing as I surrendered my marriage, my children, our losses, my fears, my very self to Jesus as my mighty warrior.

In spiritual warfare, I learned some of the most precious tenets of recovery.

---

* *It is the Lord Who goes before you; He will [march] with you; He will not fail you or let you go or forsake you; [let there be no cowardice or flinching, but] fear not, neither become broken [in spirit—depressed, dismayed, and unnerved with alarm].* DEUTERONOMY 31:8 (AMPC)

Above all, I learned that my safest place was where I stood with my God. From there, Jesus would lead me into battle. I had finally identified the true enemy. Pornography wasn't the enemy. My own weakness wasn't the enemy. My past abandonment and abuse weren't the enemy. No, my enemy was an evil adversary who would have me think that there could be no victory when in truth he had already been defeated by Jesus' work on the cross.

Identifying the enemy

> *You love righteousness and hate wickedness; therefore*
> *God, your God, has set you above your companions*
> *by anointing you with the oil of joy* (PSALM 45:7).

What type of fall have you come to detest? What types of relational assaults make your blood boil? Maybe it is serial adultery. Maybe it is an authority figure that uses their power to manipulate those who depend on him. Maybe it is pornography coming through your computer into the sanctity of your home. Or perhaps it is drugs and alcohol and their ability to replace the one you love with an angry, detached stranger. Maybe it is so called lovers who stay around just long enough to awaken the faint yearnings of love, and then suddenly disappear. Or just maybe, you fear that your own struggles are the enemy. Whatever has devastated you (or those you love), it's natural to call that the enemy.

When I first started this journey, just the mention of pornography could set off a quiet rage. My real fear was that I caused these battles. Later, as we both found long-term victory and we started ministering to other couples, we faced new temptations. Listening to Dave explain the husband's battles, I would suddenly go off on a rant how the husband was blind to how he was hurting his wife. Then Dave would explain how the wife was impossible to live with. With time, we learned that these arguments were signs that we still had healing work to do. Dave wasn't the enemy. I wasn't the enemy. Perhaps one reason our "battleship" game didn't work out so well, because it turned us into opponents.

Likewise, whatever form of addiction, abandonment or abuse you've suffered isn't the true villain.

Let me be clear here. I despise abuse. I shudder at the thought of adults using their power to prey on those younger or weaker than them. I hate abandonment. It leaves a primal wound when your loved one forsakes the promises inherent in your relationship. And I have an extreme aversion to pornography. I detest strip clubs, X-rated movies and sexual message boards, and all the other things that dehumanize and desensitize. And taking a glance at my own battles, I shudder at the depth of my codependence and love addiction and all the places these tendencies took me. Hating evil is a result of righteousness.*

But looking down on others (or despising myself) isn't a result of righteousness.

As 1 Corinthians 10:12 warns us, "So, if you think you are standing firm, be careful that you don't fall!" Just when I decide that I hate someone else's sin, I fall in another arena. Just when I think my battles are morally superior to other people's battles, pride swoops in. Just when I think I am strong enough, I falter under loads that aren't mine to carry.** When I compare myself to others, self-doubt is only a few steps behind.

123

---

* *To fear the Lord is to hate evil; I hate pride and arrogance, evil behavior and perverse speech.* PROVERBS 8:13

** *Each one should test their own actions. Then they can take pride in themselves alone, without comparing themselves to someone else, for each one should carry their own load.* GALATIANS 6:4–5

Spiritual recovery means seeking the perspective of God. Yes, God's heart is filled with pain at the places where the fall takes us (Genesis 6:6). Yet, he patiently hopes for every person to come to repentance. He longs to be gracious to us.* Eric Simmons says it well in his blog post aptly titled "I Hate Porn." After listing 19 reasons why he hates porn, he then says, "but I love Jesus." But what he says next is kind of shocking:

> I love Jesus because he loves people with porn problems.
> I love Jesus because he is powerful to free porn-
> enslaved hearts. He who knew no porn addiction
> became porn addiction so that the porn addict
> might become the righteousness of God in him.[40]

In case you are wondering, Simmons is referring to 2 Corinthians 5:21: "He who had no sin became sin for you so that you may become the righteousness of God." Of course, this scripture applies to far more than pornography. Try placing your own hurt or even your own struggle into Simmons' words:

> I love Jesus because he loves people who are emotionally abusive.

> I love Jesus because he loves people who are emotionally shut down.

> He who never abandoned others became abandonment so that the one who abandons might become the righteousness of God.

> I love Jesus because he is powerful to free codependents.

124

* ISAIAH 30:18

I love Jesus because his love renders love addiction powerless.

Jesus didn't come to earth on an anti-sin crusade, rebuking anyone who did anything that wasn't pleasing to God. Simply being with Jesus, hearing his words, and then seeing his actions was a penetrating light that illuminated the motives of those listening. When he predicted Peter's denial, he also reminded Peter that the day would come when he would use his missteps to minister to others, as the Message says, "give them a fresh start" (Luke 22:32).*

Although Jesus called his followers to leave their sin, his warfare was "against the rulers, against the authorities, against the powers of this dark world and against the spiritual forces of evil in the heavenly realms" (Ephesians 6:12). This explains so much. It explains how a Samaritan woman, who was living with a man after five failed marriages, could have become Jesus' chosen ambassador for all of Samaria.** It explains why Jesus knelt down and distracted attention away from the woman caught in adultery. He called people to radical repentance, but only after he showed them mercy.

Jesus knew his enemy and it wasn't the people he came to redeem.

Like Jesus, we need to ask ourselves, "Who is the true enemy?"

---

* *Simon, stay on your toes. Satan has tried his best to separate all of you from me, like chaff from wheat. Simon, I've prayed for you in particular that you not give in or give out. When you have come through the time of testing, turn to your companions and give them a fresh start.* LUKE 22:31–32 (MSG)

** *Many of the Samaritans from that town believed in him because of the woman's testimony, "He told me everything I ever did."* JOHN 4:39

Even as a follower of Jesus, I have relied on many worldly mechanisms to try to fight the work of the enemy. There have been so many times when I've pushed back tears and forged on like a loyal soldier who has no other option. Times where I've shifted into a *"compensation through performance"* mode. Now I see that this doesn't make sense. Someone who is chasing the wrong enemy with no spiritual armor on doesn't threaten Satan.

But when I call on Jesus, and his mighty ministering angels, when I put on *his* armor held together by faith, righteousness, boldness and prayer, Satan is clearly outnumbered, outpowered and outclassed.

True spiritual warfare keeps Jesus out in front of us, as our shield and our sword, the living Word. We look to him as our commander for guidance and clarification. And his warfare is well suited to both to a man's heart and a woman's heart because it is a mighty but gentle warfare.

Spiritual warfare

> *For the weapons of our warfare are not physical [weapons of flesh and blood], but they are mighty before God for the overthrow and destruction of strongholds [...] and we lead every thought and purpose away captive into the obedience of Christ [...]* 2 CORINTHIANS 10:4–5 (AMPC)

> *...in purity, understanding, patience and kindness; in the Holy Spirit and in sincere love; in truthful speech and in the power of God; with weapons of righteousness in the right hand and in the left...* 2 CORINTHIANS 6:6–7

In 2 Corinthians 10:4, Paul talks about how the power of God enables us to take down strongholds. The Greek word for stronghold *ochuroma*, means "a fortified, military stronghold;

a strong walled fortress."[41] It can also be used figuratively to describe "a false argument in which a person seeks 'shelter' to escape reality."[42]

What an apt description of the roots of any addiction. My love addiction and codependence were places I could hide out from all my losses. Dave's sexual addiction was built on seductive lies offering false shelter. The battleship game didn't work because it didn't remove the strongholds that guarded the ships!

Stronghold (_ochuroma_): a false argument in which a person seeks shelter to escape reality. (Strong's Greek)

How can we go against these false arguments? Since Satan builds strongholds on mirrors, illusions and lies (more in a moment), our most effective weapon is God's truth. When we hold to God's wisdom, we stand with God. When our pain overwhelms and confuses us, God's word lights up our path and shows us the way. When mourning is overwhelming, Jesus cares for us. When we're not sure what to do next, the Holy Spirit leads us. We don't need to wage warfare as the world does (praise God!). The weapons of the world lack power, whereas spiritual weapons harness the very energy of God.*

Spiritual weapons harness the very energy of God.

---

* _Therefore put on the full armor of God, so that when the day of evil comes, you may be able to stand your ground, and after you have done everything, to stand._ EPHESIANS 6:13

In the words of Paul, one of the most devoted Jesus-followers of the New Testament, I find some sage advice on how to respond when another person's behavior devastates us. We do this through refusing Satan's attempt to get us to use his tactics of war.

> *Flee the evil desires of youth and pursue righteousness,*
> *faith, love and peace, along with those who call on*
> *the Lord out of a pure heart. Don't have anything*
> *to do with foolish and stupid arguments, because*
> *you know they produce quarrels. And the Lord's*
> *servant must not be quarrelsome but must be*
> *kind to everyone, able to teach, not resentful.*
>
> *Opponents must be gently instructed, in the hope that God*
> *will grant them repentance leading them to a knowledge of*
> *the truth, and that they will come to their senses and escape*
> *from the trap of the devil, who has taken them captive to*
> *do his will* (2 TIMOTHY 2:22–26).

The chart on the following page contrasts Satan's tactics of war with the gentle warfare of Jesus. As you read through Satan's tactics (and we all are tempted to use these), examine your response to the enemy's attacks. Remind yourself that even in the aftermath of trauma, triggers and thorns, your truest identity is that of "the Lord's servant."

The warfare of Jesus is mighty, but gentle.

Satan's tactics of war	Jesus' gentle warfare: 2 Timothy 2:22–26
Shun God's standards. Find love wherever you can get it.	Shun youthful lusts and flee from them.
Be vocal with your hatred of abandonment, abuse or addiction.	Pursue all that is virtuous and good, embrace right living.
Curse others who hurt you. Use thoughts, words and deeds as ammunition.	Conform to the will of God in thought, word and deed.
Contact old friends or family members to condemn the one who abandoned you.	Pursue others who call on the Lord out of a pure heart.
Vulnerability is what hurt you. Hide behind questions no one can answer.	Refuse to engage in unedifying controversies over unanswerable questions.
Remind them of their weaknesses again and again. Show them they are nothing.	The Lord's servant must be kind to everyone, mild-tempered, preserving the bond of peace.
Fight back through name-calling, threats or accusations.	Be patient and forbearing, willing to suffer a wrong. Respond with courtesy and gentleness.
Make sure that everybody sees that you are spiritual, unlike whoever hurt you.	Pray that the one(s) who hurt you can come to see themselves as God sees them.

Putting this gentle warfare into practice can be scary. It may not seem to make sense. Before you panic, this isn't a call to perfection. It doesn't mean ignoring your pain.

Remember Stone four (tears), taught us to shed the hard belly for a softer one through mourning. It doesn't mean becoming a doormat or letting others continually abuse us. A big part of this journey is learning how to stand with God. On the very next Stone, we will claim our dignity by setting boundaries. It doesn't mean that you won't ever get angry or that there isn't a righteous anger. But it does remind us to check ourselves, lest our emotional fear overcomes us. Warfare urges us to remember that the one who is in us is greater than the one who is in the world.

Recovery in the wake of someone's fall requires time as we reach for balance. One of the most difficult is the balance of truth and grace—being able to own and reflect the depth of our pain in truthful speech, but also able to season our speech with the salt of grace. Our goal is to clothe ourselves with the spiritual armor Paul talks about in 2 Corinthians 6:6–7: "*in purity, understanding, patience and kindness; in the Holy Spirit and in sincere love; in truthful speech and the power of God; with weapons of righteousness in the right hand and the left.*"

Warfare and Re-Creation

> *Is Jehovah calling me outside the protection of the hunting shelter? As impossible as it seems, I know the answer to my own question. I don't belong shivering in the corner of a dark hunting shelter. Jehovah breathed himself into me.* Eve's Song, *p. 166*

It is helpful to keep in mind that the goal of spiritual warfare is spiritual re-creation. This helps explain why this warfare is so crucial to this journey of twelve Stones. Satan opposes new creation. Whenever he sees a new seed of conviction sprouting, he'd like to yank it out of the ground, send thorns to choke it, or keep it from receiving nourishment. To keep us from guarding this new growth, Satan sends decoys that jump up to send us running the wrong direction.

Actually, decoys are a well-known tactic of war. In recent years, a highly classified World War II "Ghost Army" came into the national spotlight, formed by the United States in the war against Nazi Germany. This group of a thousand artists, audio technicians, and designers recruited from ad agencies and art schools were commissioned to convince the enemy that U.S. troops were in one place, when they were really in another. To do this they used inflatable tanks, sound effects and works of art on the battlefield.

This "traveling roadshow of deception" opened the door for the final drive on Normandy with a "rubber army," fake equipment and ever-larger deceptions that had Germany convinced their strongest positions were secure. Actors even hung out in coffee shops, spinning tales of these deceptions for spies who might be listening.[43]

Again, isn't this how Satan works? He is a master of disguise. After all, the Bible tells us that Satan masquerades as an angel of light (2 Corinthians 11:14). The evil one is the biggest fraud of all, with the biggest rubber army of all. He has legions of demons that no doubt use their "skills" as artists, audio and video technicians to deceive. By convincing us that he is stronger than he really is, and then getting us to buy into his "coffee shop gossip," Satan convinces us that we are vulnerable in the exact areas where we are strong.

After all, it's much easier to attack someone who's fighting the wrong war, against the wrong enemy, based on untrue information.

To be honest, I buy into this travel show of deception way too often! When I exchange Satan's lie that I'm unsafe for the reality that I'm perfectly protected by Jesus, it's easy to pick up old tactics of war: running away or taking control; putting up walls to keep others out or apologizing even though I did no wrong; pretending like I'm not under attack or nursing a bitter root that I am. And although I continually struggle to engage spiritual disciplines of warfare based on surrender and prayer, when I start telling myself that I'm at risk my brain is happy to direct me to my self-protective responses. What unnerves Satan? When we face him head-on![44] When we take our stand.*

Now I see that standing firm isn't about my own strength—either asserting it through control or folding under because I'm just too weak. Standing, in and of itself, is a type of active resistance. This resistance is rooted in prayer. As I sought healing in my marriage, I began to pray, "Lord I stand against Satan's work in Dave's life. I stand against the demons of pornography. I stand with you in your power, and pray that you will take down the stronghold in my husband's life." When I saw my own great weakness, I prayed, "Lord, I am so frightened of speaking the truth. I surrender my voice to you. Give me words of grace and truth. Thank you that you are my wisdom and you will personally instruct me in the path you want me to take."** With time, God powerfully answered that prayer.

For those in recovering relationships

For those of you in a relationship where any combination of addiction, abandonment or abuse has brought devastation, here is a good place to start. Every time you are tempted to wield a worldly weapon, ask God what spiritual weapon he would have you pick up instead (see the chart on the following page).

* Put on the full armor of God, so that you can take your stand against the devil's schemes. EPHESIANS 6:11 (EMPHASIS MINE)
** Who is the man who fears the Lord? God will teach him the path he should choose. PSALM 25:12 (RSV)

Worldly weapon	Spiritual weapon
Policing —Tracking their phone or behavior to avoid risky confrontations.	Releasing —Admitting my helplessness to choose for another.
Joining —Participating in addictive behaviors	Speaking —Calling out behaviors that are not acceptable.
Disowning —Lowering my standards or compromising boundaries to keep peace.	Owning dignity — Accepting God's boundaries as my own.
Internalizing —Telling myself that this happened because I am not enough.	Humbling myself —Asking God to examine me and test my motives.
Making threats —Threatening to leave or end the relationship.	Mourning —Letting the one who hurt me into my pain, fear and devastation.
Covering —Hiding their wanderings.	Standing — Looking to God as my rock, protection, safety and self-esteem.
Shaming — Punishing them with demeaning words or actions.	Going to war —Taking a stand against Satanic schemes.

Circling back to my story of "purity battleship" at the beginning of this Stone, you may be wondering. *If I don't play battleship, how will I ever get to the heart of what's really happening with my mate or significant other?* Here are a few suggestions:

1) **Admit your helplessness:** The problem with rooting out someone else's fall is that it shifts the responsibility to you. When you receive a vague confession, try a gentle nudge, "Is there more?" Then, instead of proceeding with "yes" and "no" questions, try saying something like this:

"I appreciate your confession. But I am feeling so helpless. I have the sense there might be more, but I can't be open for you." By owning your helplessness, you put the responsibility where it belongs: with the other person.

2) **Pray first:** When I respond immediately to Dave after a boundary break, I can easily give way to hysteria. Then Dave ends up feeling controlled. Now, I seek to go to God first. Although this doesn't remove the pain, I can come to Dave with a steadier heart.

3) **Ask specific questions:** When the Spirit nudges, ask your mate direct questions instead of the yes and no variety of battleship. For instance, "When was the last time you looked at pornography? Masturbated? What specific words did you search for online? How long did you spend looking? How many beers did you have last night?"

4) **Guard your own heart:** Remember you'll have to live with whatever he tells you. Refrain from asking anything that puts a picture in your mind you'll have to live with, i.e. *What did she look like? What color hair did she have? Was her body better than mine? What did you do together sexually?*

5) **Get others involved:** If your partner is evasive, get other people praying with you. A recovery group is a great place to gather support for hard conversations, or even an intervention. Consider asking other trusted friends to get involved to help your partner open up.

Please bear in mind that this Stone just opens the door to spiritual warfare. Re-Creation, the second part of the journey is a declaration of spiritual warfare included in each of the Stones. Be patient with yourself. You'll have days when you are running for cover more than standing up and engaging. Yet as you turn your heart again and again to engage in God's gentle warfare, listen for the call of grace.

Grace calls

Spiritual warfare, like so many other arenas of recovery takes spiritual discernment. Control can easily masquerade as standing firm. To yell at someone feels like a type of standing. To withdraw feels like a type of protection. This is where grace holds us steady. Grace whispers, *Remember the grace you've received and look for ways to extend it to those who hurt you.* When you are tempted to use truth as a weapon, grace whispers, *Jesus didn't retaliate, yet he was real with his pain.*

As you examine your own life, think of the weapons of worldly warfare as coping mechanisms. Yes, your own personal strongholds have provided temporary comfort in the wake of pain. They are old friends that have been there for you in the hard times, perhaps reaching back to your childhood. But they no longer serve a purpose in this journey.

Grace can give you the courage to let go. Grace whispers, *Face the ways you've waged war as the world does with curiosity and gentleness. All of these coping mechanisms are human. As you let go, let me teach you a new way of relating that will bring forth a whole new creation.*

Your spiritual journey

Congratulations for stepping onto the Stone of warfare. You've begun to engage a key part of spiritual recovery. You may be wondering, "Why is spiritual warfare so difficult?" My answer would be one word—chaos. (Re-read the introduction for Stones 4 to 8 for a reminder of the role chaos plays in re-creation.) The chaos of warfare might cause a churning in your gut, wanting any battles to be over and yet still wondering…*why me?* You might be intrigued by the possibility of a new kind of spiritual power, but afraid that it won't work.

Stepping on this Stone may feel like you are hoisting even more responsibility on your shoulders: things you can't control. If the situation causing you pain is ongoing, you might say, "Wait one minute. What about him/her? Shouldn't they be waging war?" It may seem unfair for you to be the one getting spiritual about this. You might look at the "battleship" at the beginning of this Stone and think… *At least you were willing to know, Robin. I'm not sure I want to!* You might be tempted to feel defeated when you try to be spiritual and someone diffuses or misunderstands it. Whatever you are feeling or experiencing, please trust me that you are far from alone.

If Jesus were here, I think he might utter a word of encouragement. If you don't mind, I'll take a shot at what he might say....

> *My friend, spiritual warfare isn't for the sake of going to war. Rather it is for the sake of love. It is so you can embrace the dignity I destined for you from the beginning of your creation. Come to me with the weight of your fear and hesitation, and I will fight your battles for you and with you.*

Circle of stones: warfare

Congratulations for stepping on to yet another Stone of recovery. On this fifth stone you will write the word "warfare." Afterwards, hold the stone in your right hand and feel its weight and hidden power.

Your stone of warfare will join your other stones: trauma, thorns, triggers and tears. Again, take a few moments to put them all in front of you and take a moment to rejoice in your progress. How is this journey of Stones changing the way you think? The way you live?

Journaling: Warfare

This Stone calls you to warfare, "*in purity, understanding, patience and kindness; in the Holy Spirit and in sincere love; in truthful speech and the power of God; with weapons of righteousness in the right hand and the left*" (2 Corinthians 6:6–7).

Write down each of these words or phrases running down the one side of a page in your journal (i.e. purity, understanding, etc.). After each, write down how to use this weapon of righteousness.

For instance: purity: I will guard my own purity by watching my tongue, guarding my heart against fear-inducing media or news, and lifting my standards higher.

Now go back and circle the one you are strongest in and the one you see yourself weakest in. Where do you feel God calling you to grow?

A word from Dave — Warfare

The true objective of war is peace
— SUN TZU

Sun Tzu, a Chinese general, military strategist, and philosopher, lived in what is referred to as the Spring and Autumn period of ancient China. He wrote *The Art of War*, a book that is considered by many to be the best-crafted compilation of the strategies of war that has ever been written. One of his most famous quotations resonates strongly with me, "If you know the enemy and know yourself you need not fear the results of a hundred battles."

The spiritual reality is that becoming a Christian means entering into a battle. Jesus explained the cost of following with him with an analogy of two kings going to war (Luke 14:31-33). The message is clear, we must surrender to Jesus and give up everything we have or face certain defeat. His army is much bigger than ours! When we make the wise choice of crowning Jesus as our king, he recreates our heart. But we must then engage in another fierce war (Ephesians 6:10-17). We must fend off all challengers who conspire to take Jesus off that throne and deaden our heart.

This is a large part of what recovery is all about. Unhealthy attachments seize and deaden parts of our hearts that rightly belong to Jesus. To fully engage in recovery means going to war to reclaim this lost territory!

This is a serious conflict! Addiction, abandonment and abuse have ultimately been the cause of countless deaths: physical, emotional, and spiritual. Solomon said of the adulterous woman,

symbolic of sexual sin, that her slain were "a mighty throng."*
Ironically, being yoked with many wives that worshipped false
idols may have been the cause of his own spiritual death as
well. Becoming one flesh with women who did not know God
gradually sucked the life from his heart.

For millennia Satan has developed and perfected his
strategies for using our sexual desire as a weapon against us.
With those who know little of God's word, he often employs
a frontal assault. For people like myself, who grow up hearing
God's word, Satan will often use deception and "rubber armies"
to deaden our hearts and regain ground. Much like the Germans
in World War II who were deceived as to where the true enemy
was, I was also staring down inflatable tanks instead of facing
my real enemy.

Satan spent years convincing me that I was doing fine. He
whispered that since I was zealous for God my struggles would
soon go away and that the damage done by unfaithfulness and
its effects would be forgotten. But as I went from being a teen
to an adult, from being single to being married, and from being
young to being middle aged, this illusion—that my good deeds
would ultimately outweigh my struggles—began to fade.

Robin saw the true enemy before I did, largely because
I clung to the belief that I was basically a good guy with an
occasional lust issue. Until I was able to see that there were two
David's—David the follower of Jesus and David the addict—
my efforts were futile. This faulty view of myself, along with my
refusal to fully face my dark side, meant that I was continuously
trying to defend myself by reciting my good deeds or the ways
that God was using me.

139

---

* *Do not let your heart turn to her ways or stray into her paths. Many
are the victims she has brought down; her slain are a mighty throng. Her
house is a highway to the grave, leading down to the chambers of death.*
PROVERBS 7:25-27

With my two selves entangled, I feared that if I totally surrendered my sexually addicted self, there would be nothing left of me. My addict protested, *"Why should people in the world have more exciting sexual experiences than a Christian?"* To let go of my sexual desires (fueled by pornography) would be annihilation. With the addict and the good guy in competition, I couldn't hit the bottom and come out of denial. Once I let go of that myth, I was able to fearlessly wage war on the addict within.

You might be wondering then, what did warfare look like for me? Here are a few of the changes that Jesus, my commanding officer, called me to:

Light instead of darkness: No secrets, every part of my life in the open.

Consistency instead of intensity: No big vows, simply doing the daily work.

Connection instead of isolation: Surrendering pain rather than medicating it.

Unfortunately there were times that I treated Robin like she was the enemy. There were times when we both had the wrong opponent in our sights, leaving Satan free to continue his work of reinforcing strongholds in our hearts. Imagine the power that was unleashed when we both engaged spiritual warfare as a team.

I am now equipped for this warfare and free to love Jesus with all my heart. Like the demon-possessed man, with the chains of attachment broken, life is good. I have my wife warring for me with what she describes as "a gentle warfare."

I now welcome Robin's strength and conviction, as a God-given protection against the true enemy. I now know who the true enemy is, and through recovery I continue to deepen my knowledge of myself. Because I daily continue the practice of the spiritual disciplines of intimacy, vulnerability, confession, and boundaries, I do not fear whatever battles lie ahead!

Back to Your Journal:

Dave shares three convictions he engages in his own warfare:

- Light instead of darkness
- Consistency instead of intensity
- Connection instead of isolation

Take some time to journal about these three areas in your life. How can each of these principles help you engage spiritual warfare?

Grace will save you from
Women who throw their bodies
At men who clamor to console
Those who delight in deceit

Stone Six
Setting Boundaries: Dignity

"Strength and dignity are her clothing and her
position is strong and secure; she rejoices over the
future [the latter day or time to come, knowing
that she and her family are in readiness for it]!"
PROVERBS 31:25 (AMPC)

"One's dignity may be assaulted, vandalized
and cruelly mocked, but it can never be
taken away unless it is surrendered."
– MICHAEL J. FOX

I T WAS A WARM SUMMER DAY WHEN THE BOTTOM
fell out. We were just over a month away from a much-
anticipated trip to the beach to be with my family in North
Carolina, and I so wanted life to be good. We now understood
that Dave had a sexual addiction and with that Dave was trying
harder to get his falls into the open. He would confess to me,
but still there would usually be a gap between the act and
the confession that followed, from three to thirty days. I was
suffering from a severe case of Staggered Disclosure Syndrome.[45]
By now, there had been many confessions, spaced over a period
of twenty years. Although they shared some likeness (all having
a root in misplaced sexual desire) their origin was widely varied.

Some came because I happened into Dave's wanderings on his computer, or even awoke to him watching something racy on television right beside me in the bed. Some confessions came in the form of lists after a particularly convicting lesson or even at a marriage retreat. Some of these discoveries brought me immense personal shame, like when Dave confessed that early in our marriage, he had rifled through the suitcase of a young woman staying at our house looking for her intimate wear. *How could I be so blind?* Or when I opened our mailbox to find hardcore pornography in it. *How did pornographers get our address? What if one of our children had gone for the mail?* Others could have threatened his job, like acting out in the bathroom of an doctor's office he visited. With every confession, came nagging doubt... *is there more? Am I crazy?*

Through all of this, I saw two different men: Dave my husband—who loves God and had zealously served him since he was a teenager—and Dave the addict, a person who could manipulate, lie, hide and angrily convince me that he was the one who was suffering, while denying his anger. The problem was that the addict had become firmly entrenched. After we started counseling and Dave verbally pledged renewed sexual fidelity, he bought me a massage table for Valentine's Day. He explained, "Well, if I'm only going to get sexual pleasure from you alone, we might as well have fun!" The double-message escaped me until we talked to our counselor, who sternly warned Dave that these kind of messages (if I'm *only* getting pleasure from you) could destroy my sense of safety in our marriage.

Still there was something noble growing in my heart, a new shoot of strength springing from the spiritual warfare I had begun waging.* Gradually, I was realizing that my husband's

* *Night and day, whether he sleeps or gets up, the seed sprouts and grows, though he does not know how.* MARK 4:27

soul was at risk and that I was hurting him by allowing him to continue in our relationship with no real consequences to his actions. I was convinced that pornography was demonic and amounted to letting Satan into our home. One of Dave's most recent revelations had scared me to the core. The addiction, which up to this point had been on again and off again over twenty years, was gaining power and I was afraid, humbled and desperate.

So when Dave said he had something to tell me, something from that very morning, I was first encouraged. He is confessing right away. It went something like this: "Honey, I called a chat line flashing on the television screen. I talked with someone, realized what I was doing was wrong, and asked her to throw away my number." My heart skipped a few beats. He had made contact with a live person. He explained that he felt compassion for her, as she wanted to talk about problems with her daughter. In the past, I might have let it go right there. But, my God-given intuition told me there was more.

I began to ask questions. Did you try to talk to her about sex? (Yes, but she didn't want to talk about that.) Did you tell her your sexual desires? (Well, I tried to, but she didn't have much to say.) Did you tell her you were married? (No, we didn't get that far.) The questions began to irritate Dave, and he pled with me, "Robin, don't you see? God protected me. This was a victory!" Suddenly, righteous indignation swept over me. "No, Dave, this was *not* a victory." Dave rolled his eyes, threw his arms up in the air, looked at me with disgust and said, "I will never be able to please you. Nothing I do will ever be enough!"

At that moment I knew the end had come. I asked him to get his things and move out. He was shocked, incensed. "You've got to be kidding!" he said. "Leave, please leave," is all I could say. At long last, I was ready to draw a firm boundary.

145

I knew that this might be the end of our marriage. But over the last few months, I had come to a quiet conviction, a seed of dignity, that I could and would survive without Dave, without marriage. This wasn't what I desired, but I was finally ready to stand my ground.

Dave angrily threw a few things together and stormed out of the house. Pushing away tears, I got my Bible and drove to the nearby bookstore. I was ready to hear from God, not so much about Dave, as about me. *Who am I, Lord? What is my part in this insanity? Search me and examine me and show any unclean way in me.* God answered quickly and decisively. I would never be the same.

Setting boundaries

> *"Boundaries define what are me and what is not me. A boundary shows me where I end and someone else begins, leading me to a sense of ownership"*[46] *– Henry Cloud and John Townsend*

> *"For there is one God and one mediator between God and mankind, the man Christ Jesus."* I TIMOTHY 2:5

Anyone who seeks to recover from addiction or codependency needs to become fluent in the language of boundaries. And at the beginning, this can feel like a foreign language! Yet, understanding boundaries is a huge part of spiritual recovery. And in my experience, boundaries can be one of the most illusive parts of finding spiritual wholeness. After all, as the children's song goes, don't we put Jesus first, others second, and ourselves last? How does putting others before me fit with the idea of boundaries? If I'm married, does that now mean that my husband's boundaries are my concern as well as his?

Recently, after twelve years of recovery, I came to a new conviction that made this tricky balance so much clearer...

Setting boundaries means standing where God stands.

Please pause here and read that last statement again slowly. This is the commitment we make when we come to Christ—where you stand, I'll stand. Where you draw lines, I will draw lines (and watch myself first that I don't step over them). When I became a follower of Christ, I made the decision to accept his boundaries as my own. In fact, there would be no need for salvation if Jesus didn't have boundaries. Boundaries reflect the goodness and justice of God.[47] God wouldn't be perfectly good if he set boundaries that he didn't mean, or didn't set boundaries in accordance with his own nature. Boundaries keep us safe by preserving our dignity, while upholding the dignity of God.

To understand this better, I turned to a writer who changed my life in college with his stirring manifesto, *The Cost of Discipleship*—Dietrich Bonhoeffer. I've never thought of Bonhoeffer as a writer on boundaries, but in his treatise called *Discipleship* it turns out he has much to say about followers of Jesus and boundaries...

> *"Now they know that there can be no unmediated relationships, even in the most intimate ties of their lives, in the blood ties to father and mother, to children, brothers and sisters, in marital love...For every unmediated natural relationship, knowingly or unknowingly, is an expression of hatred toward Christ, the mediator, especially if this relationship wants to assume a Christian identity."[48]*

That means for disciples of Jesus, the only realities are those given by Christ, who has become our very identity.* So what is an unmediated relationship? Simply put, it means having a direct relationship with others that isn't lived out through Christ. As an unmarried person, it would mean dating whomever you wish, unencumbered by the Biblical mandate not to be yoked with unbelievers.** As someone who is married, it would mean taking your primary significance and security from your mate. If you have children, it would be thinking that since you own those children, you are entitled to have whatever type of relationship with them that you please. The disciple sees relationships, in whatever form they take, as a stewardship from God. Each role is to be lived out through Christ. The call to discipleship is a call to having Christ in the middle of our relationships, what Bonhoeffer calls mediated relationships...

> Christ the mediator stands between son and father,
> between husband and wife, between individual
> and nation, whether they can recognize him or not.
> There is no way from us to others than the path
> through Christ, his word, and our following him.
> Immediacy is a delusion."[48]

In his book explaining Bonhoeffer's theology, Joel Lawrence makes a stunning observation. The reason we seek unmediated access to others is because we've built our relationships on emotional love. And this love can be self-centered. Emotional

* For as many [of you] as were baptized into Christ [into a spiritual union and communion with Christ, the Anointed One, the Messiah] have put on (clothed yourselves with) Christ. GALATIANS 3:27 (AMPC)

** Do not be yoked together with unbelievers. For what do righteousness and wickedness have in common? Or what fellowship can light have with darkness? 2 CORINTHIANS 6:14

love gets translated into the desire to control. And in this system the strong tend to overpower the weak.[49] Here is my takeaway on the difference between an unmediated and a mediated relationship with another person.

Unmediated relationship: A relationship based primarily on emotion (either love or fear), and that therefore tends to rely on power to maintain it. There is the illusion of direct access to the person and therefore a type of ownership. Pleasing and/or being pleased are the primary concern.

Mediated relationship: A relationship based on and lived out through Jesus and his love.* The teachings of Jesus set the standards and boundaries for the relationship. Obedience to Jesus is the primary concern, out of faith that his way will ultimately be most pleasing and wise.

This explains so much for those of us in the wake of the fall of another person, especially as we courageously face our own struggles (more in Stone 7: acceptance) and admit that without Jesus we make a mess of things. A lack of boundaries shows that I've put emotional love over Christ-mediated love. On the other hand, building walls by using human restrictions and control can become equally unhealthy, as I use my own strength to manage the relationship rather than living it out through Christ. Dave's and my battleship game was an indication of all the ways I was trying to manage him directly instead of through Christ. I wanted Dave's love (instead of God's) to prove my worth and make up for past losses.

149

* *There is no fear in love [dread does not exist], but full-grown (complete, perfect) love turns fear out of doors and expels every trace of terror!...he who is afraid has not reached the full maturity of love [is not yet grown into love's complete perfection].* I JOHN 4:18 (AMPC)

Spiritually, this over-dependence on emotional love was confusing. When I would try to set boundaries, Dave would tell me he didn't feel respected. If I didn't set boundaries, I showed a lack of respect for God. So that brings up some good questions. How do we tell the difference between mediated and unmediated love? What warning signs show that we might be mistaking respect for an unmediated, emotionally driven relationship? And what if your response is to over-regulate your relationships, making threats to keep others in check, lest they hurt you? How does boundary setting help redeem our fear-based decisions? Clarity came as I was willing to dig beneath my struggle to set healthy boundaries.

Where did all the boundaries go?

> *"Examine me, O Lord, and prove me; test my heart and my mind."* PSALM 26:2 (AMPC)

As I shared earlier, when I finally drew a line, Dave stormed out of the house and I went directly to a nearby bookstore and begged God to examine me and show me what I needed to know about myself. Because reading helps me find healing, I asked God to give me a book. After walking down the Christian aisle, I walked down the Psychology aisle, where I found *Love Addiction* by Pia Mellody.

As I sat down to read, Dave called, desperate to talk. I knew he wanted me to ask him to come home. He was counting on me to continue the dance we'd done for years—I would explode after an addictive episode and then, conscience-stricken, be the one to apologize. This time instead, I told him I wasn't ready, that I needed time. "I don't want to talk today," I said. "I want to read."

And so, curled up in a comfy chair (and entrusting my husband to God), I plunged into Mellody's book. Very quickly, I sensed a pattern that was planted in my childhood, sprouted in my teenage years, bloomed with my boyfriend in college, and then rooted itself deeply into my marriage. Mellody identifies three central characteristics of being addicted to love:

1) Love Addicts assign a disproportionate amount of time, attention, and "value above themselves" to the person to whom they are addicted, and this focus often has an obsessive quality about it.

2) Love Addicts have unrealistic expectations for unconditional positive regard from the other person in the relationship.

3) Love Addicts neglect to care for or value themselves while they're in the relationship.[50]

Melody's book doesn't look at this through a spiritual lens. But adding the spiritual dimension brings a whole new perspective. Looking at these today, I see first and foremost, unmediated love...

1) **Disproportionate focus** – God created the covenant relationship of marriage to be lived through and with him. In fact, all of our relationships are to be lived through him (see Matthew 10:37). Either being overly enmeshed or under enmeshed reveals a disproportionate focus on the one we "love."

2) **<u>Unrealistic expectations</u>** – Hypersensitivity came from a misplaced security. Unconditional positive regard can only be found in Jesus.

3) **<u>Lack of self-care</u>** – Putting ourselves under other people isn't an act of humility. Rather it is a way of keeping control of their love. The only way to find healthy perspective and self-care is by surrendering the ones we love to Jesus.

Having Christ mediate my relationships isn't some super-spiritual religious lingo. And it doesn't just apply to recovery. It is ever so practical. For instance, I don't have the ability to control Dave. But I do have the ability to love him as my brother in Christ.

And that's the recognition that only came after I asked Dave to leave. My call to love him as his sister in Christ was more important than loving him as a husband.

Instead of immediately allowing Dave to come home, which he desperately wanted, I stood my ground with God. Meanwhile, Dave chose to sleep in his car for three nights. After three days of prayer and considering our financial and family needs, I invited Dave to come home, only to live downstairs. The bedroom became my sanctuary, a place Dave couldn't return to until there was an observable change in his behavior —things like seeing a counselor, joining a recovery group, doing recovery work or securing a sponsor. Dave was unhappy with me, and accused me of disobeying scripture and taking control. But I knew I was no longer trying to control my husband; rather, I was loving him through Christ. Through my boundaries, I was saying, "If you are going to run ahead of the commands of God,

I can't go there with you.* If you habitually bring what God forbids into our covenant relationship, I'll need you to leave, or I'll need to leave.**

Setting a boundary with Dave was the scariest and most loving thing I'd ever done. It wasn't a show of strength, but rather of my inability to control, manipulate or redeem him by my love. Most of all, it was an act of dignity, the legacy of all of God's children, and a special gift of being a woman.

Standing on the Stone: Embracing Dignity

> *"She is clothed with strength and dignity; she can laugh at the days to come. She speaks with wisdom, and faithful instruction is on her tongue. She watches over the affairs of her household..."* PROVERBS 31:25-27

Dignity: bearing, conduct, or speech indicative of self-respect or appreciation of the formality or gravity of an occasion or situation; nobility of character; worthiness.[51]

In the pinnacle of the book of Proverbs, chapter 31, Solomon declares that dignity is a marker of a virtuous woman...*she is clothed with strength and dignity.* Solomon wasn't the first to declare woman to have this gift. We find it in the beginning of Genesis, in the very creation of woman. We see it in Eve being

---

* *Anyone who runs on ahead [of God] and does not abide in the doctrine of Christ [who is not content with what He taught] does not have God..."* 2 JOHN 1:9 (AMPC)

** *Boundaries are part of every covenant relationship in the Bible. Adam and Eve couldn't eat of the tree of the knowledge of good and evil. Noah needed to build a boat in order to be saved. Abraham had to submit to circumcision, along with all the males in his household. Boundaries are required for God's church...the Bible gives instructions for how to discipline those who might pose a danger to the body.*

named a helper, in the Hebrew an *ezer*. If we go back to the earliest Hebrew language, there was a word picture for ezer—a man with a weapon and a giant eye. Thus, ezer means the eye that sees the danger.[52] Brain science has confirmed that women have better peripheral vision and are able to read body language better than men. Eve was gifted with part of God's nature that enabled her to see danger that Adam couldn't.* Solomon says… *she watches over the affairs of her household*. Dignity teaches us to discern danger and have a rightful response to it.

The sense of nobility in dignity is also found in the creation account. When God made Eve out of the dust of the earth, and part of Adam's flesh and bone, the Hebrew word used was *banah*. God *banah* (made) Eve. *Banah* is used in ancient Hebrew literature to connote making a palace. Woman was created last as the most complex part of creation, nobility. When God created Adam the Hebrew word was *yatsar*, used in ancient Hebrew to connote making a pot. Whereas estrogen broadens a woman's view (the complexity of a palace), testosterone narrows a man's view (the singleness of a pot), providing him with a dignity that translates into forward vision and leadership skills.

However, when a man is sexually aroused, testosterone narrows him to the point where his prefrontal cortex, the decision making part of the brain, shuts down. I believe God intended this to enable a man to be solely focused on his wife.

But a woman doesn't usually experience the same type of sexual narrowing as a man (unless her brain has been repeatedly exposed to pornography).[53] Women retain the ability to see danger, even when they are sexually aroused.

154   Beyond the sexual realm, women can discern danger, sexually, emotionally, physically and even spiritually!

---

* *God is our helper/ezer, see* PSALM 33:20, *"He is our* ezer *(help) and our shield…"*

How does all this work together? See the chart below.*

Gift of dignity	God's word	Brain science[54]	Proverbs 31
Eye that sees the danger	Eve was created as a helper/ezer (Genesis 2:18)	Women have better peripheral vision, read body language better	She watches over the affairs of her household (v. 27)
Nobility	God banah Eve (Genesis 2:22)	Her larger limbic system gives emotional intelligence.	She is clothed with strength & dignity (v. 25)
Broader view (including during sexuality)	Eyes that see the danger	Estrogen broadens her view. Desire doesn't close her view.	She speaks with wisdom (v. 26)

With all this in mind, I find the definition of dignity so convicting: "bearing, conduct or speech indicative of self-respect or appreciation of the formality or gravity of an occasion of situation." In the face of sexual addiction, I have handled myself in so many ways that lacked dignity...

My conduct and speech didn't reflect the gravity of Dave's actions. I glazed over the consequences of his sin just to get peace. I bartered continued affection to ensure my husband didn't abandon me the way my father did. I ran after Dave to apologize to him after he hurt me. I accepted half or heartless apologies, thrown at me in resentment just to get me off of his back. Sadly, I see so many others like me who bury dignity to keep love–who won't stand up against addiction, abuse or

---

* It is important to note that all people are not created alike. Certainly, some women feel more like a man in the intensity of their focus or trouble accessing their emotions. Some men have better peripheral vision and are more emotionally attuned. This doesn't make either abnormal..

abandonment, and say, "No more!" When we lose dignity in the face of emotional love, we buffer other people from the consequence of their actions. Dignity has a way of helping others find their own dignity.

Personally, I've struggled to find the noble, gentle heart of a woman of dignity. Remember the Stone of spiritual warfare and the gentle warfare? Dignity doesn't shame, make threats, control or manipulate, all mechanisms I've employed. Dignity requires God-given self-respect. Dignity keeps me from lowering myself into nagging, policing or trying to control another person. Dignity doesn't lash out in slander when someone abandons me or triggers me into past losses. Dignity holds grace and truth as equally important and refuses to throw either away.

Dignity requires God-given self-respect.

Ultimately, standing with God to find a way to love through Jesus (mediated love) is an act of dignity, and a beautiful expression of our gifts. With wisdom given by his Creator, Solomon aptly said that dignity enables us to laugh at the days to come.* For Dave and I, our forty-day separation became a turning point in recovery for both of us. I found a women's recovery group for wives of sexual addicts where I learned to take responsibility for my love addiction and codependency. Dave found a counselor who specialized in sexual addiction and began work restoring his own dignity. The beach vacation, which came around the 30-day mark, was turbulent in the beginning (Dave was still angry at me), but culminated in my husband walking into the ocean in deep desperation. He came

---

* *Strength and dignity are her clothing and her position is strong and secure; she rejoices over the future [the latter day or time to come, knowing that she and her family are in readiness for it]!* PROVERBS 31:25 (AMPC)

back to the beach house humbled and noticeably different. (See a "Word from Dave" for more details.) It seems significant to me that at the forty-day mark, the length of time Jesus spent in the desert being tempted,* I felt ready to invite Dave back into our bedroom so that we could begin recovering as a couple.

Let me be honest here. Learning to set and keep boundaries, and even more so, to walk with dignity has been a long process for both of us. To this day, we both have specific boundaries to protect us individually and as a couple.

My continuing quest is to love my husband (and other significant friends and family members) through Jesus, my mediator. Nothing gives me greater joy than to see how Dave leads us now in purity, seeking to have Jesus as his mediator as well.

Whatever boundaries you need, here are three simple keys:

1) **Stay away from the edge** – For each of us there is a deep pit we can fall into. For Dave it is sexual sin. For me, it is the insecurity that comes when I lean into strength and perfectionism rather than vulnerability. As a couple, there is an abyss of fear, shame and old patterns of communication that could undo us.
Your chasm might be sexual impurity, or other ways you medicate your losses, like compulsive drinking, shopping or eating. You'll want to keep your boundary wall far back enough that if you stumble, you won't risk falling in.** A boundary line right at the edge of the abyss is dangerous.

157

---

* MATTHEW 4:1-2
** *He who digs a pit [for others] will fall into it, and whoever breaks through a fence or a [stone] wall, a serpent will bite him.* ECCLESIASTES 10:8 (AMPC)

2) **<u>Keep your boundaries in the light</u>** – I know Dave's boundaries and he knows mine. We keep these boundaries so sacred that neither of us will initiate intimate time together if we have something we haven't confessed. We both also confess frequently to the small circle of men and women in our recovery groups. We both are absolutely committed to walking in the light.[*]

3) **<u>See boundaries as your friends</u>** – The need for boundaries points to losses that we didn't ask for and didn't want. Boundaries call us to confess that some situations are more than we can handle—facing our powerlessness. To *confess* means to agree with God about what is true.[55] Boundaries remind us of the truth of God's word. They teach us skills in engaging spiritual warfare. Having boundaries is a type of spiritual discipline, a true blessing.[**]

Grace Calls

> *To this you were called, because Christ suffered for you, leaving you an example, that you should follow in his steps.* I PETER 2:21

By this point in the journey of spiritual recovery, hopefully you've realized that neither extreme—chasing after someone to keep their love or erecting a tall wall of control—will bring the redemption you long for. This can bring a kind of despair...

[*] *For you have delivered me from death and my feet from stumbling, that I may walk before God in the light of life.* PSALM 56:13
[**] *The boundary lines have fallen for me in pleasant places; surely I have a delightful inheritance.* PSALM 16:6

where do I turn now? Just when we think it is too much, Jesus, the master with the gentle soul gets our attention...

> *Remember, as my follower you committed to letting me be in the center of your relationships. My path is your path, my dear one. When they hurled their insults at me, I did not retaliate. When I suffered, I made no threats. I bore their sins on my body, so that they could be healed. Why? I knew they were just sheep, gone astray.* *

The reason Jesus didn't retaliate or make threats was dignity. Truly, Jesus is our example of what it means to live nobly, especially in his response to other's hurts and sins. But this dignity didn't mean that he didn't have boundaries. Remember the time they wanted to stone him (in their own shame and angst), and Jesus turned and walked through the crowd?** Remember when his mother and brothers came to take him away, thinking he had lost his mind?*** Jesus didn't feel compelled to follow them in their fear, or even fix them. He understood that even he, the Son of God, needed to love them through his Father. He never let emotional love overtake his convictions. Grace whispers...*you too, can have dignity. Let Jesus mediate your relationships, especially the ones that mean so much to you. Don't let emotional love swing you from extreme to extreme.*

But Jesus' setting of boundaries didn't mean he put up a wall around his heart. Jesus could be emotionally vulnerable, even when others were hurting him. In the garden of Gethsemane, soldiers came to arrest him, accompanied by a crowd and led by one of his own. Seeing them, Jesus spoke with such gentleness

---

* *Paraphrased from* I PETER 2:23-25
** LUKE 4:30
*** MARK 3:21

and authority that they all fell to the ground in reverent fear, in spite of themselves.* Grace whispers...*He created you with this same dignity. Don't be afraid of being vulnerable, because it gifts you in so many ways.*

Your spiritual journey

Congratulations for stepping on the Stone of dignity. For some of you, this Stone is one of the scariest. You may wonder whether it is even safe. If you are married, standing up to an addict or to someone else who has hurt you can be terrifying. You may hesitate because you have friends who are uncomfortable with the idea (or who even think it is unspiritual). Others may be urging you towards divorce to end the pain. Be gentle with those whose opinions confuse or hurt you, but do remember that only you will live with your choices.

If you are divorced or your wounds came outside of marriage, please don't think you've passed the need for dignity. Now is an ideal time to work on these skills. Regardless of your situation, the act of setting boundaries may feel foreign, especially if you grew up in a family where there were either no boundaries or overly harsh ones. Take courage. Boundaries serve a redemptive purpose in God's plan, nudging us to face our losses, identify them, and then, in the spirit of dignity, set guards and protections.**

This Stone requires going deep with God. Your head may be spinning a little with the idea of mediated love. Do take the time to go back through it and absorb the Biblical teachings. Thankfully, you have a guide who is well versed in dignity—

---

* JOHN 18:6
** *The Hebrew writer talks about the need to guard the sanctity in marriage. For Hebrew readers, that might remind them of the temple guards, who guarded what was Holy to God. See* HEBREWS 13:4 *in* The Message.

Jesus, your great high priest. Since Jesus gave women and men unique measures of his dignity, you can rest assured he'll teach us how to use it. Jesus can help us find the tricky balance of accepting our gifts, and applying them to our trauma, hurts and even to our own struggles.

A man's gift of a narrow focus and a woman's gift of the eye that sees the danger are both expressions of God's love. However your gift expresses itself, know that as you journey step by step towards dignity, you choose love.

Circle of stones: dignity

Congratulations for stepping onto yet another Stone of recovery. On this sixth stone you will write the word **dignity**. Afterwards, hold the stone in your right hand and take a moment to think back on all you've learned in this Stone. What gifts of dignity are especially meaningful to you?

Your Stone of dignity will join your other stones: trauma, thorns, triggers, tears and warfare. Again, take a few moments to put them all in front of you and take a moment to rejoice in your progress. How is this journey of Stones changing the way you think? The way you live?

Journaling: Dignity

This Stone talks about the act of setting boundaries as standing where God stands. "Be holy, because I am holy" (1 Peter 1:16).

Picture God standing in a high and holy place. Imagine hearing his wisdom as he explains why addiction, abuse and abandonment are so damaging to relationships.

Imagine God holding out his hand and inviting him to stand with you, both in his truth and in his grace. Do you feel comfortable accepting his invitation?

161

Journal about how abandonment, abuse and/or addiction
have stolen your dignity. What it would look like for you to
embrace a Godly dignity? What changes will dignity require?

A word from Dave —Dignity

*"Self-respect is the root of discipline: The sense of
dignity grows with the ability to say no to oneself."*
– ABRAHAM JOSHUA HESCHEL

When Robin drew the line and asked me to leave the house in late May of 2003, it was an act of dignity. She was saying no to her love addicted self and yes to the woman of courage that God was calling her to be. I didn't appreciate it then, but looking back on it now, it was one of the most loving things she has ever done for me. The turmoil that was created by her saying "no more" was what I needed to force me to dig deeper and see the truth about how much I was still deceived by my addictive self. In reality, her decision was a call for me to fully respect the "clean-hearted" man God was trying to create in me, and to learn that with God's help, I could say "No" to worldly passions no matter how strong the temptation might be.*

At the time, it wasn't so easy to see Robin's decision to stand with God as the courageous act of love it was. I had just come off one of my longest stretches of purity success and my affirmation hungry soul was craving credit for the recovery work I had done. My addict self was quick to use this as a mind trick against me, insisting that Robin's response was unfair.[56] After all, wasn't calling a chat line insignificant compared to previous offenses?

This kind of legalistic thinking, trying to rate the seriousness of an offense, is common when an addict's heart is resisting brokenness. In my experience, it takes an event like what happened with Robin and I (where she asked me to move out

163

* *For the grace of God has appeared that offers salvation to all people. It teaches us to say "No" to ungodliness and worldly passions, and to live self-controlled, upright and godly lives in this present age.* TITUS 2:11-12

of the house), or something similar (being asked to leave the church, being asked to leave a job, being arrested for a crime, etc.) to bring someone into the state of reality needed to fully engage recovery.

Why does it require a crisis to evoke change? Addicts have become accustomed to living in a fantasy world. For men, living under the protective eye of our spouse (the eye that sees the danger), we become experts at dodging, weaving, and "weaseling" out of situations in order to survive the likely fallout that would come if our partner knew the totality of our actions. Robin has told me that women addicts struggle with being open with their husbands, fearing the impact their disclosures might have on his self-esteem. The answer for both men and women is walking in truth by bringing their deeds into the light (John 3:19-21).

This is why we believe that married people must confess their offenses to their spouse. Telling your offense to another believer might lead to a "thanks for being open" response. Telling a piece of the story to several different people is another common way addicts use to avoid the impact that might come if someone knew the whole story.

I could only get the reality I needed by confessing the entire story of my falls to my wife and letting her respond honestly without restriction—shedding tears of sorrow, venting anger and expressing fears. Hearing Robin's responses can be painful, but also much closer to the reality of how God sees my actions, much closer to the dignity befitting the situation. After all, I made a vow on our wedding day to keep my body, my eyes and my thoughts devoted to her and her alone.

As Robin mentioned, the timing of her asking me to leave compounded the frustration for me. Vacation usually meant more time for relaxation and greater opportunities for physical intimacy. Now our vacation would bring frustration. When we reached our ocean side retreat, my spiritual man tried to encourage me to use this separation as a time to serve my family and seek God. But my addict was desperate and angry, fearing that he might be facing extinction.

As our week on the beach in North Carolina neared its completion, Robin, fighting for her dignity, stuck to her guns. She made it clear that I wasn't welcome in the bedroom unless I wanted to sleep on the floor. My frustration caused me to pull back from her emotionally. I was acting like a child that was not getting his way, moping and using manipulative words that had gotten me what I wanted in years gone by. Robin's brother had even picked up on my mood and asked me what was going on.

Finally, when my stress and unhappiness came to a breaking point, my spiritual self convinced me to go for a walk on the beach and figure things out. It was a cloudy cool day with a strong wind blowing off the Atlantic Ocean. I walked for a long time, venting my every thought and emotion to God. Eventually a peace came over me. My narcissistic, demanding self came into full view and remorse for how I had been treating Robin weighed heavy on my heart. I felt like I needed a new start, putting to death the addict that was warring against my soul. I looked out over the cold grey turbulent sea and then a crazy thought came into my mind. Go sit down in the water and let God baptize you as a symbol of a new beginning. So that's what I did. I sat down on the beach in the freezing water and looked out into the ocean. What happened next caught me by surprise. A wave hit me so hard that it literally drug me across the rocky ocean floor. I had been "God smacked!" I pulled myself out of the water soaking, and shivering, but smiling from ear to ear. Running back to condo, I was eager to get a hot shower and share with Robin my experience and tearfully apologize.

By the time we returned home to Chicago, I had a deeper understanding of how broken I would need to become if I was ever to achieve compete victory. I was grateful that Robin had taken a stand and believed that God was leading her and me to a better place. What a blessing it is to have a wife who has willing to put everything on the line for the sake of dignity and holiness!

Back to Your Journal:

Dave shares about being "God-smacked" in the Atlantic Ocean and how God gave him the courage to face his own "demanding self."

In the wake of abandonment, abuse and addiction, it is tempting to form our own set of demands as a way of protecting ourselves from further hurt. Ask God to help you see your own demands (things you insist on receiving from God and others as a condition of your happiness).

Write a list of your demands in your journal, and then journal about how dignity and standing with God can replace a demanding spirit.

Grace reveals a place of safety
A higher path trod by the Spirit
From deepest darkness to sanity
From chaos to God's embrace

Scorning the Shame: Acceptance

All things as they move toward God are beautiful,
and they are ugly as they move away from Him.
— A. W. TOZER, *THE ATTRIBUTES OF GOD*

W E BURIED MY SISTER ON A NIPPY DAY IN early March. Before the wake started, our family, having gathered from near and far, joined in a tight circle with our arms around each other. The whole family was weeping, even my father, whom I had never seen cry. That is, everyone except me. Once again, I had shifted into my role as the strong one. *This is good for us all to be here,* I thought. Looking around the circle, I tried to push away guilt at my emotionless state. I bent my head forward, wiping at my dry eyes. As much as I wanted to cry, I couldn't. Besides, tears were inadequate to soothe the loss and all that preceded her death days before her twenty-first birthday.

Three months earlier, just before Christmas, my father had left my mother for a woman he had met in recovery for alcohol addiction. Of course, my father couldn't have known that three months after he had left mom, his daughter would be killed in a terrible automobile accident. Like the rest of us, he was helpless. I'm guessing this trail of broken fences—alcoholism, a depressed wife, an affair, deserting his family, the death of his beloved daughter—was more than one man could handle. Just

169

maybe the guilt of deserting the family filled him with shame at Jennifer's funeral. Perhaps he knew there was absolutely nothing he could do to absolve himself for the affair.

Regardless, that funeral would mark a clear dividing point in my dad's approach to me—from a father who tried to be engaged on some level to a father who no longer made an effort. To his credit, he stuck to the path of recovery, giving up alcohol completely. Yet I was stung by the personal injustice of it all. After all, I had suffered through Dad's alcoholic rages, his verbal, emotional and physical abuse, and Mom's resulting depression. Now it seemed I wouldn't reap the benefits of his recovery.

On the other hand, my relationship with my mother deepened. As I shared my spiritual journey, her heart opened. She gave her life to God and found acceptance in a circle of Christian sisters. Slowly but surely she began to heal. It was obvious that she still loved Dad and always would, even if he was with another woman. She was determined not to divorce him. He would have to divorce her against her will. He never did.

My mother wanted me to mend things with Dad. As a Christian, I wanted to heal the broken bond with him, but it seemed that this desire only ran one way. When I left phone messages, they weren't returned. When I sent gifts, they weren't acknowledged. When I would come from the Midwest to visit home, Mom would encourage me to see Dad. But Dad would only appear if I made all the effort to find him. Then he would show up for a short visit at my mother's house, say he'd be back the next day and then disappear again. More abandonment added to years of childhood losses added up to chronic shame[57]—a struggle I took into my marriage with Dave.

Now I see how marriage presses on the bruises in the heart of someone who has been abandoned. Dave knew how precious unconditional acceptance was to me and sought to give it. Yet when tests came, I responded like love was conditional. In the heat of arguments, I folded. I didn't have enough emotional fortitude to withstand his disapproval. As I sought to make up for what we both lacked, marriage became the new focus of my codependence. If I didn't hold tight, love could evaporate. I would be abandoned. My husband's on and off sexual acting out become like Miracle Grow[58] on my pesky weeds of fear. Even now, these invasive roots still find a way to send up new shoots. Perhaps this was what our counselor meant when he said, "Robin you will never entirely recover."

Recently, I read a novel about a teen girl who lost her brother to suicide and her father to guilt.[59] Reading the description of the brother's funeral and the father's desertion afterwards, I finally connected Jennifer's funeral and the loss of my dad. Death and abandonment combined to form one big blow. Facing that double loss enabled me to begin facing subtle messages embedded in my father's choices. *None of you are enough to keep me. Being your father simply isn't that important anymore. You aren't worth fighting for. It's all on your shoulders. You have to search for me if you want to find me.*

At the heart of all of this was a shame that I didn't deserve or earn. As a child I learned to be ashamed of my needs, ashamed of unruly feelings, and later on, ashamed to have an alcoholic father. Shame created misbeliefs built on "should haves" I wasn't even aware existed. I *should have* been able to keep my family together. I *should have* been enough to keep my father engaged (as firstborn daughters mistakenly act like they have power to do). My love *should have* been enough to keep Dave from straying. Underneath was fear that if I stopped over-achieving, I would be exposed as the one not worth loving. Now it makes sense why I doubled down to keep Dave's love. Why Christianity became just another place I needed to prove I was enough. I was

171

running from shame. Yet the faster I fled the shame, the more power it wielded.

It is comforting to know that I have a guide who has the antidote for shame. His acceptance is more than enough, even as I fall short daily. And if God's son needed to take a stand against shame, certainly this will be part of my ongoing journey. Here's the good news. As I've drained my wound of abandonment, the shame has followed. This has taken many tears (Stone four), spiritual warfare (Stone five), and setting healthy boundaries (Stone six). It has taken a level of vulnerability with others that I never imagined I could achieve. The healing of my heart, soul, mind and strength have come as I've put my full weight on the Stone of acceptance.

Understanding acceptance

> *Those who had seen it told the people what had happened to the demon-possessed man—and told about the pigs as well. Then the people began to plead with Jesus to leave their region. As Jesus was getting into the boat, the man who had been demon-possessed begged to go with him. Jesus did not let him, but said, "Go home to your own people and tell them how much the Lord has done for you, and how he has had mercy on you...."* MARK 5:16-19

Just recently I re-read a series of books that were among my favorites in college, Gene Edward's classic allegories, *The Singer*, *The Song* and *The Messenger*. One of the most compelling threads in this trilogy is this demon-possessed man and his odyssey from abandonment and shame to full acceptance by Jesus. Before we come back to Edward's imaginings, let's delve a little deeper into the Biblical story. *Please take a moment to turn to Mark 5:1-20 and read it out loud.*

You may have noticed in Mark's account that the man's real name is never mentioned. For ease of discussion, I will use the name Chaos (an actual name in the time of Jesus inspired by the material God used to create the earth).* Chaos' abandonment ran deep. He lived alone and alienated in the tombs. He was in immense emotional, physical and spiritual turmoil, crying out in a loud voice and cutting himself with stones. From time to time, a group of men would bravely attempt to subdue Chaos with chains, fearing the harm he could cause unbound. Talk about trauma! It would seem that shame didn't leave Chaos night or day, triggering violent reactions. In his terror, he terrorized others, sabotaging any hope of relationship.

But what is most telling to me is the tender touch of Jesus with an abandoned soul. After Jesus cast the demons into a herd of pigs who charged down a hill into the sea and died, the Bible tells us that Chaos was, "sitting there dressed and in his right mind (v. 15). I hear peace, as Chaos sat at Jesus feet instead of running through the tombs. He no longer feared being chained. I hear wholeness, as Chaos sat fully clothed, fully present, fully engaged. I hear the miraculous healing of his troubled mind, the reversing of years of messages embedded in him by the relentless accusation of a legion of demons. Thinking of Hebb's Law (Stone four), all the neurons that had fired together, and then wired together, now had been completely rewired by the touch of the Master. Chaos was basking in the complete acceptance of his maker and savior, Jesus.

173

* *In* GENESIS 1:2, *the phrase "formless and empty" is translated from Tohu va Bohu, a Hebrew phrase only used once in the Bible. This chaos was considered so staggering, that the translators created a phrase to contain it. Yet the Spirit was hovering over this chaos ready to create beauty. A key part of our re-creation is the Spirit's work in transforming our chaos into beauty.*

As Jesus boarded a boat to leave the region, Chaos begged Jesus to allow him to come. He wanted to be part of Jesus' crusade. Wouldn't Chaos have been an effective object lesson of God's power over demons? Yet, Jesus didn't allow it. Instead he told Chaos to go back to "his own people," and tell them his story of Jesus having mercy on him. Why didn't Jesus allow him to choose? After all, Chaos had been rejected for so long. The townspeople were scared of him before his restoration, and now they were even more afraid (see Mark 5:15). When they begged Jesus to leave, they assumed Chaos would go as well.

Thinking of this man in light of what we've learned about spiritual recovery can help us make some intelligent guesses of why Jesus sent him back to his people. Now Chaos, re-created by the Master, needed relational transformation—changing from someone repeatedly shunned to a tender, humble disciple who trusted others. To do so would take immense vulnerability and courage. By staying with his people, Chaos would learn to rise above being defined by his shame, regardless of how they treated him. His new identity would come from the Lord's mercy (v. 19).

And I see even more. Even though they didn't understand why, the townspeople needed Chaos. Perhaps a whole region, yet untouched by Jesus, could be evangelized. Chaos had been healed in a moment, but now he had a lifetime ahead of learning to continually accept and mirror the acceptance of Jesus. He would be tested. No doubt, Satan would try to steal back that sense of acceptance. Some wouldn't trust him. Chaos would need to continually engage spiritual warfare.

Here's where Gene Edward's trilogy is so powerful and moving. In his story, the man possessed by demons still has a propensity for shame even after his healing by Jesus. So when Jesus is crucified, the man finds himself in utter despair. The

174

authorities link him with the Singer (Jesus), arrest him and put him back in chains. He allows the arrest with no struggle, convinced that at any moment his sanity will flee. But when he hears the Singer's voice on resurrection day, he finds he can still sing the song the Singer taught him. He strains against the chains, but then remembers all that he has learned. As he stops struggling and instead calls on God, the chains just fall off. Now he understands. He will never again be that demon possessed man bound and persecuted by shame. He is not abandoned.

Like Edwards, I've got to think that one of Satan's goals in demon possession was to sabotage people spiritually *and* relationally. How could someone possessed by demons love God with all their heart, soul, mind and strength or love their neighbor as their self? Demon possession meant abandonment, and abandonment left a stinging stronghold of shame. Likewise, Satan incited the religious leaders to heap "sinners" with a destructive shame that would sabotage them relationally.

Through all this darkness comes a shining light, an antidote Satan has no defense for—the unconditional acceptance of Jesus. To understand the glory of that acceptance, let's take a deeper look at the relationship between abandonment and shame.

Abandonment and Shame

> *Shame as a neurobiological phenomenon is not bad in and of itself. It is rather, our system's way of warning of possible impending abandonment, although we do not think of it in those terms [...] However, our problem with it is generally that we tend to respond to it by relationally moving away from others rather than towards them. Curt Thompson, The Soul of Shame.*

I agree with Curt Thompson that shame warns us of potential abandonment. But where did that shame come from? Some of the most difficult-to-overcome shame floods our soul when someone abandons us. Take a look at the definition of abandonment for insight:

> *Abandonment: [...] Involves the sense that significant others will not be able to continue providing emotional support, connection, strength, or practical protection because they are emotionally unstable and unpredictable (e.g., angry outbursts), unreliable, or erratically present; because they will die imminently; or because they will abandon the patient in favor of someone better.*[60]

So how do we change our view of our personal chaos in light of the unconditional acceptance of Jesus? The journey of Stones we've been on together has much to tell us about both. First, let's look at the evolution of shame in our lives. See the chart, Stronghold of Shame (on the following page), for insight.

Feeling shame does not mean we've done something wrong.

STRONGHOLD OF SHAME

This cycle shows the interaction between shame and abandonment. This cycle revolves around what I call a "well of abandonment." This pain, laced with shame, results from abandonment wounds (or fear of abandonment). This "well" may be completely hidden. We may fear that admitting we feel shame or that we have abandonment wounds means that we have done something shameful, and therefore, that we are shameful.[61] Feeling shame *does not* mean we've done something wrong. It is healthy to admit feelings of shame. The stronghold of toxic shame is built and maintained through fear. This brew of shame and fear leads to repression, shutting people out, denying or controlling the increased impact of shame, compensating for our weaknesses, and then finding a way to medicate the pain. Let's look at each of these steps and see how they interact.

Shame enters: Abandonment comes bringing shame with it. Over time, triggers multiply our fear, as the accuser looks for ways to set painful thorns.

We repress the wound: The more we deny feeling shame, the more we are likely to repress the pain of what caused these feelings and thoughts, losing the cleansing power of tears (Stone four). Shame increases while we are on the run. Sometimes, all seems well. In the dark moments, we feel handcuffed.

We shut out others: True spiritual warfare (Stone five) gets lost in the fray as shame keeps us from opening up with others.

We deny or control: We either weaken our boundaries to become codependent, or make them so rigid that no one can enter. Instead of standing with God (Stone six), we invest our energy in feeling safe.

We compensate for our weakness: As the triggers and thorns come, they become more and more painful. We turn to performance and spiritual theatrics (putting on a mask) to convince others we are acceptable.

We medicate the shame: All of this traps shame within, in what I'll call a well of abandonment. Without a spiritual release for shame, it stores up inside of us. This internalized shame will build up, seeking a way to be expressed. Our drug of choice might include any compulsive behavior that is done in secret, promising a false relief but only creating more shame. And pockets of shame make easy footholds for Satan.

You can see why this cycle becomes self-perpetuating. The need of our soul, strength, heart and mind to cope with the deep well of abandonment turns us inward. Our relationships suffer. A little like our friend Chaos who was caught inside the tombs, we live running from accusations thrown at us by the evil one. Vulnerability becomes a foe rather than a friend.

So what is the answer?

When I first charted this out, it thrilled my heart to see a beautiful simplicity and clarity to the ways of the Spirit. See the chart below (Victory of Acceptance).

Victory of Acceptance

Acceptance is the path to draining the well of abandonment and its accompanying shame. As you can see there is a similar circle to the Stronghold of Shame chart. But this one has channels leading outward from the center that allow the abandonment wound to drain. As Christians, we already have the radical acceptance of Jesus. What remains is for us to adopt the discipline of acceptance into our spiritual recovery. That looks something like this:

Shame comes – Being on a path to recovery doesn't prevent shame from showing up at our door. We get triggered into our core wound of abandonment.

We accept the wound – By letting our wound speak, we access God's plan of mourning and comfort. As we do this habitually, in some mysterious way, it seems that our neurons rewire. A spiritual discipline begins to form.

We accept help – Part of spiritual warfare is letting go of old friends like denial and control. Instead, we surrender our pain and confess the resulting shame to others. We choose vulnerability over self-protection.

We accept the change – Bit by bit, we accept that we are no longer chained by shame. We learn to scorn shame (more in a moment). With that, we embrace healthy boundaries that are balanced and God-driven.

We accept our weakness – Perfection is no longer needed. Our spirits are freed as we say to the evil one, "Yes, I am weak, sinful and still struggle. But the Son of God fully and freely accepts me. Away from me."

We accept our true value —We come boldly to his throne of grace knowing he understands our weakness and pain. That means we are accepted. We are completely valued. Now instead of being plagued by shame, we rejoice in a double-portion of acceptance—our initial salvation and his ongoing redemption of our battles.*

Toxic shame versus Godly sorrow

Obviously, a big part of this battle is identifying the voice of the accuser (Stone two: thorns). One of his most potent weapons is to shame us over our sinfulness. This can be especially deceiving, because there is a healthy type of shame talked about in the Bible, a shame that leads us to change. To find this higher, holier perspective, we need to separate toxic shame (the kind Jesus calls us to scorn) from a healthy sense of falling short. I find clarity in the Biblical principle of Godly sorrow:

> *Godly sorrow brings repentance that leads to salvation and leaves no regret, but worldly sorrow brings death. See what this godly sorrow has produced in you: what earnestness, what eagerness to clear yourselves, what indignation, what alarm, what longing, what concern, what readiness to see justice done. At every point you have proved yourselves to be innocent in this matter.* 2 CORINTHIANS 7:10–11

Godly sorrow is directed at my own behavior and its effects on other people's lives. It is far different from the toxic shame that says I am defective and unable to do anything about it.

181

---

* *Instead of your shame you will receive a double portion, and instead of disgrace you will rejoice in your inheritance. And so you will inherit a double portion in your land, and everlasting joy will be yours.* ISAIAH 61:7

Instead, this godly sorrow empowers me to face the ways I strike out, withdraw or shame others. It gently exposes my sinful responses when the possibility of abandonment seems more than I can bear. Take a look at the chart below for insight.

Toxic shame	Godly sorrow
I am a failure in the eyes of God and/ or others.	I constantly fall short of God's glory (Romans 3:23). In my pain, I also hurt others.
Reflects our deepest fears: I have made an irreparable breach that cannot be repaired, so I should hide.	Reflects reality: God/others were hurt by my actions/words/behavior. Yet God's grace allows me to face myself.
De-motivates. Why should I try? I'll never satisfy you.	Leads us towards transformation. I see I've hurt you. What can I do?
Full of despair. Extreme reactions could range from suicide to murder.	Full of godly desperation. Leads our heart towards recognition, and repentance.
Weakens us spiritually.	Refreshes and cleanses as we remember the acceptance God extends (Acts 3:19).

This chart fills my heart with joy. You see, one of the ways Satan attacks me is to taunt me about my sinfulness. Now I see that godly sorrow is motivated and sustained by the acceptance of Jesus. Hallelujah, he accepts me! I am free to be curious about what took me to sinful places, instead of throwing toxic shame on myself.

With its rising and falling, this journey has thrust me on the potter's wheel so that new air bubbles could be pushed out of the clay of my heart. But as Jesus has done his work of probing and examining, I've come away with less shame instead of more. God's acceptance has become more precious, grace more indispensable. Through this I've learned an essential lesson. *If I look at my life through me, I see mess. If I look at my life through Jesus, I see blessed.*

> *If I look at my life through me, I see mess.*
> *If I look at my life through Jesus, I see blessed.*

As Jesus holds out his hand to bring us onto this Stone, he also reminds us that the true power to overcome the shame surrounding abandonment is to follow him to the cross. Here we learn the power of scorning the shame.

Standing on the Stone of Acceptance

> *Therefore, since we are surrounded by such a great cloud of witnesses, let us throw off everything that hinders and the sin that so easily entangles. And let us run with perseverance the race marked out for us, fixing our eyes on Jesus...For the joy set before him he endured the cross, scorning its shame...* HEBREWS 12:1–2

What we really need is a way to process shame that makes us more resilient, while reducing shame's sticking power. To do so, we need to look no further than our guide, Jesus. We need to learn from Jesus how to scorn the shame.

Scorn: *kataphroneo*

Jesus scorned [kataphroneo] *the shame.*

Kataphroneo comes from two root words: *kata*, meaning down, and *phroneo*: regulating behavior from an inner mindset. In other words, to scorn the shame like Jesus did would be to repel it. Although we can't control the wounds that have already happened, we can choose whether to let new shame penetrate. This powerful Greek word gives the sense of esteeming shame lightly, deciding that it is of little account.

Knowing how hard it is for me to esteem shame lightly, I am moved by Jesus' example, especially in all the events surrounding his death on the cross.

Jesus scorned the shame of dishonor. Throughout his ministry, others called him names, accused him of being demon-possessed, held councils to talk about his behavior, made public denouncements and, eventually, plotted his demise. He was dishonored at every turn, yet *he scorned the shame.*

Jesus scorned the shame of disgrace. His own people condemned him to a shameful death. His disciples fell asleep and then ran away in his moment of need, while a mob of fellow Jews screamed for his crucifixion. Surely he felt like a leper being excluded from his people, yet *he scorned the shame.*

Jesus scorned the shame of disfigurement. In the Old Testament law, a man couldn't serve as a priest if he was blemished (Leviticus 21:21). Satan, knowing God's plan to institute Jesus as our Great High Priest, wanted to convince Jesus that he wasn't qualified. No doubt Satan incited them to scourge Jesus (rip his back to pieces), and the soldiers to strike him in the face repeatedly and then hammer a crown of thorns into his scalp. Jesus was one "from whom men turned their faces,'" yet *he scorned the shame*.

Scorning the shame cost Jesus internal agony expressed in tears, loud cries and prayers to God in the Garden of Gethsemane. It cost him extreme stress (to the point of his sweat being mixed with blood) as he surrendered to God.** Yet scorning the shame gave Jesus a gift, one which each of us on this journey so desperately need. Through scorning the shame, Jesus was able to lift his eyes beyond his own pain to God's working in his life.

You may be thinking...*wait, only Jesus could do that perfectly.* You are right, my friend. You have just discovered a clue to a critical connection. We are not enough to overcome shame. We need a guide that is higher and holier than us. And that requires seeing his holiness as perfectly meeting our need. We stand on this Stone, as we make Jesus our true high priest.

Grace calls

> *Accept one another, then, just as Christ accepted*
> *you, in order to bring praise to God.* ROMANS 15:7

Facing down your shame is a large task of re-creation and prepares your heart for opening the sanctuary door of sexual healing (Stone eight). This part of recovery has circled you back to your coming to God—his acceptance given at a great price. You trusted he would forgive. Now it's time to once again claim that acceptance as your own. The chains of shame have no power over you. Yet, as with the other Stones, facing our

---

* *He was despised and rejected by mankind, a man of suffering, and familiar with pain. Like one from whom people hide their faces he was despised, and we held him in low esteem.* ISAIAH 53:3

** LUKE 22:39–46

shame can bring fear. Grace calls. *I'll help you take yourself less seriously, own your flaws and mistakes, and laugh even more. Trust me.* If you are like me, you long to be past shame once and for all. When it pops its ugly head up again and fills your heart with dread, it can be overwhelming. Grace calls. *As you scorn the shame, I will help you change what Satan intends for your harm into part of God's goodness…a sacred altar where you learn the true meaning of holy living.*

Your spiritual journey

Congratulations for stepping on yet another stone of the journey. Stone seven, acceptance, is one of the most difficult stones to navigate. It takes balance. Don't be surprised if you feel a bit wobbly on this stone like the stone might tip and send you to the depths of darkness at any moment. It is perfectly acceptable to allow another Stone to help hold your weight. Do remember to lean on your guide, Jesus, for support.* He will help you stand. As you unwind your own shame, you'll find a growing compassion for the one(s) who hurt you. At the same time, you are learning to embrace Godly sorrow as an antidote to shame. Are you finding these skills far easier to talk about than to implement? Afraid that there's more to recovery than what you bargained for? Hang in there, my friend. With time and patience, you'll find a beauty that far outshines the pain in this journey—the joy of re-creation.

* *Then Asa called to the Lord his God and said, "Lord, there is no one like you to help the powerless against the mighty. Help us, Lord our God, for we rely on you, and in your name we have come against this vast army.*
2 CHRONICLES 14:11-12

Circle of stones: acceptance

There is only one more stone before you complete the second part of the journey. Congratulations! On this seventh stone you will write the word **acceptance**. This is a sacred stone indeed. In fact, you might want a smallish stone that you can easily take with you everywhere.

Your stone of acceptance will join your other stones: trauma, thorns, triggers, tears, warfare and dignity. Again, take a few moments to put them all in front of you. What victories have you had thus far?

Journaling: Acceptance

Curt Thompson sheds some light on shame, (see his quotation on page 175) that…

1) Shame is intimately attached to the fear of abandonment.
2) The problem is that when we feel shame we move away from people instead of towards them.

Asking Jesus to be your guide, make a list of circumstances or ongoing struggles that currently cause you shame. Then write by each one, "away" or "towards" meaning how you relate to others when shame comes.

Choose a friend you feel safe with and go through what you discover. Pray together that you'll remember the acceptance of Jesus the next time shame attacks.

A word from Dave — Acceptance

*A positive sense of self precedes any possibility of closeness
or intimacy. Without that fundamental acceptance
of self, nurturing and intimacy can be closed out.*
— PATRICK CARNES, *OUT OF THE SHADOWS*, P. 171

For me, and for the numerous men I've counseled, the paradoxical relationship between shame and acceptance is one of the trickiest yet most important balances to maintain during recovery. On one hand, indulging lustful desires is shameful. Ephesians 5:12 states, "It is shameful to even mention what the disobedient do in secret." For those seeking to recover from addiction, shame is a barrier to true intimacy. On the other hand, acceptance and intimacy are possibly their greatest needs. The evil one is aware of this and masterfully uses toxic shame to keep people trapped in the darkness of isolation. Understanding the difference between shameful acts and being a shameful person is the key to unlocking this door of understanding.

Sexual shame started early for me and soon became etched into my heart in ways that have been difficult to overcome. When I was about six, an elderly relative suffering from a skin disease came to our house to sunbathe in the nude. We lived in the country and she thought the large mounds of construction dirt behind our house would give her the privacy she needed. My parents warned me, but curiosity got the best of me and I climbed up one of the mounds to sneak a peek. She saw me and told my parents. They scolded me for disobeying and looking. I was left feeling like I was bad. Unfortunately this was reinforced by other sexual violations during my pre-teen years. Reading an article my mother gave me was the extent of my sexual education.

188

Because I had little training about sexuality, the connection in my brain between sex and shame grew stronger. Sex and shame became synonymous to me. I felt deficient because of my lack of knowledge and dirty because of my inability to control my sexual urges. In junior high, Satan's whispers grew louder, but they now added defectiveness to their chorus. I had no idea until many years later in counseling, that all this was the perfect trap. My craving to be accepted would fuel my sexual addiction for years to come. *Why am I repeating behaviors that bring grief to others and myself? I must be totally sinful!*

In my late 20's when I became part of a church where regular confession was encouraged, I hoped that this might bring the end to my sexual sin. It didn't. Now my sin was coming into the light, but those trying help me were alarmed and frustrated. In desperation, they tried heaping shame on me to help me repent.

How can you say that you love God and continue doing this?

Can't you see how this is hurting your wife?

You don't really hate the sin; you just hate confessing it!

They reasoned that if I could really see how disgusting my actions were to God, I would stop. They did not understand, nor did I, that the emotional pain of shame is one of the primary drivers of the addictive cycle. This journey of shame lasted for 36 years embedding thorns deep into my perplexed heart. As someone well acquainted with the Bible and Jesus teaching about purity, my biggest accuser was my own corrupted conscience. What I didn't yet understand was that Jesus had the perfect answer for my fear and shame.

189

You see, at just the right time, when we were still powerless, Christ died for the ungodly. Very rarely will anyone die for a righteous person, though for a good person someone might possibly dare to die. But God demonstrates his own love for us in this: While we were still sinners, Christ died for us. ROMANS 5:6-8

Although my actions were sinful and shameful, God accepted me for who I was. He loved and desired me, and his plan was for me to be in real relationships that would meet the needs of my heart. As I entered into a counseling relationship with a mentor in 2002, the shame began to lift. He helped me see that my acting out, while illegitimate, was driven by my emotional pain and desire for acceptance and affirmation. Two years later, when I attended my first recovery group, I felt like I had come home. As the men there listened to my whole story and offered me acceptance and hope, more shame was lifted. Twelve years later, I still meet with men weekly to drain any new emotional pain.

When I was first asked to speak publicly, sharing purity struggles and what I was learning from recovery, I feared I would be seen as a sinful pervert and that people might be afraid to be around me. But instead, I was showered with appreciation and grace, as men and women stood in line to tell their stories.

Twelve years of speaking, and having my life story told to thousands through Robin's books has actually produced more acceptance, affirmation, and respect than I dreamed possible. I still cringe when I am reminded of how far I had fallen and how much pain I caused. But with Jesus as my guide, I now scorn the shame and let the power of his amazing acceptance be seen through my testimony. Here are a few shame-busters I've learned through my journey:

- Find a recovery group where you can be totally open and accepted.
- Seek counseling if persistent shame is haunting you.
- Learn to identify the language of shame and ask significant other's help to banish it from your conversations.
- Go to the scriptures and study out how God sees you.

Back to your journal

Dave found power to overcome sexual addiction as he discovered the true need of his heart was to be valued and accepted. What are the needs of your heart when it comes to acceptance?

Make a list of areas where you haven't always felt accepted, for instance: my health (do people believe I'm really sick?) or my intellect (my father called me stupid, and now I silently call myself stupid).

How are you tempted to compensate? Find one scripture like Dave did (Romans 5:6-8) that speaks to your heart and commit it to memory.

Grace can save you from adultery
Center you after abandonment
Comfort you as you face abuse
Renew the beauty of covenant

STONE EIGHT
Healing Sexually: Sanctuary

But for you, the ones who tremble at the sound of
My name, a warm sun of righteousness will come
forth with healing in its rays, and you will go out,
springing from the stalls like calves in open pasture.

— MALACHI 4:2 (VOICE)

D AVE PULLED OUT A CASSETTE TAPE AND
waved it. "Would you like to listen to this together?"
he asked with a smile. "What is it?" I asked. "It is
Catherine Smith's* talk about sexual intimacy for wives.'" I
sighed. We were driving along a backcountry road on our
way to a family event. Having been married twelve years, and
having had sexual addiction rear its head again and again, our
sexual relationship had become a sore point. When Dave had
first found Catherine's message in a pile of old cassette tapes,
he listened to it several times by himself. *If Robin only knew*
these teachings, surely it would be better for us. Dave asked me on
multiple occasions if I would listen to the lesson. My replies over
time went something like this...*sure, later, maybe, we'll see.* Sure
enough, the speaker was a faithful follower of Christ with good
things to say. To Dave it meant hope of a more sexually engaged
wife—a potential answer for his many purity battles. To me

193

---

* *Made-up name, but a real lesson.*

it represented Dave's insistence on making me into someone different, fueling my insecurity that I would never be enough. In one particularly charged moment, I said, "Well then, you should have married her!"

Driving along that lonely road, I finally drew a line. "Dave, just so you know, I will never listen to that lesson."

Dave was left defeated while I was left hurt and stuck. (And true to my word, I never listened to it.) The sheer risk of sexual intimacy had turned into a great revealer of my own need for additional emotional, mental and even physical recovery. These wounds showed themselves as I deflected being present with my own body. Body image issues resurfaced tracing back to my eating disorder in college. I even strategized how to undress when Dave was occupied in another room.

Sexual fantasy (retreating inside my head) became a way to respond without the risk of communicating how I really felt. I lived out the paradox of being far away in a fantasy, so I could appear to be fullly engaged. I wondered what it would be like to completely shut down my sexual self—even though in our early marriage I cherished this part of our relationship.

Sometimes I fed myself romance through television or movies. It pains me to admit it, but I especially enjoyed the two days after Dave and I had intimate time together...days free from unpleasant encounters or pressure to perform. Then as day after day would pass, I would procrastinate, look for clues that he wasn't needy and convince myself that tomorrow would be better. Dave was sure that I never thought about sex. Actually, the opposite was true. I fretted about it endlessly. There was a lost little girl inside of me crying out for value.

194

These wounds showed themselves often. Times where I divorced myself from my own desires in trying to manage his. Nights when Dave would pronounce our encounter over when

I wasn't showing enough interest. Weeks where I compromised precious boundaries in return for peace. Nights when Dave went downstairs to sleep on the couch because things hadn't gone as planned, and then I went after him to apologize. Our unhealthy patterns became well-rehearsed dance steps. Dave and I were both tempted at times to elevate each other to the status of, "my biggest problem in the world," a sign of mutual codependence and making each other our "higher power."[62] By the time we entered recovery after our forty-day sexual separation, we both yearned for something new—being re-created by God himself. Our marriage depended on it.

Recovery allowed us to begin healing this thorny tumbleweed made up of miles and miles of repressed pain. In addition, we needed tools for diffusing the ongoing pain of trauma, triggers and thorns. This all would require introducing a different kind of chaos—a healing chaos. Growing through this chaos meant Dave giving me the safety of weeping in his chest over wounds he had caused. There were times when we made love with tears running down my cheeks. It meant me staying gently engaged with Dave when, feeling spurned sexually, he confided he wanted to curl up in a ball and weep.

As our struggles led us back to the cross of Jesus, I learned to pray rather than get hysterical, explode or say something difficult to undo. Dave learned that a difficult conversation could provide an entrance into intimacy instead of an exit. Through listening to my body, I was rediscovering sexuality as a holy place. At the same time Dave no longer wanted sex as a medication— he dealt with pain through shedding tears often. His emerging tenderness and humility softened my heart. As God's warm sun of righteousness melted away fear, insecurity and blame, we learned to skip like calves in a pasture. Play, laughter and eye contact became more important than techniques, tricks and performance. Oneness became our supreme value.

If you aren't currently married, you may be wondering if sexual healing is for you. *Does it matter at this place in my life? Should I skip this Stone?* My answer would be, *Yes, it does matter my dear friend.*

This second part of the journey has been building towards this very pinnacle. Do understand that in this tender realm, each of our stories is unique. I tell mine to help you access yours. Regardless of our situation, to understand how abandonment, abuse and addiction wreak havoc on our sexual and spiritual selves, we've got to get to the heart of why God gave us sexual desire. What can turn our desires from a sore point into a sanctuary?

Entering the sanctuary

> *For this reason a man will leave his father and mother and be united to his wife and the two will become one flesh. This is a profound mystery—but I am talking about Christ and the church.* EPHESIANS 5:31–32

After God selected the Jews as his chosen people, delivered them from slavery and gave them his law, he asked them to build a sanctuary where he would live (Exodus 25:8). This traveling tabernacle would be a holy place where God's people could find solace, fellowship and forgiveness. Within the Holy Place, stone tablets were housed contained God's sacred covenant with his people. This sacred space was an object lesson of God's desire that his people allow him, and him only, into their own most holy place, their souls. Just as the tabernacle was an object lesson pointing them to God as their true sanctuary, it can help us understand God's plan for sexual intimacy and sexual healing.

You see, long before the tabernacle existed, there was another spiritual sanctuary that God created. It was between two people—a man and a woman (Genesis 2:22–25). This covenant was sealed by one life-giving act—the two becoming one flesh. Unlike animals, whose copulation is purely physical, it culminated in a spiritual act of oneness.

Why only in marriage? When man and woman became one flesh, their spirits become entwined. Your mate has access to a part of your spirit that only God had access to before.[64] Thus God only allows sexual contact within the sacred sanctuary of marriage.* In this intimate union, one man and one woman enter a covenant relationship where they give their bodies (and hearts) to each other and each other alone. If you are not currently married, sexuality still points to this inner place where you and God meet. You see, the most valuable treasure isn't marriage, even for those of us who are married—the real treasure is a deep, intimate relationship with God.

No matter what your battle, tearing down the walls you've erected between body and spirit requires careful attention and sacrifice. To do this, I'm convinced we need to see sexual desire in a whole different light. You see, although Satan wants you and me to believe he owns desire, desire is actually embedded within the very nature of God. We have desire because we are created in his image.

---

* *Now for the matters you wrote about: "It is good for a man not to have sexual relations with a woman." But since sexual immorality is occurring, each man should have sexual relations with his own wife, and each woman with her own husband.* 1 CORINTHIANS 7:1-2

Making peace with desire

The world is little, people are little, human life is little. There is only one big thing – desire.
– WILLA CATHER, *THE SONG OF THE LARK*

Now let's get really honest. In the wake of addiction, abandonment and abuse, it's easy to get mad at desire. My angst about desire first rooted in my parents' marriage. My father worked constantly, as an engineer by day and math professor at night. When he was gone more and more, my mother shut down her desires for years, convincing herself it didn't matter. The medication of alcohol blunted his natural desire for his family and his children, who also desired him…the good parts of him. When he was intoxicated, he abused us verbally and emotionally. A mishmash of desire culminated in his adultery, distorting his desire for his family. This blunting of his good desires stole precious moments where his presence was needed and eventually led to full emotional abandonment.[65]

Dave's sexual addiction and my own love addiction both came from misplaced desire. As Thomas and Beverly Bien say in their book, *Mindful Recovery*,

> *Each moment contains a potential fullness—a simple satisfaction in living—that refreshes the spirit [...] But this opening is difficult for the addicted person, for addiction is about blunting your perceptions, about closing off [...] Addicted individuals seek the easy way out. They learn to turn off their pain by dulling it, rather than face it, learn its lessons and do something to make things better.[66]*

So you can see why I developed some attitudes about desire. Desire hurts! Desire has delivered some of my most fundamental wounds. Even after we entered recovery, when Dave told me he desired me, my heart no longer raced with joy. *What does that even mean after all you've done? When your desire has broken my heart?*

But you see it wasn't just what Dave had done. It was my past catching up with me, so that in God's grace and mercy I could be healed. I had learned as a young adult that I needed to create desire in men, yet desire was dangerous, unsafe. I was vulnerable to the hijacking of my desire through the various coping mechanisms I'd picked up: repression, displacement and attachment.

Repression: Cut out or numb desire. I can't desire this, so I don't. Life is easier without desire.

Displacement: Throw the unfulfilled desire onto something else more predictable, like work, performance, beauty or fitness.

Attachment: Nail my desire to something or someone. The turning of desire into addiction.[67]

So how do we make peace with desire? We've got to ask where desire comes from. This once again takes us back to the beginning of creation. In the Old Testament, *teshuquah*, the Hebrew word for desire, means a stretching out after, a longing. God created Adam in his own image, with the longing for companionship. We see God stretching out after Adam— coming down in the cool of the day to walk with Adam and Eve (at a time best suited to their needs).[68] And then we see desire's first betrayal in God's haunting cry after Adam and Eve disobey, and then hide: "Adam, where are you?" Of course God knew where Adam was hiding, yet desired communication with Adam, intimacy.[69]

Desire for his creation prompted God to choose the Jewish nation to prepare the way for his ultimate bid of desire—sending Jesus. Did God give up on desire when the Israelites hurt him, abused his grace and eventually gave themselves over to idols? Israel went after other lovers, but God pursued her. Then he brought Israel to the desert, the place where he originally covenanted with her in order to woo her. Listen to the words of Hosea 2:14 in several different Bible translations:

> *I, the Lord, will lure you into the desert and speak gently to you* (CEV).
> *So I the Lord will speak romantic words to her. I will lead her into the desert and speak tender words* (ERV).
> *That is why I'm going to win her back* (NOG).
> *So I am going to attract her...* (NCV).
> *But once she has nothing, I'll be able to get through to her* (VOICE).

The language of desire is loud and clear in God's intention: allure her, charm her, speak romantic words, woo her, win her back, persuade her, court her again, start all over again, attract her and entice her.

I find this so instructive as one who has been in the wake of addiction, abandonment and abuse. First, my God understands the pain of unfulfilled desire. I've got to believe that when God planted desire in our very essence, he knew the pain it could bring himself. Desire meant we could either choose him or not. I relate to God's anguish over how his people acted out their desires with idols:

You have set up statues to remind you of your gods. You have put them behind your doors and doorposts. You deserted me. You invited other lovers into your bed. You climbed into it and welcomed them. You made a deal with them. And you looked with desire at their naked bodies. ISAIAH 57:8 (NIRV)

God understands the anguish of knowing your mate has looked at other people naked. He knows how much it hurts to desire someone and have them reject you outright. He understands the wrenching pain of abandonment. He gets the betrayal of adultery, even the primal wound of having it committed in your own bed. This comforts me.

Yet, in God's way of seeing, the glory of desire was (and is) worth the pain. God continued to desire, even as he watched his people suffer the consequences of their own choices. He didn't let his people's unfaithfulness change his own character. Wow! Please read this again.

> *God never let his people's unfaithfulness change his own character.*

God is love and love is full of desire. If God ceased to desire, the whole nature of his love would be altered. Desire makes God yearn for us. It is much the same for us.

Desire causes us to reach for a deeper knowledge of God.

Desire gets us up early in the morning and on our knees to pray.

Desire allows me to put my soul above the clamor of the world.

Desire helps me push past emotional fatigue to risk loving someone who has the power to hurt me.

201

God embedded desire in our very nature. On Stone six (dignity), we talked about the differing relational gifts of women and men and how each imparts dignity. If you look closer, you'll see that these are empowered by desire. For women, as the eye that sees the danger, our desire for other people is what gives us the strong protective impulse. Our emotional intelligence comes from our larger limbic system, the bonding center of the brain.[70] We desire to bond. In fact, our very complexity is reflected in female desire. Desire is the fuel for a woman's relational engine.

It's no wonder then that Satan seeks to hijack desire from women. God cautioned Eve that this would happen after she gave into temptation. "Your desire will be for your husband and he will rule over you" (Genesis 3:16). In other words, he was saying, "Eve now that you let desire win over my word, your desire will be so great for Adam that it will rule over you."

God also gifted man with desire in his most essential nature. As we discussed earlier, the powerful hormone testosterone narrows a man's focus, allowing his desire to be a safe haven for his mate.

From our marriage counseling experiences, men can be even more confused and befuddled than women by their mate's infidelity. They feel betrayed in the very essence of their manhood. Rejection, abandonment or abuse from a woman is difficult to process.

After the fall in the Garden of Eden, God had a similar prediction for Adam (Genesis 3:17). Now that he had forgotten his truest desire for God himself, he would be tempted to throw all his desire towards providing the physical necessities of life.* Or, similar to Eve, throw his desire onto woman, seeking a fulfillment that could never come from a human being.

* *...through painful toil you will eat food from it all the days of your life. It will produce thorns and thistles for you.* GENESIS 3:17-18

Part of my healing has been releasing the power of misplaced desire. As I have learned to stand with God, fear has lessened and love has grown. By throwing my heart at God with unbridled desire, I have learned baby step by baby step, to reignite the beauty of desire within relationship. Honestly, I still have days when desire tests me to the core, yet I've found peace. This re-creation has come as I've refused to budge from the Stone of sanctuary.

Standing on the Stone: Healing Sexually

> *Together, we tenderly take the myrtle blossom, bursting with buds and a healthy wad of root, and plant it in the ground in a barren place where I can encourage it up the side of our house. I know it will produce thorns, but I say a prayer that will also give us the glorious blossoms I've come to treasure.* Eve's Song, *pp. 173–174*

The night before I started fleshing out this Stone, I had a haunting dream. It was my first night in Lake Tahoe, California, where I had driven to spend a week finishing this book. Knowing the previous spiritual attacks I had suffered on earlier writing trips, I prayed thoroughly about my dreams. The dream came early in the morning.

> *I was preparing to speak at a huge conference and had no Bible or notes. After I wheeled my bags into a corner, the conference leaders gave me a Bible and a short book on love right as I was introduced. Walking up the podium, I faced a huge hall full of faces hoping to hear me redefine love. All that came to mind were cliché sayings. Shame washed over me. I would need to bluff.*

203

The dream then transitioned into a second scene. I was curled up on a bed asleep but fully dressed with covers over me. The bed was in the middle of the same large hall. Suddenly, I stirred to see something happening on the far left of the room. Dave was lustfully leaning over another woman, whispering words I could hear clearly. "I'm thinking there might be something between the two of us. We could have some really good times together." He was seducing her. As they got up to leave together, I sprung up out of bed and went to him. She disappeared. I was agitated. "Dave, I saw and heard everything you just did. What you are doing is…wrong! I am so hurt and so angry!" Dave's lips curled in a defensive sneer. "You have never been able to satisfy me. Do you think I can keep going on without my needs being met? I will see you at home." After he left, I began searching for my bags so that I could leave the conference center and leave Dave. No, I would not follow him home. Instead, I would catch a flight to Virginia (where I grew up) and there build a new life without him. Suddenly, I saw some old friends in a corner. Running to them, I started crying, telling them what had happened. Then as quickly as it started, the dream was over.

Jerking awake, I put on my tennis shoes and noticed the sky streaking red in the windows of my hotel room. It was 6:30 a.m. I trudged outside into the sleepy town, heading towards the lakefront where the sky was pink with billowing purple-blue clouds. As I walked I first felt a bit shaken. The thought traced through my skull…*Am I still at risk with Dave?* Determination followed quickly. *No, the healing is real that God has given us. This is an attack from Satan.*

Suddenly clear images came back to me from my previous trips. How a storm that shut down the electricity in the middle of the night in a lonely bed and breakfast became the storm scene in *Eve's Song*. How the satanic dreams I had in a condo in the wilderness transferred into deeper resolve to stand my ground. How a rabid bat showing up in my bathroom (more in Stone twelve), showed me the reality of spiritual warfare. After God comforted me, he used the attacks for my good, helping me engage spiritual warfare and minister from a deeper place.

But what about the dream's content? As far as scene one, it is a miracle that God chose me with all my struggles to minister to women in the arena of sexual intimacy. In the dream's first act, I was the performer and the audience was there to see my weakness, part of the evil one's plot to steal my confidence in this calling (more in Stone twelve: hope).

In the second act, Dave and the woman were the performers. I watched my trauma (Stone one) acted out before me. Thorns sprouted (Stone two) as Satan shrieked… *You can be sure, this happy time won't last. You will never really be safe!* Triggers fired (Stone three), taking me back to the day Dave called the dating hotline. No longer afraid of tears (Stone four), and ready to wage warfare (Stone five), I reminded myself of my dignity (Stone six). Acceptance (Stone seven) provided a growing security that lessened my fear. Most of all, the healing work I'd done on intimacy had turned sexuality from a threat into a sanctuary.

Now it's time to figure out what stepping on the Stone of sanctuary means for you. How has Satan dug his ugly accusations into the depths of your sexual experience or in your views of sexuality? As you work through this, take heart! I've found that the very losses that have come through addiction, abandonment and abuse become paths to re-creation in the hands of God. See the chart on the following page for insight.

Type of loss	Damage to my sanctuary	Role in re-creation
Addiction	The genuineness of intimacy comes into question. I put barricades up. I push into my own addictive patterns to escape the pain. I forget how to be present with my body and emotions.	As I let God into my inmost parts I find spiritual safety to risk intimacy again. Seeing my losses gives me a new way of seeing others' losses. My deepest wounds reveal themselves as I view them with tenderness and curiosity.
Abandonment	I lose a sense of who I am, my dignity. I don't tell the truth lest I am abandoned again. I am stuck in a pattern of control; I become over-responsible for the other person to ensure he can't abandon me.	As I engage in spiritual warfare, I learn to stay present when I used to flee. I gain dignity by engaging the battle and setting healthy boundaries. As I let go of control, I find my senses sharpen. Instead of being protective, I become more creative and playful.
Abuse	I develop a fight-or-flight response. Since I don't always read others correctly, I often feel at risk. Spiritually, I become defensive at the first sign of abuse. I fold inward when conflict threatens.	When my sensitive spots are triggered, I find myself able to stay present. I listen more deeply. Spiritually, I process my abuse and shift my security to God. I feel worthy and am able to speak up even if it causes conflict or defensiveness.

What is your vision of sexual healing? Do you believe God could completely re-create you with this intimate terrain as the pinnacle? Here are a few suggestions for you as you test this Stone with your full weight:

1) **Invite Jesus into your desires** – Being in the wake of addiction, abandonment or abuse may have left you with your own sexual struggles, including sexual anorexia, fantasy or ways you act out your desire outside the covenant relationship of marriage. Invite Jesus to lead your healing in this arena.

2) **Usher recurring fantasies out** – When an old fantasy appears, I refuse to give in to shame. Instead I say, "Hello old remnant of my sexual abuse as a child. Thanks for stopping by but you are no longer needed." Then I exhale, symbolizing letting go.

3) **Let deferred desire train you** – If you are in the midst of your mate's battle with addiction, the pain of waiting is great. *Why would I choose this life?* If you aren't currently in a relationship, you might be tempted to shortcut God's plan for a companion. Yet deferred desire is an opportunity to understand the heart of God better.

4) **Be honest and curious with your mate** – Recovering in this area as a couple takes risk upon risk. For me it meant telling the truth about why I didn't want to be intimate, learning to ask difficult questions, and lightening up in our discussions about sexuality. Laughter has truly been medicine for my soul.

5) **Trust the slow growth of recovery** – Growth in this tender area will be incremental, step-by-step. Entrust the pain to a small circle of spiritual friends, but also be sure to acknowledge the ways you are slowly changing.

No doubt, in this area, as with the other Stones of Part Two, we will have more confidence to engage the sanctuary buried underneath our deepest wounds as we listen to the call of grace.

Grace calls

> *Therefore he is able to save completely those who come to God through him, because he always lives to intercede for them.* HEBREWS 7:25

Just as in the other Stones, we have a guide who understands our sexual losses, Jesus. As an agent of creation, Jesus is well acquainted with our inner sanctuary, the holy place inside where our most sacred desires live—the place where his Holy Spirit inhabits God's children. As his powerful word divides soul and spirit, he can redeem our innermost struggles.

One of my early victories in embracing sexual healing was going to God with my angst about sexuality. I remember a prayer walk where I begged God, "Father, I don't understand why you created sexuality. Why is it so painful? What am I missing?" God answered in a powerful way several hours later when I entered a bookstore with my mother. Walking down the Christian book aisle, I noticed a book bathed in light from a skylight directly ahead. It was called *Sacred Sex*,[71] and that book would usher Dave and me into new depths of healing. Grace calls…*As you cry out to God with your specific fears, know that I will be there to cover you.*

My guess is that this Stone, even more than the others, has a way of reflecting unhealed wounds. You may not be sure if you are ready, but do remember that each of the previous Stones of re-creation have prepared you well. You've stepped on the Stones of tears, spiritual warfare, dignity and acceptance. Sexual healing is a natural outgrowth of mediated love—letting Jesus the Great Physician into our deepest parts. Grace calls...*I am a gentle guide. Take my hand and let me show you how facing these intimate wounds can bring renewed joy and hope*

Your spiritual journey

Congratulations, my friend! You have stepped on the last Stone of the second part of the journey. I rejoice with you that you've come this far. Soon, you will begin the part of the journey you've been longing for—the Stones of rest. Above all the levels of spiritual recovery, I personally believe covenant requires the strongest stand against Satan. It is clear that the evil one wants to own sexuality, and fomenting sexual confusion, chaos and separation is his goal. And so, spiritual recovery calls each of us to take a stand against this spiritual oppression and hijacking of our desires. In doing so, we embrace desire as a gift from our Maker, a fountain of hope, spilling forth from the depths of our soul. This hope won't disappoint us because it comes from admitting that our deepest need is for God to reign in these parts.

As Augustine said, "Thou hast made us for thyself, O Lord, and our heart is restless until it finds its rest in thee." Or in the words of the apostle of love, John... "All who have this hope in him purify themselves, just as he is pure" (1 John 3:3).

Circle of stones: sanctuary

On this eighth stone you will write the word **sanctuary**. With a nod to the pain, I'd suggest that you find a stone that moves you with its beauty. Let your heart guide you.

Your stone of sanctuary will join your other stones: trauma, thorns, triggers, tears, warfare, dignity, and acceptance. Put them in a circle in front of you and then take a moment to rejoice at your accomplishment. How have the earlier stones prepared you for this stone of sanctuary?

Journaling: Sanctuary

What unique sexual wounds do you bring to your spiritual journey? Ask Jesus your Guide to join you, and then journal about what wounds you carry today. Let Jesus' presence remind you to be gentle and curious as you reflect. These starters can help:

1) I wonder if...
2) I worry that...
3) I'm afraid that...
4) I'm angry about...
5) I question whether...

Then let Jesus talk to you about your answers. What perspectives does he offer?

A word from Dave — Sanctuary

*In my inner being, I delight in God's law; but I see another
law at work in me waging war against the law of my mind
and making me a prisoner of the law of sin at work within
me.* ROMANS 7:22-23

Antonyms (opposites) of sanctuary: massacre, risk, hazard,
wreckage, peril and war zone.[72]

When I was twelve, some young men came to preach at our
tiny church in my hometown in central Illinois. It was the first
time I had seen teens that were zealous for God. A seed of desire
was planted in my heart, desire for obeying God and doing his
will. About the same time my sexual desire was beginning to
emerge. Riding on a school bus every day with much older kids,
deposited words and thoughts in my head that were new to me.
Watching their coarse gestures fueled my sexual curiosity and
eventually led me to discover masturbation. An opposing seed
of desire had been planted. A war had broken out, a conflict
of desire. Lacking the understanding I needed, there was no
safe place to hide. As the years passed, what began as a normal
sexual curiosity skirmish escalated into an all-out combat zone
within my heart. There was a clash going on inside of me, but
no one I talked to could explain what it might be. Everyone,
including myself, thought it was simply my hormones or
possibly a spiritual battle that could most likely be remedied
with more prayer, Bible study, and getting married as soon as
possible. After all, didn't Paul say, it is better to marry than to

burn?* *Yes, that's it! Marriage will be my sanctum, a safe place to channel all my sexual desire.*

So that was my plan. I prayed fervently that I would find a mate who loved God and who wanted to go into the ministry. I hoped that she would be eager to meet my sexual needs. Although my showdown against sexual sin was raging and I was continuing to lose ground during the months leading up to our wedding, I was still hopeful that sex in marriage would be the ultimate safe place that would protect me and end my decade-long conflict of desire!

You know by now that this is not what happened. Within months of our wedding, I was defiling the beautiful sanctuary of our marriage by looking at pornography. The war resumed unabated and the bloodshed to Robin's sensitive soul began. I had no idea why Robin, in spite of her best efforts, was unable to pacify my sexual desires. I searched for answers and plotted new lines of attack:

- *Frequency:* If we had sex more often…
- *Enthusiasm:* If Robin was more excited and energetic about sex…
- *Spontaneity:* If our sexual encounters were more unique and risky…
- *Novelty:* If we purchased some sexy lingerie or toys…

These ideas, obviously inspired by the world of pornography, led to many tearful exchanges and battle scars that sadly linger even to this day.

---

* *But if they cannot control themselves, they should marry, for it is better to marry than to burn with passion.* 1 CORINTHIANS 7:9

I had brought into marriage one of the core belief of sexual addicts: *Sex is my most important need.* Where did this come from? I grew up in an era where it was not common to acknowledge, let alone share deeply about, emotional wounds or disappointments. I was unknowingly carrying around a backpack full of wounds that needed to be mourned and healed, and I was using sex as my painkilling medicine. As Patrick Carnes says in *Out of the Shadows*...

> *"Addicts confuse nurturing and sex...sexual activity*
> *never meets the need for love and care, but continues to*
> *be seen as the only avenue to meeting those needs. Addicts*
> *have a high need to control all situations in an effort to*
> *guarantee sex." p. 115*

Instead of medicating my losses through lust and sex, I would have to face head on my need for love and connection. First, this would require going back to my youth and mourning my losses. As a young boy, my need for nurturing and affirmation was often unmet. I longed for time with my father, but was turned away repeatedly. He was too busy to play catch, go to my sporting events, or spend time with me one-on-one. He was doing many good things like building us a house and helping neighbors, but my tender heart did not feel like I was a priority.

Later, in junior high school, when I longed to have the attention and desire of girls, this was also illusive. I saw my friends making out with their girlfriends and wondered why this wasn't happening for me. Again, behind my sexual acting out were wounded desires, the desire to be...

213

- Acknowledged by my father
- Desired by women
- Successful in my career

- Strong and self-disciplined
- Spiritually powerful

Through the guidance of the Holy Spirit working through various books (like *Sacred Sex* which Robin mentioned) and mentors in addiction recovery, the answers I longed for finally came. More sex and more varied sex wasn't the vehicle to healing. Sexuality was to be a celebration of the healing power of oneness. The big "O" wasn't orgasm. It was *oneness* established through eye contact, laughter and a nakedness that encompassed our minds, motives, emotions, bodies and souls.* What my heart was really longing for was this true sanctuary, a safe place of communion and acceptance in the presence of God and others. I believe that David paints a picture of this place in the 23rd Psalm. He calls his soul's sanctuary "green pastures." Within this place of freedom, we are protected and nurtured by the great shepherd and safe from the attacks of the wolves. Likewise, sexual peace comes when we align our desires with God's desire for sexuality—a sanctuary of connection, intimacy, and oneness.

What's more, helping Robin craft journeys of the heart for women and men has helped me to heal my relationship with my father on a deeper level. As I've talked through these losses with him (wanting his permission to share deeply in these pages), his humility has been breathtaking and his unconditional acceptance has mirrored the beauty of true intimacy in all its messiness. I thank God for the healing that has enabled Robin and me to end the "sex wars" in our marriage and that now allows me a heart that runs free—a true place of sanctuary!

---

* *Adam and his wife were both naked, and they felt no shame.* GENESIS 2:25

Back to your journal

Dave describes… "carrying around a backpack full of wounds that needed to be mourned and healed and using sex as my painkilling medicine." This visual can help us in the wake of abandonment, addiction and abuse.

Asking Jesus to join you, draw an outline of a backpack in your journal or on a piece of blank paper. Inside this backpack, write wounds that have influenced your sense of sanctuary. Don't worry about whether the wounds are "worthy" of being mentioned, or whether they are "too small" to be significant.

After writing these wounds in your backpack, go back and write an associated loss for each. For instance, "Wound: my father's ridicule about my weight; Loss: the sense that my body defines my worth." "Wound: sexual abuse; Loss: a deep sexual insecurity that caused me to distrust my body."

If you feel mourning nearby, invite it to join you. Remember that mourning is a way of releasing wounds and losses.

Now imagine Jesus offering a healing balm. Journal about what the balm looks like for you. Is it acceptance? Sanctuary? Grace? Explain why this balm is needed.

PART THREE
Rest

On the seventh day,
God had finished the work he had been doing;
so...he rested from all his work.[*]

Stones Nine to Twelve
Rest

*Most of the things we need to be most fully alive
never come from pushing. They grow in rest.*
— Mark Buchanan, *The Holy Wild:
Trusting in the Character of God*

WELCOME TO STONES NINE TO TWELVE: the Stones of rest. Yes, we've finally come to the part of the journey that we most long for, sweet rest. How do you envision rest? You may picture a time when pain is replaced by victory after victory spilling into your life like a spring stream cascading down the side of a mountain. Or at least, rest would promise a time when struggles aren't quite so potent. As the clouds of despair roll away, suddenly you see God better. Rest certainly holds elements of peace and provision, but yet it isn't as much about an absence of struggle as it is a way of seeing. For insight, let's take a glance at the terrain we've already crossed.

Stones one to three—the Stones of darkness—helped us to look inward and take stock of all the hurts we brought into this journey. We entered into the chaos of trauma, triggers and thorns and found God's redemption in all three. Trauma, a tearing of the soul, reminded us to embrace our humanity by acknowledging past traumas that have stretched or torn the fabric of our faith. Thorns brought to life God's ability to bring good out of Satan's accusations, reminding us that the power comes from God, not from us alone. And then triggers pointed us to Jesus as the great potter, a master craftsman who sincerely cares about our healing. As types of signposts, triggers point us toward buried pain within, a veritable roadmap to healing.

Part two of the journey took us to the heart of re-creation. We saw God's Spirit hovering over the chaos, ready to turn our losses from abandonment, addiction and abuse into investable talents. To do this, we claimed the power of tears, declared our dignity and marveled at the true and complete acceptance of Jesus. Lastly, we went to the holy place, the inner sanctuary, where God dwells. Unafraid to admit our need for sexual healing, we opened up to rethink the beauty of desire. In all of these ways, we've released old coping mechanisms, learned to stand with God and speak his truth, while switching our security from our circumstances to our guide, Jesus.

All of these milestones are grounds for celebration. Yet, there's a third group of Stones to be crossed. And as you have most likely experienced, the Stones of rest can be the most elusive. Strangely enough, it takes moving through more layers of pain to stand on these Stones. Each of them are Stones of surrender, and in my experience, this level of letting go doesn't come without testing. Yet the view from these Stones can be absolutely breathtaking.

The call to rest asks us to cease from human striving (markedly different from spiritual warfare) and put out new roots that go deep into the character of God.

The path to rest

Cease striving and know that I am God.
PSALM 46:10 (NASB)

Strive: To exert much effort or energy; to struggle or fight forcefully (from the Old French *estrif,* to quarrel).

The Hebrew word for strive (*rib or rub*) has four meanings that are instructive for our journey of spiritual recovery: to rub, to wrestle, to wrangle or to contend.[73] I see glimpses of my natural tendencies in all four of these! I learned striving at a very young age from a variety of circumstances. The loss of innocence from sexual abuse opened the door to more abuse. The loss of worth through verbal abuse taught me to rely on performance as a place to find worth. The loss of dignity through my dad's alcoholism and my mom's depression formed the roots of codependence and love addiction. My own loss of purity translated into me giving more and more of my body away to find love. The loss of the fairy tale in marriage caused me to double down to be a better wife or turn Dave into a better husband. Then there were other losses: the deaths of my sister, mom and dad, and other ones dear to me. There were brushes with my own mortality. My striving grew and swelled as I sought to outrun these pains. Clearly, the Hebrew explanation of the word strive resonates with my own journey. And I'm thinking each is a temptation in the wake of abandonment, addiction and abuse.

To rub – We rub when we hold a magic lamp (performance or perfectionism for instance) and furiously rub it, in order to get the genie (changed circumstances) to appear.

To wrestle – We wrestle when we roll this way and that, using human mechanisms in order to pin down whatever it is that distresses us.

To wrangle – Wrangling is a good old Idaho kind of word, meaning to get all of our horses back into pasture after they've torn down an old fence. We wrangle when we seek to manage those who hurt us by taking control of their battles.

To contend – We contend when (like Job in the Bible) we turn our losses into a bone of contention with our Creator. We hope he'll finally figure it out that he's got it all wrong, and pull away all the pressure on us.

How does rest speak to each of these? Remember our vision of spiritual growth as a spiral? (See *Preparing the Ground* at the beginning of the book, if you'd like a reminder.) Picture rest as the process of keeping God at the very center of your spiritual journey. In every decision, every circumstance, you keep an eye on God, seeking his higher path through the challenge.

Going back to Psalm 46:10, this is a process of knowing that God is God, and that we aren't! How does this merge with the Stones of rest? Let's take a look in preparation for these life-transforming Stones.

Stone of rest	My striving	Knowing God
Pain trading	Burying my pain, fearing that God doesn't understand.	I invest my story knowing that in truth it is God's story, and that he will allow me to share in his joy.
Forgiveness	Making the one who hurt me prove they are absolutely safe. Refusing to let go.	As I release judgment, self-doubt and retaliation, I show my trust in God's providence.
Empathy	Seeing weakness in others or myself causes me to flee connection.	I accept God's empathy for my battles and seek the higher path of empathy for others.
Hope	Only embracing hope when I'm convinced it cannot disappoint me.	As I allow hope to bloom and grow, I find myself ministering to the wounds of others.

You'll notice that standing on each of these Stones of rest requires an effort to let go of striving. Since I sought self-esteem from striving, it could pop up its head in any given situation. Sometimes the risk of letting go seemed more than I could manage. I changed as I listened to and responded to God's call to rest. *Robin, will you stop striving and know that I am in control? Will you slow down, be still, know me and trust my sovereignty? If I rule over the nations, can't I make sense of your journey?*

Here's the good news. Within the freedom of letting go, you'll find new energy and compassion that will help you to extend a renewed grace to others.

Our guide for the journey

Are you tired? Worn out? Burned out on religion? Come to me. Get away with me and you'll recover your life. I'll show you how to take a real rest. Walk with me and work with me—watch how I do it. Learn the unforced rhythms of grace. I won't lay anything heavy or ill-fitting on you. Keep company with me and you'll learn to live freely and lightly. MATTHEW 11:28–29 (MESSAGE)

I love Eugene Peterson's paraphrase of Matthew 11:28–29 found within *The Message*. You'll notice that the rest he deciphers from Jesus' words are not a rest from any type of labor. Rather he urges us in his rewriting of Jesus words to "walk with me and work with me—watch how I do it." Perhaps this is what Jesus meant when he told his disciples (and us), "Come follow me." How I wish I could have been with Jesus in the flesh. I'm guessing that those who could embrace the sheer gift of being in his presence found deep refreshment. Even when his teachings were disturbing or their meaning unclear, his followers found their hearts burning within them as he talked with a supernatural energy.*

No doubt, Jesus had a way of working that led to deep rest. He didn't strive, contend, wrestle, wrangle or rub in the human sense. His working came as his Father worked in him, and within that was deep rest, the kind he offers to us.

On these four Stones, it will be more important than ever to keep an eye on our guide, Jesus. Are you ready to get started? Even as I write these words I am praying for God to give you the strength to persevere...

224

---

* *They asked each other, "Were not our hearts burning within us while he talked with us on the road and opened the Scriptures to us?"* LUKE 24:32

*Look to yourselves (take care) that you may not lose
(throw away or destroy) all that we and you have
labored for, but that you may [persevere until you]
win and receive back a perfect reward [in full].*

2 JOHN 1:8 (AMPC)

Friend, if you accept my call
Trust me to invest your pain
Set your heart on my value
Cry aloud for my lessons

Investing your Suffering: Pain Trading

Everyone has talent. What's rare is the courage
to follow it to the dark places it leads.

— ERICA JONG

G LANCING AT THE SMALL HOTEL ALARM clock, I saw it was three in the morning. Two of my adult children were sleeping soundly. Having just returned from travel abroad, I had an infection that just wouldn't go away. My skin was crawling. But even worse, my heart felt like it was about to burst out of my chest. The pain was worse than when Grave's Disease violently jolted me from my sleep, like someone had reached into my chest and jerked me into a sitting position. It was worse than an anaphylactic reaction to an allergy shot that brought hives over every inch of my body and almost took my life. Those pains were acute pains. Their trauma caused damage to body and soul. They formed triggers attached to doctors, medical tests and diagnoses. But this pain was different. It wasn't a body wound. It was a crushing blow to my heart.

It started three days earlier with a phone call. My son's name flashed across the screen. Silence. "Hello, Caleb?" I said. "Are you okay?" I heard him struggle to choke out a word and knew the answer to my own question. Just a week before, his girlfriend of two years had been in the hospital on suicide watch. "Is it

Cassie?" I said. More silence. "Caleb, are you okay?" Then the words that took my breath away, "She's dead, mom. I found her dead... The ambulance is here. I have to go." Pain rose up like a tsunami leaving wreckage scattered everywhere. Dave watching Caleb weeping his eyes out as he tenderly placed yellow roses on her bed. Excavating the mounds of clothing on her bedroom floor that her parents couldn't find the strength to touch. Painful discoveries—how she had left the hospital in good spirits, then offered a ride to a young man in her recovery group. Wanting in his own way to repay her, a couple days later he offered her some heroin. *One time won't hurt...*she thought. That drug combined with an undiagnosed heart condition, combined with other medications for a disabling disease and an anxiety disorder, stopped her weak heart. The night before she died, she confessed to Caleb what she had done and promised...*never again.*

The hotel room in Ohio was the pinnacle of my trauma. With my heart pushing against my chest, I took a spiritual book and went into the tiny hall leading to the bathroom where I could find a little light. Placing my forehead on the carpeted floor, I began to weep. "God, who could handle all this? This is more than I can do!" Thinking of 1 Corinthians 10:13, a scripture that promises we won't be tempted more than we can bear, I rehearsed those I loved who had died over the last twenty years—my sister, my mother, my dad, multiple dear friends. Recounting the years of suffering in the wake of my father's alcoholism and Dave's sexual addiction, I whispered, "God if this is within what I can handle, then I'm right at the limit. Enough!" I wanted the pain to be over. But then guilt came. *I know better.* After all, I had well-developed recovery tools, including a book I'd authored on finding security in God alone. But now the sorrow threatened to engulf my body and soul.*

Sitting up, I lifted my eyes and whispered, "Lord I need a word from you. Please Lord." My eyes found the book on the floor beside me...*Secrets in the Dark* by Frederick Buechner. Opening the 300-page book randomly, I landed in the middle of an essay called "The Adolescence of Pain," a reading of the parable of the talents (NIV) or the bags of gold (2011 NIV) in Matthew 25:14–29. Please take a moment to read this passage before you continue.

Buechner's take on this parable jolted me. I had heard many people suggest that the talents in this parable represent our innate gifts. I had never heard anyone propose that this parable relates to pain, and, even more so, that there is a sense in which God calls each of us to trade in pain...

> *To trade is to give of what it is that we have in return for what it is that we need [...] The good and faithful servants were not life-buriers. They were life-traders. They did not close themselves off in fear, but opened themselves up in risk and hope [...] [T]he parable seems to suggest: We are never more alive to life than where it hurts—never more aware of our powerlessness to save ourselves [...] We are never more aware of our need for each other, never more in reach of each other, if we can only bring ourselves to reach out and let ourselves be reached.*[74]

---

* *Be merciful to me, Lord, for I am in distress; my eyes grow weak with sorrow, my soul and body with grief.* PSALM 31:9

God's message for me was clear. *Robin, you have been entrusted with much pain. Please don't bury your pain in the ground. Become a pain trader. This loss is part of your story, a story that other women will need.* Tears of repentance streamed down my cheeks. My God had heard and seen me.

I awoke the next morning prepared to trade in pain at Cassie's funeral. God used me to console her family—her mother and I weeping in each other's arms. She reassured me: "Just so you know we don't blame Caleb for any of Cassie's issues. He made her happy in a way that nothing else ever had." Although watching Caleb carry her ashes down the aisle was devastating, I was moved by his raw courage. The priest explained how Cassie's favorite saint was Jude—the saint of lost causes. Cassie had borne so much in her short life. She had watched her mother be crippled by a disabling disease, knowing she had the same fate ahead. She fought depression. Yet she was brilliant. Her tender heart brought joy. After the funeral, our family was invited to a meal at a relative's house. I was fully present, fully allowing my story (and my pain, present and past) to be merged with that of her family and other people who loved her. As much as it hurt, my ability to give was a miracle from God.

While I still mourn the devastating loss of Cassie and hurt for the pain that my son and her family continue to live with, I can see now how experiencing this tragedy has better equipped Dave and me to be healers for others through what the Bible calls treasures of darkness.* My husband, who for the longest time couldn't shed a tear over his sin, now couldn't stop crying over this young woman we had welcomed into our hearts. Those tears helped him weep over all of his losses, and eventually helped us learn to weep together. My heart swelled with compassion.

---

* *I will give you treasures hidden in dark and secret places. Then you will know that I, the Lord God of Israel, have called you by name.* ISAIAH 45:3 (CEV)

Through all this, I glimpsed how trading in life's most horrible and seemingly unredeemable pains transforms our hurts into a pathway of healing. In Buechner's way of thinking, I have given and continue to receive back comfort and perspective I didn't even know I needed.*

What will pain trading mean for you? And how will it produce rest? Let's go a little deeper into the idea of trading in pain.

Pain trading

> *"He who had received the five talents went at once and traded with them, and he gained five talents more"*
> MATTHEW 25:16 (AMPC).

When I think of trading, I think of a new phenomenon happening in my city. It's called the Treasure Valley Real Foodies. All the women who participate are into natural living and grow, craft or bake different natural items—from vegetables to soap, breads and bakery items to yogurts and fermented goods. Once a month or so, the women get together for a time of trading. A woman who brings an armful of homemade soaps leaves with a selection of items made by others that would be costly to purchase or time-consuming to make on her own. She has no experience with fermented products, but she benefits from the hard-won knowledge of others, as others benefit from her labor (it took years to perfect her soaps!). Every woman leaves with her offering multiplied. And there's an additional benefit.

231

---

* *It is better to go to a house of mourning than to go to a house of feasting, for death is the destiny of everyone; the living should take this to heart. Frustration is better than laughter, because a sad face is good for the heart. The heart of the wise is in the house of mourning, but the heart of fools is in the house of pleasure.* ECCLESIASTES 7:2-4

The Treasure Valley Real Foodies has become a community of like-minded people who lean on each other for advice, recommendations and more. The community has become as important as the trading.

I see something similar in Matthew 25 and its application to our hurts and losses. Picture Jesus' audience. As they sat listening, how were they applying his words? In the newest version of the NIV released in 2011, the word "talents" that I am accustomed to has been translated into "bags of gold," since a talent in Jesus' time was a monetary unit. Although Jesus had much more in mind, perhaps his listeners first assumed he was speaking literally of money. I'm pretty sure they weren't thinking of their innate and developed gifts (how many of us apply the scripture). But then it must have dawned on them, why would this man who carried everything he owned on his back be talking about entrusting us with money? And what about the poor? Were they excluded? By now, they knew that these stories always had an alternate meaning. He was talking about their lives, asking, *What do you do with what you've been given? Good or bad? Do you invest it? Do you share the heartbreaking wounds? Do you allow God to bring a return from your mistakes and missteps?*

We need each other to trade in pain. Addiction, abandonment and/or abuse have brought us onto common ground, even in our differences. Just as each person in the parable had a different portion, we each possess our own unique pains. Our losses vary in expression, magnitude, duration and consequences. These can't be compared because they are so individual. But all are potential receptacles for grace.

As in Matthew 25:16, trading is what multiplies the grace received in the pain. When I share my pain with tears, others get teary-eyed as they connect with their own losses. When they tell their story that resonates with mine, even if it is completely different, my heart is lifted...*I'm not alone.* I always find an insight, a new way of seeing that I couldn't have envisioned without them. Grace is multiplied. Problems have a way of changing into perspective as I trust the giftedness of pain trading.

Pain trading: Using your pain to be a healing salve for the hurts of others, while at the same time receiving comfort and perspective for your own trials. Listening to the Spirit's call, to risk investing past and present pains, believing that God will bring a rich return.

Pain trading doesn't come easily. Going back to Jesus' parable, the servant with one talent reminds me of where many of us start with pain. We haven't learned pain's mysterious graces yet, so we bury it, afraid that owning it will generate even more pain. This stuffed away pain isn't tradable. It would be like our soapmaker staying home, afraid to trade because she's convinced she'll be misunderstood. Nursing her insecurities, she misses out on a treasure trove of blessings! And the other traders don't receive the unique benefits that only her soap brings.

Likewise, when we sit on our pain others miss out and we miss out! As Buechner says, "The universal experience of pain is what makes us all brothers and sisters, the parents and children of each other, and the story of one of us is the story of all of us. And that in itself is a pearl of great price."[75] When you sit in a small group of women and risk owning your pain, they are emboldened to tell the truth of theirs. Their story redeems yours, yours redeems theirs, and Satan runs as you dispel his evil lies.

So take heart! This journey of Stones has prepared you (yes, you) uniquely for this type of trading. You've allowed tears in order to receive the sweet comfort of God (Stone four). From

233

Stone five, you know how to engage in spiritual warfare, incredibly essential for pain trading because the *last* thing Satan wants is for you to benefit from your pain. Pausing on Stone six (dignity), you've learned to stand with God to claim his dignity. On Stone seven (acceptance), you've been ushered to the very throne of Jesus and learned to move towards others instead of away in fear of abandonment. And on Stone eight, you've prepared for some of the most risky trading, involving the sanctuary deep within. You are now on a journey of sexual healing, reclaiming losses in this tender arena.

You would not hold this book in your hands without my own faltering steps towards becoming a trader in pain. When I wonder, *why continue trading in pain? Ah, Lord, at times the risk seems more than I can bear,* I can go back to a hotel room in Ohio where God transformed pain into a spiritual revelation.

What will pain trading look like for you? Take a look at this chart contrasting burying our pain and becoming a pain trader (on the following page). Be sure to acknowledge the ways you are changing from a pain burier to a pain trader.

*God can transform pain
into a spiritual revelation.*

When I bury my pain, I...	As a pain trader, I...
Constantly talk about who is to blame.	Own my hurt, my concerns, my fears, my spiritual battles. 1 Peter 5:6–7
Polarize others...to be for me, you need to be against the one who hurt me.	Acknowledge the complexities of the fall of the one who hurt me. Proverbs 20:5
Look for ways to bury pain. Make sensitive areas untouchable.	Look for ways to process pain spiritually as I mourn my losses. Isaiah 43:2, Psalm 119:50
Constantly manage how others see me, secretly afraid I am less than them.	Take risks to trade pain knowing God will multiply grace. 2 Peter 1:2 (AMPC)
Proudly insist that I am strong or accuse others of judging.	Humbly allow others to sit with me in my pain, even (when appropriate) with the one who caused it. Proverbs 27:6
Shut down when others (especially the one who hurt me) suggest ways I am responsible.	Ask for others' perspectives, even being open to learn from the one who hurt me. James 1:21
Fear that my pain means that God shows favoritism.	Trust God's ability to pour out grace into my heart. Psalm 34:18, Romans 5:5
Fight to move forward as quickly as possible in order to appear spiritual.	Fight to process my pain in order to grow spiritually. 1 Peter 2:19
Only talk about pain long past.	Willing to invest past and present pain in order to help others. Matthew 25:19–23

When I review the pain trader column of this chart I see spiritual growth. Do you remember the spiral of spiritual growth we discussed in the introduction to the journey? I explained how…

> "…sometimes in the middle of re-creation or rest, darkness will descend out of nowhere. But this doesn't make God farther away or take away from all you're learning. Each time you circle back onto an earlier Stone of recovery, you'll go there with new perspective, seeing that the journey is more about God and less about you."

Our goal in spiritual growth isn't to get past certain struggles in order to never, ever see or talk about them again (linear growth). Rather, through God's Spirit, we continually process our struggles, humanity and pain so that each time they circle around (or are triggered), we respond to them from a deeper well of comfort. Trading in pain allows for a healthy circling back, and with it a changed perspective and more resilient hope—the raw materials of spiritual rest.

Standing on the Stone: Pain trading and Rest

> The telling goes late into the night, yet darkness never comes. It seems as if our stories have the power to shed light into every crevice of our souls, turn the rough places into smooth and make way for goodness, hope and truth—not only in our own lives, but in the lives of all who will follow. Eve's Song, p. 235

In processing all of this, you may find yourself thinking…*I thought the Stones of rest would be happier. Why is the first Stone of rest one that has to do with our pain?* In the introduction to these stones of rest we talked about a type of rest that is worth the battle. But this battle isn't against pain (although none of us want to prolong pain through poor boundaries or codependence). Instead, it's a battle to process our losses spiritually from past/present abandonment, addiction or abuse. What I've found is that the sweetest rest comes not from the absence of pain but from the working through and resulting redefinition of it.*

> *Rest comes as we move through our*
> *pain to process it spiritually.*

To understand this, we can look to how God knit us together physically. I just read an insightful article by American meditation expert Shinzen Young on how to transform physical pain into spiritual growth. He says…

> *In order to understand how pain becomes suffering, you*
> *need to know a deep truth about the nature of suffering.*
> *Most people equate suffering with pain, but suffering*
> *is a function of two variables, not just one. Suffering is*
> *a function of pain and the degree to which the pain is*
> *being resisted (S = P x R).*[76]

One of the miracles of our nervous system is the body's ability to transmit pain signals. But because pain hurts, we resist it. Our body sends pain signals flooding through our nervous system and instead of simply listening to and heeding these vital messages, we seek to cut them off. We beat the pain messages back, deny them and repress them. Again…

237

---

* *And after you suffer for a short time, God who gives all grace, will make everything right. He will make you strong and support you and keep you from falling. He called you to share in his glory in Christ, a glory that will continue forever.* I PETER 5:10 (NCV)

Suffering = Pain x Resistance

Resisting our God-given nervous system doesn't bring rest. Instead, as Young says, this creates "a kind of violent conflict, a veritable civil war between the two parts of the same system." He calls this pressure "suffering." Hmmm. Makes me think of the servant in Jesus' parable who went and buried (repressed) his talents in the ground in fear. Those endowments from his Master weren't meant to be a curse—rather they were meant to allow the servant to participate in the Master's work. By running from his pain, the servant ran from the Master's work.

Young's solution for physical pain is to open up to it rather than fight it. Stop holding our breath and instead practice being present. Let go of self-judging thoughts and relax into whatever hurts. Let pain inform us and motivate us, rather than allowing pain to take us to a place of suffering, and then trigger past addictive coping mechanisms.[77]

Personally, I am most aware of the way I repress pain when I visit a massage therapist. First, I only end up there after a long cycle of physical symptoms. I've put off getting help, thinking these hurts will go away by themselves. As I finally walk through her doorway, I'm still wondering whether I really need this, even though I used to write for *Massage Therapy Journal* and know the benefits.

But then, the instant I lay on the table, my body begins to speak to me. My left shoulder begins to throb and then radiates into my elbow and thumb. Then my right hip begins to speak... *There's a big knot here. Don't forget about me.* Soon more and more parts of my body are chiming in. And then as the therapist lovingly puts pressure on tight muscles, I lovingly tell my body that it is safe to release, let go and trust her ministering touch. (Yes, it is helpful to give your body permission to accept the therapist's touch.) By the time my massage is over I am in a deep state of rest.

What gives my therapist this ability that goes beyond book learning? One of the musts of massage therapy training is receiving massage from other trainees. As another therapist's hands press deep into her own hurts, she learns how to minister to others, what needs to be released and how. The best therapists practice what they preach, i.e., receive regular massages. This ongoing commitment to her own healing allows the experienced massage therapist to work from a place of rest. As she trades, rest multiplies.

Likewise, my rest has been multiplied by trading in the pain. Every time I trade in pain in my small recovery group, insights appear that weren't present before we entered the deep places together. Afterwards, my dignity is greater rather than less.

Some of you might reply, "Robin, when the worst pains of sexual addiction, abuse and abandonment are firmly in the past, I'll be a trader in pain. I'm too devastated now!" I hear you. We all would rather trade in past pain…and we'd like the past to be as far away as possible! But, here's a lesson I've learned from years of leading recovery groups. My past pains are valuable for lessons learned, but my present pain is even more helpful in the day-to-day work of helping other women recover. In fact, my past pain is most relevant in how it impacts me in the present. One more time…

My past pain has valuable lessons to impart, but my current pain holds special value in helping other women.

239

If you went to the Treasure Valley Foodies, would you prefer some handcrafted soap that a woman made twenty years ago, or the soap she made last week? Just as natural products (that contain no preservatives) are best current, our pain is similar. Biblically, this makes sense to me. The Hebrew writer encouraged the current sharing of pain and sin, in fact, as long as it is called today:

> *See to it, brothers and sisters, that none of you has a*
> *sinful, unbelieving heart that turns away from the living*
> *God. But encourage one another daily, as long as it is*
> *called "Today," so that none of you may be hardened by*
> *sin's deceitfulness.* HEBREWS 3:12-13

So what current pain do I trade in? I have a wide selection! The pain of applying all that I've learned in recovery to the full-time ministry. The exhaustion of having just moved to the third house within five years, after living in nineteen different homes in our thirty-five years of marriage. Ways I give in to perfectionism and start hyper-controlling everything. Getting triggered on vacation and dramatically throwing my Bible on the bed with all my might, followed by the file folders containing a draft of this book—thankfully they stayed intact—while proclaiming my complaints about ongoing trials with great disgust. I am grateful that this third leg of the journey, rest, doesn't depend on having arrived. You might want to write this on an index card and post it on your bathroom mirror:

Rest doesn't depend on perfection.

I find this liberating! But if we are to trade in our own imperfection, we'll also have to allow for the imperfection of others. Sometimes the honest sharing of ongoing pain can be difficult for those who listen. Why?

> *When you are so crazy vulnerable you might expect me to follow…and I'm not sure that I'm ready.*

> *I'm afraid that my "small" pains might not be mentionable in the light of your "big" pains.*

> *Since you are married, you might not think my pain as an unmarried woman is valid. Since you are unmarried, you might not think I have the right to be in pain in my marriage.*

> *I am the one in our marriage who has a healthy view of sexuality, while my husband constantly withdraws. I feel like no one understands.*

> *Purity is my biggest battle and my husband struggles with codependence. How will others relate?*

When we examine the root, I think our deepest fear is what our pain means about us. In the past, I've had other Christians tell me that they didn't want to follow me because of ongoing situations in my life. Eventually, I came to understand that their angst wasn't really about me. It was about hanging on to the illusion that their righteousness spares them from pain. In other words, if I was suffering because I did something wrong, then as long as they weren't doing anything wrong, they didn't have to worry! As a pain trader, I'm learning to be curious about what fear my story raises for others, instead of shrinking back

241

into my old habits of withdrawing. To be sure, this trading in imperfection is only possible through calling on our guide.

I can't count how many times I've cried out to Jesus, begging for help, relief, wisdom and cleansing as I've walked in the wake of addiction, abandonment and abuse. As I've begun pain trading, I've cried out again and again for the strength to expose my vulnerable places, my scars. Every time a woman contacts me who feels she just might be able to share a burden she's never shared, I feel blessed. Let's turn one more time to Young's thoughts on pain and suffering…

> *Pain informs and motivates; suffering drives and distorts.*
> *Pain experienced skillfully brings us closer to our spiritual*
> *source; suffering alienates us from our spiritual source*
> *and our fellow human beings. Suffering obscures the*
> *perfection of the moment; pain experienced skillfully is*
> *the perfection of the moment.*[78]

These are the same skills you will develop as you trade in pain. Instead of running, you'll let your hurts inform and motivate you. Instead of burying away from others, try digging deeper into your spiritual source. In the trading, you'll touch the hem of the garment of God's perfect love.*

All this circles us back to the parable of the talents where there is a phrase I've read right over. After the five talent and two talent traders came, having multiplied what they were given and after God commended their faithfulness, God added, "Enter into and share the joy (the delight, the blessedness) which your

* *Just then a woman who had been subject to bleeding for twelve years came up behind him and touched the edge of his cloak. She said to herself, "If I only touch his cloak, I will be healed." Jesus turned and saw her. "Take heart, daughter," he said, "your faith has healed you." And the woman was healed at that moment.* MATTHEW 9:20–22

Master enjoys" (Matthew 25:23b AMPC). Wow! Could it be that God instructs us to trade in life, its highs and lows, for us to share in the joy of a Father who delights in seeing his children overcome? God wants his comfort to flow to others like us…in a cascade of comfort.* As this solace flows from God to me, to you and back again to me, it brings spiritual rest and fresh grace.

Grace calls

Make level paths for your feet, so that the lame may not be disabled, but rather healed. HEBREWS 12:13

Sanity lies in somehow opening to the chaos, allowing anxiety, moving deeply into the tumult, diving into the waves, where underneath, peace simply is.
– Gerald May, Simply Sane: The Spirituality of Mental Health

Stand assured that it doesn't take abandonment, addiction or abuse to become a pain trader. It only requires your unique story. And of course, you may have quite an assortment of different types of pain to offer, from long-term singlehood (especially if you're not thinking this is your gift), to physical trials, to the pains of broken friendship, rejection by a family member or having children in painful circumstances. You may have experienced physical or sexual violence, been falsely accused or suffered financial losses. All of this is investable in God's power. Rest assured that pain trading is the call of every follower of Jesus. Grace whispers…*Oh, the rich comfort in knowing that your*

243

* *Praise be to the God and Father of our Lord Jesus Christ, the Father of compassion and the God of all comfort, who comforts us in all our troubles so that we can comfort those in any trouble with the comfort we ourselves receive from God.* 2 CORINTHIANS 1:3–4

God walks you through your suffering to a spacious place. Surely as you share his glory, other women will catch a glimpse of the healing he offers.

Even with these precious promises, trading in pain can be deeply humbling to outright painful. Humbling, as you are reminded of your weakness. Painful, as you tap into the pain in order to help others. Grace speaks to your own journey... *Trade your pain with others and you'll each better scorn the shame of your own hurts.* It also promises redemption for others. Grace whispers...*There will be a day when you shout for joy, carrying a harvest as God himself reveals all the ways that your trading in pain has multiplied his grace to others.*

Your spiritual journey

> *Blessed* and *enviably happy [with a happiness produced by the experience of God's favor and especially conditioned by the revelation of His matchless grace] are those who mourn, for they shall be comforted!*
> MATTHEW 5:4 (AMPC)

Congratulations for stepping onto Stone nine: pain trading. By stepping on this Stone, you claim God's promise that all you've learned through abandonment, addiction and abuse is now an investable talent, a conduit of comfort to others. Remember that you aren't venturing into this trade alone. Jesus leads your way for us as the supreme pain trader of the universe. Jesus allowed God to press suffering into every part of his being so that he could understand ours. He traded his pain for our redemption. Remember Stone seven? Jesus scorned the shame for the joy set before him—the joy of our salvation, our restoration, our growing into and towards our Maker. Through

244

him we see the preciousness of this Stone. It is a rare Stone that God esteems greatly.

Circle of stones: pain trading

Are you ready to find your first stone of rest? On this ninth stone you will write the words **pain trading**. Let your heart guide you. As you hold the stone in your hand, say a prayer for God to send you others who need your story to help redeem their own. Say a prayer over their journeys towards recovery.

Your stone of pain trading will join your other stones: trauma, thorns, triggers, tears, warfare, dignity, acceptance, and sanctuary. Put them in a circle in front of you and then take a moment to rejoice at your accomplishment. How have the earlier stones prepared you for true spiritual rest?

Journaling: Pain Trading

Close your eyes and picture yourself as a pain trader. What does this look like for you?

Take your journal and make a list of all the pains you currently have to trade. Be sure to include past pains that are triggered by current circumstances.

1 Thessalonians 5:18 says, "give thanks in all circumstances; for this is God's will for you in Christ Jesus."

Write a prayer of thanksgiving over these pains, entrusting each of them to God for his use in other people's lives.

A word from Dave — Pain Trading

"I cannot undo the damage I caused by my sin, but if by sharing my story I can help someone else break free earlier, it gives me a sense of peace and redemption."

During the past decade, I have repeated this phrase over and over again. I'm really not sure if I share it more for the sake of others or if it's because I need to hear it. I will never forget the first time I was asked to speak at a seminar on the topic of sexual impurity. Actually I was not their first choice, but was asked to speak at the last minute because the person who was supposed to speak had relapsed. Still, as someone who loved to preach, I was always excited for the opportunity. However, while preparing the lesson it dawned on me...*If I hope to have an impactful message, I will need to be brutally honest about the specific ways I have fallen short.* My joy about being asked to speak quickly turned into fear. What would people think of me? Is this talk going to be recorded? After sharing my concerns with Robin, I decided to make my first investment on the pain trading market.

When the day arrived, I had a pit in my stomach. *Maybe some kind of general confession would be enough?* As I stood looking out at a room packed full of people, Robin looked at me with reassuring eyes and I found the courage to boldly share my story. I can't remember any of the points, but I will never forget the response. Instead of being shunned or rejected, people were waiting in line to thank me, encourage me, and confess their own sins to me. The investment had paid instant dividends! I had no idea at the time how many transactions were ahead, even trading in foreign markets! God has allowed Robin and me to trade pain in Africa, Asia, Europe, Eurasia, the Caribbean and even in New York City just a few blocks from Wall Street! I've seen the same response over and over again. "Thank you for being so vulnerable! When I heard how you now run free after 30 years of trying and failing, it gave me hope."

I smile as I remember a very special pain trade we made in the African market. While conducting a marriage seminar in Uganda, Robin and I were told that there would be a high ranking government official and his wife in the audience that day. I couldn't help but scan the audience during our very open discussion of sexual healing. We were brutally honest about how we almost lost our marriage due to damage caused by my many years of sexual addiction. I could not tell by the expressions on their faces how this couple was receiving our message. (By African standards we were stepping way outside of the box with our vulnerable approach to this topic.) During the next break we were told that the official had requested a private audience with us for lunch. Before I had time to get nervous, the hotel staff had readied a secluded place for us to dine. Soon they would be sharing with us their own painful journey and asking for our advice! When the conference was over, we were even invited to a dinner on the veranda of their highly secured private residence. Another successful transaction had taken place in the pain trading market!

This is the mystery and beauty of pain trading. Over and over again, as we have traded our pain, God has opened doors for healing and connection. I am convinced that trading pain makes you real. People want real, especially if they are in the midst of their own pain. The Apostle Paul told the Corinthians that he came to them in weakness and fear.* Every time he told the story of how he held the coats of those who were stoning Stephen, he was trading in pain. No doubt, it was a story that   247

---

* *I came to you in weakness with great fear and trembling. My message and my preaching were not with wise and persuasive words, but with a demonstration of the Spirit's power.* I CORINTHIANS 2:3-4

brought back memories that he would like to forget, yet he kept telling the story, over and over again, because he saw people come to understand the amazing riches of God's forgiveness when they heard it. He, no doubt, had people tell him, "I thought that my sexual acting out was so bad that it could never be forgiven, but when I heard your story, it gave me hope."

Still, both Robin and I have had moments of fear in releasing as much vulnerability as you are finding in these pages. There is pain in the trading of personal pain. It would be easy to say, "Pain trading is for others who are further from their pain. Let others, specialists, do this." It would certainly be easier to fill a book with the stories of people we've counseled. Yet in doing so, I'm convinced we would miss a blessing. As Robin mentions, this kind of pain trading is a participation in the work of the Master. In pain training, our suffering becomes investments placed in our Father's loving hands. In investing (instead of burying our sin and loss), we find joy. Beyond that, there is a sweet cleansing and refreshment that comes from deciding to see God in our stories, even our most wretched ones. As we see through his eyes, we don't find judgment; rather we find mercy and grace being poured through our lives to the lives of others.

As you have read this book I am sure you have mourned and wept over many painful events in your own life. I'd like to encourage you now to embrace the God-esteemed role of pain trading. Start small by opening up (investing) with someone today about any pain you may have experienced today. As the scripture says, "He who is faithful in a very little thing is faithful also in much; and he who is unrighteous in a very little thing is unrighteous also in much (Luke 16:10)." If we bury the small pains, losses and sins, we will likely be tempted to also hide the larger ones, preventing others from learning from our losses. But if we are faithful as pain traders today, God himself will propel us towards more faith-demanding transactions to come. Your trading like ours may have greater impact than you ever imagined. I look forward to hearing your stories of pain trading and how God is using your investment in suffering to inspire many more.

Back to your journal

Dave suggests that we start small in the arena of pain trading, by starting with today and being willing to share the small pains of each day. Read Hebrews 3:12-13. Here we are encouraged to, "encourage one another daily as long as it is called 'Today.'"

People in recovery groups often participate in something called "daily renewal." In these scripted conversations, people check in with a recovery partner daily to "surrender" pain instead of medicating it. This is a type of pain trading.

What small pains have you suffered over the course of the last 24 hours? Make a list, including even the insignificant irritations. Beside each pain, write how the event made you feel. Then call a trusted friend and explain that you are learning to invest your pain instead of burying it. Then ask for permission to share your pains from the last 24 hours. If they agree, briefly share your list.

If they've never participated in this kind of exercise, you might also let them know that you aren't asking for solutions, just for a listening ear.

Journal afterwards about your phone call or personal encounter. How did you feel afterwards? Did they reciprocate by sharing their pains of the day?

Grace will lead to wholeness
Treasures you're yet to know
A guard for all that's sacred
Redemption in letting go

Learning to Let Go: Forgiveness

To be a Christian means to forgive the inexcusable
because God has forgiven the inexcusable in you.
— C.S. Lewis

ABOUT FIVE YEARS AGO, I WAS ASKED TO speak at a women's day in Las Vegas, Nevada. Arriving in the afternoon, I bonded over dinner with the team of women running the event. As one of the women drove me to my hotel, I noticed a big sign with the word, "Rehab" over the Hard Rock Hotel. She explained that Rehab is a "party pool," kind of a giant orgy, its name a jab at the idea of recovery. A little shocked, I nodded, silently grateful I was staying away from the strip in a sprawling (safe) hotel complex. Arriving in my room just after 9:00 pm, I flipped through a magazine on the coffee table. Page after page featured ads with scantily clad women. Surprised, I threw it in the trash and set a wake up call for early morning. Even after praying myself to sleep, I tossed all night with memories spurred by an event 15 years earlier…

We were in Las Vegas for a sales award trip my husband won through his company, spending most of our time in the beautiful countryside, riding bikes through a canyon and visiting Hoover Dam. To honor my love of theatre, we budgeted for one show, and on our last night found one advertised as a "family show." Dave called ahead to make sure it was G-rated. Due to getting delayed by our adventures, at the last minute we changed our tickets to the 9:30 p.m. show, unaware that the late show was "spiced up." As we walked in, Dave tipped the doorman to get us a seat near the front. The show started with women diving into a giant pool, a few of them topless. We both covered our faces. I asked if we could leave. Dave mumbled, "Maybe it changes after this." Sure enough, the next two numbers were variety types, one having motorcycles chasing each other through giant, flaming metal loops, and another with a stage full of talented tap dancers. I relaxed a little. *This is going to be okay after all.* Then suddenly, the stage filled with girls in see-through mesh tops. Stunned, Dave couldn't take his eyes away. I whispered, desperate, "We should leave… now!" Unable to accept that what he meant for good was turning into a fiasco, he said, "It will get better." Suddenly, a buxom blonde sauntered on to the stage barely covered by a bikini top. I glanced over at my husband who looked like he was in a trance. Deeply disturbed, I got up and marched out with Dave following behind me. Going straight into the women's room, I fell on my knees in a lonely stall sobbing while Dave got a refund. The only words I said afterwards were, "Why didn't you lead us out?" Dave's posture crumpled as a dark cloud drifted across his face…

So when my alarm sounded the morning of the women's event, my heart was heavy. *God, why did you bring me here again? Will I be able to speak to these women?* Anguished, I put my face to ground and prayed for the women's day, for the visitors preparing to come, and for Dave's continued victory over sexual temptation, ending with the prayer that guided me as I wrote *Secure in Heart…Test me and reveal any unclean way in me.* Leaning against the couch, I picked up my Bible. It fell open to this passage:

*If anyone has caused grief, he has not so much grieved
me as he has grieved all of you to some extent [...]
The punishment inflicted on him by the majority is
sufficient. Now instead, you ought to forgive and comfort
him, so that he will not be overwhelmed by excessive
sorrow. I urge you, therefore, to reaffirm your love for
him [...] Anyone you forgive, I also forgive. And what
I have forgiven—if there was anything to forgive—I
have forgiven in the sight of Christ for your sake.*
2 CORINTHIANS 2:5–8, 10

Recognizing God's calling, I dressed and put on my tennis shoes. The sun was just beginning to light up the horizon. For over an hour, I walked around pools and gardens, interceding for Las Vegas. Thinking back to that show fifteen years earlier, I prayed for the salvation of each of the women in the see-through mesh tops, and that the buxom blonde would sense God loving her. I forgave the promoters, those who built the billboards, the ushers and ticket takers. Lastly, I forgave any who would come to the women's day who had participated in these industries. I thanked God for his desire to redeem them. By the time I headed back to my room, I was ready to be God's messenger.

A few hours later in a room bursting with women, I told the story of the night before, and then what happened to us fifteen years earlier. With tears streaming down my face, I read 2 Corinthians 2:5–10 to them, and told them of my prayer of forgiveness. Then I shared a story about another woman, Eve, who was tricked by the evil one. Intermingling Eve's story with my own, I told of my sexual abuse as a child, my husband's sexual addiction, and God's redemption. Afterwards, many women signed up to know more about spiritual redemption.

253

Forgiveness was the weapon of righteousness needed in a city that boasts in its dark legacy of lust.

You see, as a follower of Jesus I was his representative. Satan whispered...*It's too much for you!* He wanted me to forget God's promise that he would never tempt me beyond my ability to bear.* In his love, God allowed these triggers to lead me to buried pain—pain that God wanted to release in order to bring rest. True rest could only come from wrestling to stand with God in a place of mercy.

What past hurts has God circled you back to in this process? Just even saying the word *forgive* may bring up fear on your part. You may find yourself resistant or even wondering whether this could possibly apply to your personal devastation. Know you are not alone. But do remember that this process of forgiving on a deeper level is meant to bring spiritual rest. And, looking to the heart of God, we can see that this type of letting go comes at an extremely high price.

Letting go—the beginning of forgiveness

One of the most mysterious forgiveness ceremonies in the Old Testament had to do with letting go. It took place only once a year on a day aptly named the Day of Atonement. God's instructions were very specific:

> *Aaron is to offer the bull for his own sin offering to make*
> *atonement for himself and his household. Then he is to*
> *take the two goats and present them before the Lord at*
> *the entrance to the tent of meeting. He is to cast lots for*

---

* *The only temptations that you have are the same temptations that all people have. But you can trust God. He will not let you be tempted more than you can bear. But when you are tempted, God will also give you a way to escape that temptation. Then you will be able to endure it.* 1 CORINTHIANS 10:13 (ERV)

the two goats—one lot for the Lord and the other for the
scapegoat. Aaron shall bring the goat whose lot falls to
the Lord and sacrifice it for a sin offering. But the goat
chosen by lot as the scapegoat shall be presented alive
before the Lord to be used for making atonement by
sending it into the wilderness as a scapegoat [...] He is
to lay both hands on the head of the live goat and confess
over it all the wickedness and rebellion of the Israelites—
all their sins—and put them on the goat's head. He
shall send the goat away into the wilderness in the care
of someone appointed for the task. The goat will carry on
itself all their sins to a remote place; and the man shall
release it in the wilderness. LEVITICUS 16:6–10, 21–22

Two goats. One was sacrificed. One was let go. God offered
his people a two-part cleansing: one goat symbolized the blood
needed to redeem them, the agent of their cleansing. The other
goat symbolized the legal consequences of their sin, what they
deserved. The first goat was sacrificed on an altar. The second
goat was driven far into the wilderness so it would not return.
Scholars have dissected this passage in many different ways, but
I hear God pointing to a simple beauty that was to come. I
sinned. Jesus was sacrificed. I was released. Instead of driving me
out of his presence along with my transgressions, God drew me
closer.* Then he escorted me into the most holy of places,** while
my sin went to dwell in remote places from which it could never
return. The Psalmist tried to explain the sheer magnificence of

---

* *He is able to save forever those who draw near to God through him...*
HEBREWS 7:25
** *Therefore, brethren, since we have full freedom and confidence to enter*
into the [Holy of] Holies [by the power and virtue] in the blood of Jesus...
HEBREWS 10:19 (AMPC)

this thought when he said, "as far as the east is from the west, so far has he removed our transgressions from us" (Psalm 103:12).

But, there's still more to learn from this Day of Atonement ceremony. To ensure that this goat never returned (and perhaps to ease the minds of those participating in this holy ritual), God instructed for someone to usher it far into the wilderness.

Another beauty pierces my heart. We help usher other people's sins away. As Solomon writes: "Whoever would foster love covers over an offense, but whoever repeats the matter separates close friends" (Proverbs 17:9). Similarly Peter says: "Above all, love each other deeply, because love covers over a multitude of sins" (1 Peter 4:8).

As time passed, the Jews modified this law of the scapegoat. You see, they were having trouble letting go of that live goat. Even though they put it far into the wilderness, couldn't it potentially wander back? Someone suggested wrapping red wool around the goat's horns so it could be identified. Hallelujah! This new practice eased their minds. But this false sense of security wouldn't last. Eventually, a scapegoat that had been led out into the wilderness returned to Jerusalem with his red crown intact. The people were horrified, declaring it a bad omen.[79] Fear spread across Jerusalem like wildfire.

Why were they so overwhelmed by the return of the goat? Perhaps they missed the bigger picture—the goat was only symbolic of what God did with their sin. Wouldn't it have been easy enough to escort the goat back to the wilderness? My guess is that fear, superstition and the legalistic interpretation of the law took everything out of focus.

Emboldened by their earlier modification to the law, the leaders decided to fully change God's law. From that point on they would not only wrap the red wool around the goat's horns, but they would also usher the goat to the edge of the wilderness and then push the scapegoat off the side of a mountain to ensure its death. Surely the people would feel more forgiven if the goat died. And once they began to quantify forgiveness new contingencies would arise.

Now they had a different dilemma. How would they know if the goat was dead? *What if we push it off the cliff and it survives?* They needed some way to verify the goat's death. Finally, they decided to station multiple men up and down the path, all with signal flags. Once the first flag went up from the bottom that the goat was dead, then the flags would continue to the people on top, on through other signalers stationed along the road to Jerusalem until the signal reached town, and the people could shout with joy, "Our sins are now forgiven!"

No goats returning to town on them again and *triggering* all their fears or misbeliefs about forgiveness. Only one sacrifice was needed, and now, in their fear, they instituted a double sacrifice of sorts.[80]

How does this historical practice figure into the New Testament call to forgive? God's requirement of the second *live* goat being sent into the wilderness foreshadows New Testament forgiveness. One of the Greek words for forgiveness—*aphiemi*—means "to send away." It was used in ancient Greek writing talking about forgiving (i.e. sending away) a financial debt, but it was also in the prayer Jesus modeled for his disciples: "Forgive [*aphiemi*] us our sins, for we also forgive [*aphiemi*] everyone who sins against us. And lead us not into temptation" (Luke 11:4). When God forgives us, he sends away our shortcomings and cancels our debt. When we forgive another person, we cancel their debt to us even while the pain of their actions remains.

This is where these combined teachings slice into the depths of my soul. Those of us in the wake of addiction, abandonment and abuse want guarantees that we won't be hurt again. So

257

what do we do? We usher out the possibility of relationship with anyone who reminds us of these hurts. Or we put the possibility of deep intimacy to death lest the pain of whatever it was that hurt us chases us down and shows up again like that pesky goat. We make up elaborate "signal systems" to figure out if people are safe. Like the red wool in the goat's horns, we might even crown the person who hurt us with disgrace through shame-based accusations.[81] Like the Jews, we want guarantees! (Believe me, I'm speaking to myself here.)

And no longer sure that the one sacrifice of Christ is enough, we demand a double sacrifice—somehow the one who committed such atrocities against us has to pay!

But I think there's another way of seeing, also embedded in the Old Testament law, that enables us to let go of bitterness, while releasing others to make real changes. To forgive is to participate in the joy of the Father. This forgiveness means we refuse to retaliate, enact revenge or constantly remind them of their shame. Instead of condemnation we offer mercy. We no longer consider them slaves to their past actions. In doing so, we tap into a spirit of Jubilee.

To forgive is to participate in the joy of the Father. Instead of condemnation we offer mercy.

A Jubilee of forgiveness

Within the Old Testament law, God declared every fiftieth year to be a Year of Jubilee, a year of rest. At the beginning of this year, liberty would be proclaimed by releasing slaves and reinstating any property that had been sold during the previous forty-nine years to its original owner. The translators of the Septuagint (who translated the Hebrew Bible into Greek) called this "the year of *aphiemi*," meaning to let go. And so, Jubilee was a year of forgiveness. Imagine the joy of being released from mistakes with drastic consequences such as the loss of property or even personal slavery.[82] (Oh, how I relate.) For other people, this was a costly year. They gave back property someone had sold to them in order to pay a debt. They let go of a slave who had become a trusted helper.

Here's my question for you. Who received the greatest blessing during the Jubilee? The one who gained freedom from slavery or debt, or the one who pardoned them?

I think the greatest blessing came to those who chose to obey God…the ones who forgave debt and/or released slaves. In doing so, they received a precious chance to understand God in a whole new way. Imagine watching a man you just freed run into the arms of his family. Picture removing the heavy burden for a family whose financial mistakes followed them wherever they went. Jubilee (the day of *aphiemi*) was an invitation to God's people to join in his work of forgiveness and therefore his rest. And that was worth celebrating!

Let's bring together all these teachings in order to apply them (see the chart on the next page).

Bible example	Our human instincts	Call to rest
Old Testament example of the scapegoat. One goat sacrificed. One let go.	Make the one who hurt me the scapegoat. Crown them with shame. Demand proof that it couldn't happen again.	Rest from your own efforts to guarantee redemption and trust God's plan.
aphiemi: to release from debt. Jesus told us to pray daily to forgive other's sins.	Constantly remind them of their debt. When triggered, heap shame on them.	Rest from the heaviness of carrying another person's sin. Celebrate your own release.
Old Testament law: year of Jubilee. Set slaves and debtors free.	Hold the debtors captive until they prove themselves 100 percent innocent. Consider addicts worthy of slavery.	Join in God's blessedness and joy by displaying *his* heart to those who hurt you.

So the question begs to be asked. How do we stand on this holy Stone? We know that this extravagant grace of our God cost him everything. What will it cost us, those who have submitted ourselves to be re-created by God with Jesus as our guide?[83] Please read this prayer out loud, trusting the Spirit to translate it perfectly to your spiritual journey…

> *Father in Heaven,*
> *I was thrust on this journey of Stones largely because of other people's decisions. I never would have chosen the trauma of addiction, abuse or abandonment. Father, you've collected my every tear, heard my every cry and given me gifts I could not have imagined. You've called me to spiritual warfare and then equipped me for the battle. You are my dignity. But Lord, this forgiveness you call me to is painful. It reveals my deepest fears. Teach me to forgive as*

you forgive. Reach out and steady me, Father of comfort, as I place my full weight on this Stone. As I step, I trust. I pray through Jesus my guide. Amen.

Standing on the Stone: Forgiveness and Rest

When I lift my hands, it feels like a burden has been lifted. Adam takes the cord off the goat's neck and gives him a swift slap on the rump. Startled, the goat takes off running to who knows where. But this I know, Jehovah will not permit him near us again. Eve's Song, *p. 228*

Understanding forgiveness requires a deep dive into the heart of God. And even as we step on this Stone, I can testify that I am trembling just a little at what this might require. Yet within me is a call growing stronger and clearer. It is a call to surrender to God's plan of release and rest. That looks something like this:

Lord, I release my rights. I esteem mercy above judgment (SEE JAMES 2:13).

I release retaliation. Striking out will not mend me (SEE 1 PETER 2:23).

I refuse self-comfort. You are my comfort and my rest (SEE 2 CORINTHIANS 1:4).

Although our rights, retaliation, self-righteousness and self-blame are heavy burdens, I've found that releasing them isn't always easy.

In Stone eight (sanctuary) I shared about my codependent propensity to promote Dave to "my biggest problem." Just like what happened in Vegas, when new hurts surface old pains, it's easy to shift my gaze entirely onto Dave. Perhaps in my own long line of hurts starting with my sexual abuse at age six, I made a subtle modification to God's law. I no longer wanted to let one goat be set free. I wanted guarantees, even if I had to turn my gaze away from God to construct them. But please hear me out. When I stopped running from the pain, and asked Jesus my Guide to join me, precious knowledge came.

As I stand on this Stone and turn my eyes to my guide, Jesus, I catch a glimpse of the power of releasing. I choose to accept the one sacrifice of Jesus for my sins and the sins committed against me. I let go, allowing the Master Potter to reach his hands deep into the clay of my heart to mold me into the character of his son…making me into one who forgives.* This is the Jubilee rest I long for.

Rest from blaming.

Rest from holding on to burdens too big for me.

Rest from constantly reinforcing the walls that don't protect me.

Rest from Satan abusing my pockets of shame.

Sweet, glorious rest.

---

* *Bear with each other and forgive one another if any of you has a grievance against someone. Forgive as the Lord forgave you.* COLOSSIANS 3:13

This rest cuts across our circumstances, losses and unique fears. Someone told me recently...*Your situation is different, Robin. You are still with your husband, the same one you've had for 35 years. How could you possibly understand how difficult it is for me to forgive while I'm in the ashes of a broken relationship? You didn't get divorced. Your world was righted again.*

I do think that all of our situations are different and the path we each will individually have to take to reach forgiveness will be unique. I also hear a question here. Can you forgive from the midst of great pain?

Forgiveness does not depend on restoration of the relationship—that would make it depend on two people rather than one. The forgiveness we are exploring is an outgrowth of *your own* spiritual recovery. This process of forgiveness will happen over time, enabling you to let go of much of the confusion and fear contained in your past trauma. It is a way of claiming your own spiritual journey. Letting go today won't look the same as letting go tomorrow. God will perfectly tune his grace to the needs of your heart day by day. And so the Stone remains the same.

Forgiveness calls both you and me to let go of the burden of carrying another person's fall *today*. God wants this for us so that we can run free. You see, even if you are no longer in a relationship with the one who hurt you, a lack of forgiveness can bind your heart to the pain and lessen your dignity. Read this again, slowly.

A lack of forgiveness binds my heart to the pain.

263

In their 2014 book excerpt in *Spirituality and Health* magazine, Desmond and Mpho Tutu explain how the conditions we set for forgiveness act as chains to bind us spiritually to past trauma. They use a simple illustration of someone stealing your pencil. (As an author, my pencils are important!) To take the Tutu's illustration a bit further, let's just say it is a Smythson Viceroy Pencil of solid sterling silver worth $540. It seems logical to withhold forgiveness until the pencil is returned. The problem is, this condition becomes a string that binds us to the pain of having our favorite (or even irreplaceable) pencil stolen. As we are held hostage by another person's free will, the string becomes a chain. The Tutu's go on to say...

> *Those are chains to which the perpetrator holds the key. We may set the conditions for granting our forgiveness, but the person who harmed us decides whether or not the conditions are too onerous to fulfill. We continue to be that person's victim.*[84]

Releasing conditions is not the same as having no boundaries. No doubt, I'll guard my pencils more vigilantly after the loss than before. But releasing does validate the power I have to choose who I am, regardless of anyone else—even a pencil thief!.

What's more, without this deeper work of forgiveness, we may attract more abandonment, addiction or abuse. We fear that forgiveness makes us more apt to be hurt. The truth is that forgiveness makes us more resilient. If you are married, forgiveness sets the stage for healthy vulnerability with your husband. If you are unmarried, you'll create vulnerability in friendship, free from fear of abuse. As you engage forgiveness, you can depend on a day-by-day outpouring of grace, tailored to your needs.

264

Whatever your circumstances, you'll find forgiving takes entrusting your spiritual journey to your faithful Creator. As you continually let go of what isn't yours to carry, he'll soften your heart. Forgiveness then becomes the salt that seasons your words,* actions and heart, filling your eyes with light so you can see as God sees.** As you suffer in order to forgive, he will suffer with you, making your burden light and even beautiful. More than any of the other Stones, you'll find that forgiveness tunes your heart to Grace's call.

Grace calls

Just as it cost Jehovah the skin of an animal to forgive me, letting go will not come easily. "I forgive," I say, breaking loose a trickle of forgiveness [...] Then I hear Jehovah's prompting as clearly as if he whispered it in my ear. Eve will you forgive yourself? Eve's Song, *p. 178*

To find rest in forgiveness, we must call on the previous Stones in this journey. God doesn't ask us to skip over the pain and pretend we are strong enough. Instead he calls us to plant our tears as we cry out in prayer (Stone four). To forgive does not mean going back to a boundary-less existence. No, it means reclaiming our dignity (Stone six). It doesn't mean keeping yourself in a pattern of addiction, abandonment or abuse with no indication that the other person is willing to change. On the Stone of warfare (Stone five), we learned to take our stand against the evil one. Talking about forgiveness isn't meant to cause you shame, rather to release you. Do remember that Jesus himself will uphold you after you forgive (Stone seven: acceptance). Grace calls... *I know your fears about letting go.*

---

* *Let your conversation be always full of grace, seasoned with salt, so that you may know how to answer everyone.* COLOSSIANS 4:6
** *The light is sweet and pleasant, and it is good for the eyes to see the sun.* ECCLESIASTES 11:7, AMP

Trust that my grace is able to perfectly equip you for what's ahead. As you release other's sins, you also release my healing power.

Like me, you might find this Stone a call to a revolutionary new mindset that doesn't always make sense to those around you. Do remember God's promise that repentance and forgiveness of sins brings "seasons of refreshing from the Lord" (Acts 3:19). This promise is saturated with rest. A good starting place is forgiving yourself. Grace calls...*you were never meant to bear the weight of sin—even your own. Pray to forgive yourself so that you can rest from the burden of your own sin.*

Your spiritual journey

Congratulations for stepping on to the second Stone of rest, and the tenth Stone of this journey: forgiveness. Truly you are standing on one of the most holy places of the Bible. I pray that your heart thrills a little. We couldn't pass to another Stone without remembering our guide, Jesus, and the literal outpouring of forgiveness from his life. Sitting here, I am suddenly reminded that Jesus came to forgive. He lived to forgive, died to forgive, and was resurrected to complete the work of forgiveness. In this, he guaranteed our eventual resurrection free from sin, fear and doubt. Hallelujah!

For those in recovering marriages

Addiction, abandonment or abuse almost took your relationship down. Perhaps you are just seeing beginning fruits of your mate's desire to change. Or perhaps, like me, your partner has made large strides, but the duration and/or intensity of pain has left you with a pronounced limp. There may have been a time when divorce was a legitimate consideration. But now you've committed to work on the relationship. Still, the thought of divorce can be an old teddy bear you are used to snuggling with on the down days. Sometimes you may be tempted to use divorce like the red crown on the goat's horns, letting your spouse know that he or she is marked for life and that if the bad behavior returns, you will file for divorce. We threaten divorce to leverage power in the relationship. Although this is understandable, is it healthy? Will it help you recover spiritually?

When the Pharisees asked Jesus about divorce, he drew on the covenant status of marriage to answer them:

> *Some Pharisees came to him to test him. They asked, "Is it lawful for a man to divorce his wife for any and every reason?"*

> *"Haven't you read," he replied, "that at the beginning the Creator 'made them male and female,' and said, 'For this reason a man will leave his father and mother and be united to his wife, and the two will become one flesh'? So they are no longer two, but one flesh. Therefore what God has joined together, let no one separate."*

> *"Why then," they asked, "did Moses command that a man give his wife a certificate of divorce and send her away?"*

> *Jesus replied, "Moses permitted you to divorce your wives because your hearts were hard. But it was not this way from the beginning."* MATTHEW 19:3–8

What does this mean to you and your recovering marriage? Here's how I see it. The fantasy of divorce, or a new "less-flawed" man, or even not having to face the one who caused the pain everyday, has the ability to harden my heart. Mulling over divorce creates emotional distance, while triggering deep-rooted

267

fear of abandonment. If divorce becomes a routine friend I call out to on the hard days, I'm very unlikely to walk vulnerably before my mate—the very thing needed to work through challenging conflicts. This will make me more likely to move towards old patterns of love addiction, control or codependency. And if I continually allow a hardening of my heart by feeding and nurturing the idea of divorce, I may end up hardening my heart toward the very one I have decided to recommit to. What's more as they see me pull back, they will be tempted to pull back, sabotaging our renewed attempts at a healing intimacy.

The skills we've learned on the earlier Stones can be helpful here. Thinking about divorce can become a type of automatic negative thought. If you've formed this habit, it's important to let your brain know that this thought is no longer needed. That might look something like this...

> *Divorce. There you are again. I know you were seeking to comfort me in the most chaotic moments in my marriage. But now we are healing our relationship. I'm walking in forgiveness. So here's the door.*

As you habitually usher out divorce as a coping mechanism, you'll find that the thought diminishes in power, allowing forgiveness to spread out and send out new tendrils of spiritual growth.

Circle of stones: forgiveness

Are you ready to find your second stone of rest? On this tenth stone you will write the word **forgiveness**. Your stone of forgiveness will join your other stones: trauma, thorns, triggers, tears, warfare, dignity, acceptance, sanctuary and pain trading.

Put all of your stones in a circle in front of you (leaving room for the last two) and then take a moment to rejoice at your accomplishment. How have the earlier Stones prepared you for this Stone of forgiveness?

Journaling: Forgiveness

What did you learn about forgiveness growing up? Journal about these questions:

- How did your parents treat you when you committed a wrong?
- Were your wrongs acknowledged and cast away? Stored up to be used against you later? Overlooked as if you didn't matter?
- Were you forced to apologize before you were ready?

Ask yourself: how does this help me to understand what's underneath my reluctance to forgive? What fears does forgiveness still raise for me?

How can you reassure your inner child that it's safe now to let go? Spend some time journaling about this.

A word from Dave – Forgiveness

Fully grasping the depths of God's love and forgiveness is far beyond my human ability. But the role of forgiveness in forging healthy relationships compels me to try. Certainly, I owe a debt to God from my years of wandering that I could never repay. The forgiveness God has graciously extended me makes me think of a parable Jesus told about two servants (Matthew 18:21-35). Both of these servants had debts they could not pay. The master of the first servant called him into his presence to pay his debt—the equivalent of 20,000 years of wages.[85] You would think the credit card of the first servant would have been rejected long before he accumulated that much debt! When the servant fell on his knees and begged the master for forgiveness, the master was moved with compassion and released him from the entire debt.

Immediately afterwards, this servant went and found a fellow servant who owed him the equivalent of 100 days of wages. Although the servant begged him for forgiveness, he refused. Instead, he had him thrown into jail. When the master heard what his servant had done, he ordered that the first servant be thrown into prison until he could pay all that he owed. Jesus ended the story with these words, "This is how my heavenly Father will treat each of you unless you forgive your brother or sister from your heart."

Jesus uses this ridiculous comparison to help you and me understand our need for grace and our need to be forgiving of others. When I think of the number of offensive and abusive behaviors I engaged in, including every lustful thought, over the 30-year span of my addiction, I realize that my debt was enormous. The fact that both God and Robin have forgiven me is staggering. Remembering this brings me to a perpetual place of gratitude and humility. Truly Jesus atoned for my sins in a marvelous way.

Yet when I dig into the heart of the Old Testament atonement ceremony that Robin beautifully details in Stone ten, I find something that fills me with awe. I will call it, "The Why of Atonement." The Day of Atonement is the most important of all the Jewish holy days. Leviticus 16 details the events that God prescribed for its observance. Ultimately it was a day of fasting and repentance as people were called to acknowledge and turn from their sin. The most significant event of the day was the high priest entering into the Most Holy Place and sprinkling blood on the mercy seat of the Ark of the Covenant to atone for the sins of himself and for the people of God. The Most Holy Place was considered the closest one could get to God himself. The high priest would even try to fill the room with the thick smoke of incense to somehow shield him from the intense light of God's glory. They believed that if anyone got a full dose of God's glory they would die. Of course, this ceremony was meant to usher them into the spiritual realities that take place when we are forgiven…

> *Therefore, brothers and sisters, since we have confidence to enter the Most Holy Place by the blood of Jesus, by a new and living way opened for us through the curtain, that is, his body, and since we have a great priest over the house of God, let us draw near to God with a sincere heart and with the full assurance that faith brings, having our hearts sprinkled to cleanse us from a guilty conscience and having our bodies washed with pure water.* HEBREWS 10:19-22

271

While it is amazing to think that God would give the blood of his son to pay our debt and forgive our sin, the "why" behind this is truly magnificent! This was all done so that we could "draw near to God." Because God is holy and cannot be in the presence of sin, our sins had to be dealt with, but God's heart to do this wasn't just to satisfy the legal requirement. His motivation was that, having removed the barrier between us, we could walk close to him—be in an intimate relationship with him. To me, that gives God's forgiveness a whole new depth of meaning. Even after all I did to hurt him, the God of the universe wants to walk with me in a father-son relationship!

In the same way, while I appreciate Robin's forgiveness of the offenses I committed against her and our marriage, what moves my heart most is that she really loves spending time with me. She often states that she longs to be by my side until we leave this life. This is an amazing thought in light of how many times I have sinned against her by striking traumatic blows to her heart. In my shame I was convinced that the wounds I inflicted made me permanently unworthy of her love. Now her greatest joy is walking beside me.

This God-like forgiveness goes beyond a legal removal of a debt and takes us to a place where we actually, love, pray for, and potentially even desire the opportunity to walk with those who have wounded us (Matthew 5:44-45). This is a revolutionary teaching that, when lived out, makes us "children of our Father in heaven." The heart of our God, who calls us to draw near to him despite our weakness and sin, is worthy of celebration and imitation.

At the end of the day of fasting during the Day of Atonement, this most holy day is brought to its dramatic conclusion with a blast of the shofar (ram's horn) and a massive celebration feast. The blast of the horn served as a kind of seal, pointing towards the overflowing of God's forgiveness into the year to come and the happiness that comes with it. When we experience true forgiveness from God or from those we have sinned against, we can blast the horn with rejoicing, then draw near with grateful hearts and full assurance of the good that lies ahead!

Back to your journal

God forgives us so that we can draw near to him. Jesus calls us to draw near to those who hurt us through praying for them and through loving actions.

How often do you pray for those who hurt you through abandonment, addiction or abuse? Make a prayer list of those you need to pray for more, and commit to seven days of praying for them. At the end of the seven days, journal about how this transformed or encouraged your own heart.

For Jesus came full of grace
From his mouth comes truth
He shields our tender places
His hands hold the victory

Renewed Tenderness: Empathy

*"The most beautiful people we have known are those
who have known defeat, known suffering, known
struggle, known loss, and have found their way out
of the depths. These persons have an appreciation,
a sensitivity, and an understanding of life that fills
them with compassion, gentleness, and a deep loving
concern. Beautiful people do not just happen."*

– ELIZABETH KÜBLER-ROSS

D AVE AND I WERE SPEAKING AT A SINGLES
conference in Zagreb, Croatia. People traveled from
across Europe to hear us talk about sexual purity.
After our workshop there was an outpouring of joy, openness
and repentance. Afterwards, we had scheduled five nights in
the Croatian city of Rovinj to celebrate our anniversary. When
we crossed onto the tiny island city, the sight took my breath
away. Imagine weatherworn foundations of white, pale yellow,
tan and orange homes plunging straight into blue-green water,
with terra-cotta roofs staggered up the hillside. After checking
into our flat, we wandered the rolling cobblestone streets until
we found a little seaside restaurant on the side of a cliff. Glowing
in the sunlight, the tables staggered down the steep cliff side as
waves slapped lazily at the rocks twenty feet below. My heart
thrummed with joy. We couldn't have found a more perfect

place to celebrate. About ten minutes after we settled in at our table, my breath caught in my throat. A woman was sunbathing topless on the rocks right below us.

Dave saw my eyes go to her and quickly diverted his. We positioned ourselves facing away from her, but after about fifteen minutes the sun overpowered us. When we moved into the shade, she switched her position to a place with better sun and in a more direct sightline. Dave turned his body away from her, but as we nibbled at our appetizer, I couldn't shake the feeling of being unsafe.

After an uneasy conversation debating whether to stay or go, we paid our bill and left. Dave was visibly saddened to give up the view that thrilled me. After poking our heads in and out of restaurants, we finally found a dining room with a sea view. Although the meal was lovely, the earlier experience cast a cloud on our night together.

The next day, making a mental note about the liberal culture of Croatia, we determined to be more careful. After inquiring with a tour guide, we rented bikes to ride a seaside trail through the Zlatni Forest Park. As we rode, the scenery was soothing. The trail went for miles with forests on the left and the sea on the right. I felt completely free. We found a little restaurant for lunch and then turned back. After we had ridden a bit, a woman on the left came into view…

Again sunbathing topless.

She only caught my attention because Dave was ahead of me and I saw him divert his eyes away from her. When we stopped to rest, I asked him about her. He admitted that he had also seen her in on the way in and had taken a second glance. He took a deep breath. "That's not all honey. When we were in the restaurant on the cliff yesterday, while you were in the bathroom, I took a second look…I'm really sorry."

"Thanks for sharing," I said, my heart racing with adrenaline. "But I'm angry."

He was humble, "I understand why you are angry." Then seeing my hurt, he tried to help me feel better, saying, "I didn't ask for any of this honey."

His words sounded close to a justification. Rage exploded within me, and I whacked him in the shoulder with all my might. I caught myself and willed myself to breathe. *Calm down Robin. Be merciful.* I apologized, but the damage was done.

The next day we took off in the car to explore the hilltop cities through mid-Croatia. That afternoon, we visited the Coliseum in Pula where at least one famous Christian was rumored to have been sentenced to death. Both experiences were deeply spiritual, lifting our hearts. Afterwards, we drove to Split for more seaside views. As we walked around the coastline, immodesty was just a glance away. Once again, I shifted from deep peace to high alert.

When it came time for dinner, Dave wanted a grand finale, something to make up for the first night. I preferred something modest. Dave allowed me to choose, but seemed disheartened. Finally, after we finished eating, I pressed, "Dave, what is it? Please honey. Help me understand." He sat silently and then lifted his eyes to mine, "Robin, I feel like no matter what happens my sin will always ruin things for you. I'm afraid it will always be this way, no matter how hard I try." I protested, but knew my words couldn't speak as loud as my actions on the bike trail.

Moments like these are testy for me. Resentment comes... *Why do I have to be the one to initiate these talks?* Hurt follows close behind...*What about me?* Instead, as we sat quietly waiting for our check, I began to pray. Then an ember sparked inside, warmed by the very breath of God. *God loves us. He used us powerfully on this trip. His love hasn't changed.* Suddenly, I realized that Dave's shame was triggered because of his desire to give me nothing but good and then seeing it tarnished by a temptation he didn't ask for.

On our hour-long drive back to Rovinj, I was ready to extend empathy. "Honey, this trip has had some difficult moments. Yet, the purity workshop you led was amazing. God worked powerfully through you." I took a deep breath and plunged in. "I know you don't want sexual temptation. You didn't ask for the losses you had as a young boy. I'm thinking that this battle is a thorn in the flesh. You've agonized with God for it to be removed. Maybe the reason it remains is because your weakness opens men's hearts to learn from you. They know you understand. Maybe God needs this thorn in the flesh to use you as powerfully as he does." I paused, both of us quiet. And then I added, "And you're not the only one with a thorn. My ongoing battles with insecurity make me relatable to other women. *Secure in Heart* and *Eve's Song* wouldn't have been born without my insecurity and love addiction. Other people trust us because of our struggles."

Dave smiled, reached over and squeezed my knee. "Thank you sweetie," he said.

Later on, we identified our experience in Rovinj as a turning point in our relationship. It became easier for us to identify and talk about shame. Personally, asking for the Spirit's lead, I became more intentional about letting go of a deep-seated anxiety that quenched my empathy in volatile moments. Dave reached towards a new level of emotional availability, astounding me at the levels of risk he took.

278 What does this mean for you? Abuse, addiction and abandonment have left each of us with a particularly sensitive fear meter. Fear has a way of distorting our vision. Beyond that, we have an accuser, Satan, determined to press on our

fears at every turn. Yet if we listen very closely, we'll hear Jesus our shepherd and guide, urging us through his Holy Spirit to treat others with empathy, just as he extends empathy to us. His aim is not only re-create us after the darkness, but gift us with sweet rest.

A renewed tenderness

Where denial darkens our path and compulsions hide and confine us, the light of God's love gently and compassionately penetrates the layers of our most ingrained defense mechanisms and coaxes us out of the tomb into the light. This light opens us to the possibility of intimacy.[86]

Why do we all need empathy? Simply said, it's because we all need human connection. Connecting with someone else in our moments of despair gives us a sense of worth. *I am worthy of someone else understanding.* Empathy modeled after Jesus strengthens our moral fiber by nourishing a life-giving connection to others. Certainly, empathy does coax us out of our caverns of despair into the glorious light. It's no wonder then, that empathy is one of the gifts Satan most wants to steal. But, there's good news! God can use abuse, abandonment and addiction to transform our empathy—both for the wounded one and the one who inflicted the wounds.

One of the most moving stories of the renewal of empathy in the Bible comes from God's dealings with David—yes the king and shepherd of Israel, musician and writer of Psalms. But his preparation for this legacy came in the remote grazing fields of Palestine. David's early schooling in empathy first came in the fields, where he developed a meaningful relationship with his

279

beloved sheep who knew and trusted his voice. In these fields, David learned the cost of empathy—requiring a shepherd to risk great danger for his sheep. With a slingshot, David took on both a bear and a lion (1 Samuel 17:36) to defend his sheep.

But David's empathy was even greater because it sprang from his close walk with God. In Psalm 23, David painted a beautiful picture of how he related taking care of sheep to his own relationship with God. In his sheep's need for water, he saw his own need for spiritual refreshment. When wild animals mounted attacks against his sheep, he saw his own vulnerability and need for the protection of a shepherd.

This precious empathy defined David in the challenging years when King Saul chased him relentlessly. By being the one who needed a shepherd (God) to defend him against a wolf (Saul), David grew in humilty, the building block of empathy. His shepherding experience grew as he hid in the Cave of Adullam. Seeking David's leadership, a band of men came to the cave. They were all either in distress, in debt or discontented (1 Samuel 22). No doubt, they desired to follow someone who understood. Left to themselves, they could have become a rebellious band of embittered men. Instead David took them and created a band of mighty warriors, men of principle.*

The far opposite of empathy is entitlement. And David wasn't immune from this temptation. After the deaths of Saul and Jonathan, becoming King suddenly meant that David's needs now trumped anyone else's. Empathy shifted to the side as a subtle foe began to take hold—entitlement.

Somewhere around David's 20th year of reigning as King, he made a fateful decision. He had been known for fighting besides his soldiers. This particular year he stayed home, sending the Art of the Covenant, the sign of God's presence, with his men.

* I SAMUEL 22

Entitlement. Restless and idle, one night he spied on Bathsheba (estimated at half his age), becoming a voyeur. More entitlement. As King, he could have whatever he desired, and he desired her. This desire would lead to adultery, pregnancy and then murder of one of his most loyal soldiers, Bathsheba's husband Uriah.

Satan's insidious plot to hijack David's empathy had now come to fruition. Instead of being out in the battlefield with his soldiers (sheep) and the Ark of the Covenant (God's presence), he sent them into harm's way without him. Instead of seeing Bathsheba as a precious young ewe entrusted to him by God and her husband, he preyed upon her vulnerability like a wolf. Instead of being honest with Uriah, David brought him off the battlefield and tried to manipulate him into having sex with his wife by getting him drunk. Instead of being a commander/shepherd who laid down his life for his soldiers/sheep, he became a hired hand, purposely abandoning Uriah in battle where he would be killed. Can you imagine more un-shepherd-like behavior?

When Nathan confronted David, he appealed to his sense of empathy.

> *Then the Lord sent Nathan to David. And he came to him, and said to him: "There were two men in one city, one rich and the other poor. The rich man had exceedingly many flocks and herds. But the poor man had nothing, except one little ewe lamb which he had bought and nourished; and it grew up together with him and with his children. It ate of his own food and drank from his own cup and lay in his bosom; and it was like a daughter to him. And a traveler came to the rich man, who refused to take from his own flock and from his own herd to prepare one for the wayfaring man who had come*

*to him; but he took the poor man's lamb and prepared it
for the man who had come to him."*

*So David's anger was greatly aroused against the man,
and he said to Nathan, "As the Lord lives, the man who
has done this shall surely die! And he shall restore fourfold
for the lamb, because he did this thing and because he had
no pity."*

Then Nathan said to David, "You are *the man!"*
2 SAMUEL 12:1-7 (NKJV)

In this confrontation, I see God's mercy. God appealed to David's truest identity as the empathetic shepherd boy that God had chosen as King. I can't even imagine the devastation of this rebuke—how clearly Nathan showed David the grossness of his sin. Yet there was love. It was as if God was saying, "Remember? You don't belong to Lucifer. You belong to me." Then God the shepherd crippled David, by taking the son Bathsheba was carrying. (Shepherds have been known to break the legs of a wandering sheep and carry them around on their shoulders until they heal.) Likewise, God would also carry David on his shoulders, using his horrible fall to re-create him as a man of empathy.

Perhaps the most convincing evidence of David's rebirth of empathy is the book of Psalms. Multitudes have looked to Psalm 23 — "The Lord is my shepherd, I shall not want…" — for comfort and perspective. When I read Psalms, I feel David sitting beside me, validating my distress and angst and then reminding me (with him) to look above.

I see my husband Dave in the story of King David. Dave grew up in the farmlands of Illinois. From a young age he was a passionate, tenderhearted shepherd-leader who impacted

282

hundreds of other young people. Satan used pornography to strip away Dave's truest essence, taking him places and inciting him to do what is too shameful to mention.* Dave's empathy decreased as entitlement raised its ugly head. There was a huge price Dave paid for his lapses in sexual purity. He endured years of stepping back from public leadership (one of his strongest gifts) to focus on his repentance. God broke Dave of deriving his self-esteem from the full-time ministry by having him work as a sales representative for twenty years. Relationally, Dave weathered the pain of separation from his wife and the sheer chaos of my responses when I was triggered. He watched his children suffer in the aftermath of his sin.

After such a steep fall, God's re-creation of my husband as a man of boundless empathy has been nothing short of spectacular. Much like his renouncing of false intimacy, this hasn't happened all at once. It has been a progressive change. I've listened to Dave freely give countless hours of empathy to men who feel like they have no one else to turn to, even while we are on a much-needed vacation. I've seen his heart stirred by the underdogs of God's Kingdom—those who tend to be pigeonholed because of their deep plunges into sexual immorality. Under his leadership, I've seen man after man grow into mighty men of integrity.

But my husband isn't the only one who has needed a rebirth of empathy. Going back once more to King David, in what the Bible calls "the last words of David," I see a breathtaking example that stirs my own heart…

> *The God of Israel spoke,*
> *the Rock of Israel said to me:*

283

---

* *It is shameful even to mention what the disobedient do in secret. But everything exposed by the light becomes visible—and everything that is illuminated becomes a light.* EPHESIANS 5:12-13

"When one rules over people in righteousness,
  when he rules in the fear of God,
he is like the light of morning at sunrise
  on a cloudless morning,
like the brightness after rain
  that brings grass from the earth." 2 SAMUEL 23:3–4

In the wake of addiction, abandonment and abuse, I've ranged from being buried in my pain to throwing out accusations. I've been tempted to develop a spiritual superiority complex…*I'm above you.* What would it look like instead for me to be, "the brightness after rain that brings grass from the earth"? Here in Idaho, the most beautiful skies come right after a storm. *Now I see!* An emotional storm that washes through can cleanse me. As I surrender to his way of seeing, God re-creates me to become light after a long night or clarity after a soaking rain. This is the cleansing power of empathy.

Going back to that beach bike ride in Croatia, by striking out at Dave I sent him an unintentional but clear message… *you are not worthy of empathy.* This wasn't helpful. Dave's greatest fear was that if anyone truly knew him, they would reject him. I thank God that he inspired that conversation on the way back to Rovinj, when I released Dave from the heavy burden he carried. In that moment, I glimpsed the power of empathy…a lesson I still carry with me and seek to live out in my marriage and ministry.

Again, for my husband, the re-creation of his empathy has been spectacular. At first, I thought this process might drive me crazy. Dave now had feelings about everything, especially things I did and said! When I would treat him wrongly, he would speak up, "No, Robin. I can't accept that. I have feelings about that!" It seemed like I was forever hurting him. Yet I had to remind myself, *Robin, this is what you've longed for. Don't run away. Stay engaged.*

But as Dave's self-empathy grew, so did his empathy for me. Dave was now able to tenderly sit with me in the ashes of the pain he caused. Do you see the miracle of empathy? My empathy nourished Dave's empathy, and then his empathy bolstered mine.

Going back to the last words of King David in 2 Samuel 23, I hear a man who made God's story his own. Let's continue with verse 5:

> *If my house were not right with God, surely he would not have made with me an everlasting covenant, arranged and secured in every part; surely he would not bring to fruition my salvation and grant me my every desire.*

As King David accepted God's empathy, he was able to extend empathy to others. Let's rephrase that for you and me.

*As I accept God's empathy for my weakness,
I grow in empathy towards others.*

This empathy is costly, but precious. How do we find this expansion of our wounded hearts? Growing in empathy will require redefining weakness to see as God sees. It will take Standing on the Stone of Empathy.

Standing on the Stone: Empathy

> *While your father and I were apart, Jehovah took me*
> *back through my most beautiful and my most painful*
> *memories. He taught me a truth I hope I'll never forget."*
> *I pause, waiting for Cain to give me permission to share.*
>
> *It takes a long moment, but Cain finally mumbles, "What*
> *is that, Mother?"*
>
> *"I learned that in the midst of my pain, even when it*
> *seemed I'd been cut off from all I loved, God wanted me*
> *to trust him, to believe he was speaking to me through the*
> *pain. Like God wanted his way of seeing things to flow*
> *through me."* Eve's Song, *p. 208*

Why do I have to fight so mightily to climb off of my high
perch and sit on level ground with the very people that hurt me?
Perhaps it's because I've been conditioned by my circumstances
to see weakness as a threat. Recently, I found two concepts in
the Greek language contained in one powerful scripture that
has revolutionized my thinking about empathy and weakness:
sumpathes translated sympathize (only appearing twice in the
New Testament, both occurrences in Hebrews); and *astheneia*
usually translated as "weakness."

> *For we do not have a high priest who is unable to*
> *empathize with our weaknesses, but we have one who has*
> *been tempted in every way, just as we are—yet he did*
> *not sin."* HEBREWS 4:15

Part of God's reason for sending Jesus was that he could empathize with us by sharing our experiences, including our human weaknesses. First let's take a look at the word empathy. Does it have a different meaning than sympathy? Commonly, the word sympathy is used to connote having compassion on someone's situation. In contrast, the word empathy describes actually entering the feelings of another person, being "in" their feelings. So we could suggest that sympathy comes from the outside in, whereas empathy comes from the inside out.

Jesus empathizes (*sumpathes*) with our weakness. The Greek word *sumpathes* comes from the Greek *sumpascho*, which means to suffer with someone.[87] Since pathos means illness, we could think of Biblical sympathizing as understanding another's predicament because we have suffered the same illness. In my way of thinking, this is a revelation. Jesus doesn't sit outside of us, stirring up a little compassion for our weakness and sin. No, he entered our temptation and carried our sin, at the cost of great personal suffering.* He experienced our illness firsthand in order to redeem it. He has felt with us. So when we come to Jesus, he isn't just trying to understand, he enters our feelings, as the old hymn says, "Jesus knows all about our troubles. He will guide 'til the day is done."

Secondly, Jesus empathizes with us in our weakness, our *astheneia*. According to Strong's Greek Dictionary, *astheneia* holds many meanings, including:

> *without the strength of capacity to understand a thing;*
> *an ailment/weakness that deprives someone of enjoying or*
> *accomplishing what they would like to do; the handicap*

---

* *Surely he took up our pain and bore our suffering, yet we considered him punished by God, stricken by him, and afflicted. But he was pierced for our transgressions, he was crushed for our iniquities; the punishment that brought us peace was on him and by his wounds we are healed.* ISAIAH 53:4-5

that goes with that weakness; the weakening influence of the problem.[88]

Jesus understands when we struggle to make sense of our weaknesses left in the wake of abandonment, addiction and abuse. He hurts with us when we can't accomplish all that we hope for because of these flaws. And he understands that we've been left with a limp in our relationships.

In this way, our emotional handicaps form a bridge between us and Jesus, our guide for this journey. Jesus doesn't require moral perfection. He encourages you and me to bring our foibles and flaws that we fear most to his throne to find grace and mercy. He wants our weakness to move us towards him, instead of away from him. And then he works to create in us *his* character—including a beautiful empathy.

> *Empathy has a unique power to change us and help redeem those who've hurt us.*

Now we are ready for an important task of rest, integrating this renewed empathy towards weakness into our daily lives. We've needed each of the previous Stones to be ready for this one. Empathy is a high calling to be like Jesus, who found the power to suffer with others even in the wake of their oppression, verbal abuse and abandonment of him.

But whatever it costs us, empathy is worth it. You see, empathy has a unique power to change us and help redeem those who've hurt us. It opens up common ground, common feelings, and uses them to increase our compassion. Growing in empathy is progressive, taking us from one degree of glory to another. Here are a few suggestions to get started:

Examine yourself: With a gentle curiosity, dig beneath situations that expose a lack of empathy on your part. What weakness do you fear?

Confess a lack of empathy: Triggers may tempt you to pull away and shut down any sense of empathy. Talking about it with a friend who understands (empathizes) will help refill your personal reserve of empathy.

Start small: Remember that listening is the foundation of empathy. Practice the discipline of withholding words, even if you have to bite your tongue. Then be brief… *I hear you. You aren't alone. Thank you for sharing.*

Remember Jesus: Learning to see weakness differently takes time and practice. When you fall short, move towards Jesus instead of away from him. Trust that he understands your weakness. Ask him to give you empathy (like his) towards the weaknesses of others.

See commonalities: Spirituality isn't meant to divide us from others. *I've repented, but you haven't. I'm trying to be like Christ and obviously you aren't.* Rather, like Jesus, we can find the common roots in our humanity and theirs. By facing our own repression, denial, and addictive habits, we will learn to feel with those who have hurt us.

Rest: developing a Shepherd's Heart

There's one more final task on this Stone of empathy. As rest turns us outward, we are ready to develop a shepherd's heart. To do this, let's circle back to Psalm 23. As you read this meditation out loud, think of Jesus our Guide who has faithfully walked us from Stone to Stone of this journey.

> *The Lord is my shepherd, I lack nothing.*
> *He makes me lie down in green pastures,*
> *he leads me beside quiet waters,*
> *he refreshes my soul.*
> *He guides me along the right paths*
> *for his name's sake.*
> *Even though I walk*
> *through the darkest valley,*
> *I will fear no evil,*
> *for you are with me;*
> *your rod and your staff,*
> *they comfort me.*
> *You prepare a table before me*
> *in the presence of my enemies.*
> *You anoint my head with oil;*
> *my cup overflows.*
> *Surely your goodness and love will follow me*
> *all the days of my life,*
> *and I will dwell in the house of the Lord*
> *forever.* (PSALM 23)

By trusting Jesus as our shepherd, we find the courage to embrace true empathy. This gives perspective for every other Stone. See the chart on the next page for insight.

Trauma	My primal fear	My Shepherd (Psalm 23)	Stone of empathy
Abandonment	I will be left behind	Leads me in paths of righteousness	I choose righteousness
	No one will provide for me	Prepares a table that meets my needs	I listen for others' needs
	I'll be deserted in heated moments	Leads me beside quiet waters[89]	I peacefully connect with their pain
Abuse	Others will take advantage	Comforts me with his rod and staff	I sit with them and simply listen
	My faith doesn't protect me	Restores my soul	I am protective of others
	I cause things to go wrong	Floods my life with goodness and mercy	I choose mercy over judgment
Addiction	Another person's losses define me	Promises spiritual abundance	There is enough in my cup to share
	I will never get over it	Anoints my head with oil	My prayers anoint others
	I can only deliver myself	Walks me through each situation	I look beneath others' actions

Now, go back through the chart noting the primal fear and corresponding action of empathy. Do you see how empathy neutralizes your primal fears? No wonder empathy is so redemptive! Now you are ready to follow the good shepherd into a renewed empathy, the foundation for the next Stone, Hope. More than ever, for this Stone, you will need the reassurance of grace.

Grace calls

> *I do not ask the wounded person how he feels;*
> *I myself become the wounded person.*
> – WALT WHITMAN, *SONG OF MYSELF*

Earlier in this Stone, we talked about the renewal of empathy experienced by King David. I believe that David was able to infuse his relationships with empathy because he had learned to let God sit with him in his own pain. With that came security in God alone. Do you see how your security has grown on this journey? Grace comforts you...*Your Father is right by your side. His heart bursts with pride. He will honor the covenant you made with him. In fact, it is secure down to the very last detail!*

But we have an even greater witness to the power of the empathy. By now, you are well familiar with our Guide. Jesus gives the resounding "amen" that at last can free us from the fear surrounding weakness, whether ours or that of other people. Grace whispers...*Jesus, Lord of Heaven and Earth, calls you to come into his presence with your weaknesses. He wants to be near you and for you to feel his empathy. He will keep you safe as you risk extending empathy.*

Your spiritual journey

*And I will give them one heart [a new heart], and put
a new spirit within them. I will take from them the
heart of stone, and will give them a heart of flesh [that is
responsive to My touch]...* EZEKIEL II:19 (AMP)

Congratulations for stepping on the next to the last Stone:
empathy. As I imagine you standing on this Stone, tears of
joy gather in my eyes. You see my friend, the thought of you
has helped carry me this far. If I may boast in the Lord for a
moment, there's a sense where your progress redeems my own
search for this Stone. You are part of the spiritual reward of my
journey and God's calling for me to become a messenger of hope
(Stone 12). And now, you have the same joy to look forward to.
Stone twelve will call you to a sacred status, to decide how you
will use this growth and new knowledge for the sake of others.
As a wounded healer, the ways you reach out will spring out of
your weakness and your empathy.

Do remember that Jesus understands your weakness, your
astheneia. In fact, he was crucified in weakness. And the miracle
is that his weakness mirrors your own, and your weakness is
redeemed through his:

*For to be sure, he was crucified in weakness [astheneia],
yet he lives by God's power. Likewise, we are weak in
him, yet by God's power we will live with him in our
dealing with you.* (2 CORINTHIANS 13:4).

Circle of stones: empathy

Are you ready to find your third stone of rest? On this eleventh stone you will write the word **empathy**. Your stone of empathy will join your other stones. Your stones of darkness: trauma, thorns and triggers. Your stones of re-creation: tears, warfare, dignity, acceptance and sanctuary. Your stones of rest: pain trading and forgiveness.

Take each stone and lift it to your lips for a kiss. Were some of the stones harder to kiss than others? Were there some you chose not to touch at this time? Honor your sense of what you are and aren't ready for.

Journaling: Empathy

Empathy is a Stone that turns your vision outward towards other people, even those who have wounded you with their decisions.

Hold the stone in your hand and ask God to bring to mind who ever most needs your empathy now. Say a prayer for God to increase your empathy for them as you hold the stone. Then write a prayer in your journal for the person(s) you have in mind.

As you are ready, add prayers for others as needed.

A word from Dave — Empathy

"No one heals themselves by wounding another."
– AMBROSE OF MILAN

The Stone of empathy brings to mind two pivotal moments in our recovery journey—moments that I believe could have only happened by the power of God as he extended his grace to me through Robin. The first was when I was caught looking at the sunbathing women in Croatia. Robin could have put me in the doghouse and heaped shame on me. That might have spoiled our much-anticipated get away. Certainly, this would have been the instinctive thing to do. When we are wounded, everything in us wants to strike back, hoping that the inflictor of our pain can feel what it's like to be hurt.

By Robin patiently waiting in the restaurant in Split for me to process my fear that I would forever taint every cherished experience by giving into temptation, she allowed God to work. On the drive back to Rovinj, I was ready to hear what she had to say. As she extended empathy to me, I sensed the Spirit moving. Robin was able to discern the Spirit because she was in touch with her own longstanding weaknesses and fears. She understood how persistent and disabling these can be. Her empathy melted my heart and inspired me to not give up, but to fight even harder to win my battle with lust. I thank God that my wife was willing to battle to find empathy.

You see, extending empathy is risky business. *What if my abuser never gets it and keeps on hurting me, and others? It seems so unfair that I should be left with another wound and they should go away without any consequences.*

Jesus surely had to fight off similar thoughts as he hung on the cross, being insulted and wounded over and over again. Yet he didn't wound those who wounded him. He didn't retailiate. (If he had called down angels from Heaven to defend him, the retaliation would have been epic!*) Instead, he chose to empathize with them, entrusting both himself and his abusers to God.

On the cross, Jesus was able to be empathetic to the greatest degree possible. Since at that moment he was carrying the sins of all mankind, he could empathize with the thief hanging on a cross beside him. After all, Jesus was carrying the weight of every theft that had ever been committed. In essence by becoming sin (2 Corinthians 5:21) Jesus felt the accompanying shame, guilt, and remorse just as if he had committed those acts himself. He felt the bitterness, hostility, and emptiness of those who mocked him. Having shared in their condition through bearing their sins (Isaiah 53), he then prayed that they be forgiven and set free from their toxic state. What an inspiring thought! Jesus knows exactly what I felt like each time I fell sexually. Because he took up my infirmities, he understands the loneliness, regret and frustration that came from being caught up in addictive sin.

The second event that comes to mind, one that was not recorded in this Stone, was the day I shared my entire sexual history with my counselor and Robin. I slowly read through eight single-spaced pages of details about events that spanned forty years from my childhood until that moment. The most embarrassing and disgusting acts I had ever committed were all brought into the light. Robin wept that day, but not tears of rage. Rather, when she heard my whole story, she empathized,

---

* *Do you imagine that I could not appeal to my Father, and he would at once send more than twelve legions of angels to defend me? But then, how would the scriptures be fulfilled which say that all this must take place?* MATTHEW 26:53 (PHILLIPS)

seeing the similarities between my trauma and shame and the trauma and shame she carried from her losses and sin. She set aside her own pain caused by the new revelations in order to enter my pain. Her tender and vulnerable response was a balm to my soul. She resisted the temptation to pull her heart away, but rather came toward me with empathy.

Had Robin not begun her own journey into grace, I do not believe that this would have been possible. I knew she was not lowering her standards or expectations for me to continue in my recovery. Rather, her empathy provided a place of safety where I could risk total honesty. Her empathetic response gave me a glimpse into the heart of my Heavenly Father who through Jesus was able to go with me to my greatest moments of weakness. Instead of abandoning me, Robin dared to continue to be with me. In this she followed the example of Jesus, who calls us to draw near carrying our weaknesses with us.

So how can those who have never personally experienced addiction be truly empathic to people like me? Please listen carefully to the words of Gerald May:

> *I also learned that all people are addicts, and that addictions to alcohol and other drugs are simply more obvious and tragic than other types of addiction. To be alive is to be addicted and to be alive and addicted is to stand in need of grace.*[90]

When you come to understand that an addiction/idol can be defined as anything that you use over and over again to fill the empty spot in your heart reserved for God, you then can begin your journey to becoming empathetic. Since breaking free from my addiction to pornography and masturbation, multiple other addictions have come to taunt me. At times, food (i.e. sugar), sports, TV, video games, travel, gardening, work, talk radio, etc.

have all taken over God's rightful place in my heart. I know that they are becoming addictions when I crave them more than I crave my time with God and when I don't feel complete without them. Their addictive hold is revealed when I try to give them up and a wrestling match ensues in my brain, bringing withdrawal symptoms.[91]

I relate to May's words, "To be alive is to be addicted and to be alive and addicted is to stand in need of grace." If you take some time to think about it, I'm guessing you relate to May's words as well. When the humbling reality of this sinks in, you will then be moving toward the empathic heart of Christ, who "is not unable to empathize with our weaknesses… but one who has been tempted in every way, just as we are" (Hebrews 4:15).

Back to your journal:

Influenced by Gerald May of *Addiction and Grace*, Dave gives us a simplified definition of an addiction that can prove instructive to all of us.

- Anything that you use over and over again to fill the empty spot in your heart reserved for God
- Things you crave more than you crave time with God.
- Anything that creates withdrawal symptoms when you step away.

Using this definition, make a list of past and present "addictions" that you have wrestled with. Circle the ones that are still problematic for you and then journal about their addictive power. What pains are you medicating? How can you use this understanding to build empathy towards those who have hurt you?

To take it higher: See the list of "Attraction Addictions" and "Aversion Addictions" on pages 38 to 39 of *Addiction and Grace*. Circle the ones that apply to you. Take some time to read the entire chapter. How has your understanding of addiction been broadened?

Plant your feet on my stones
Accept hope as holy ground
Extend the healing of Jesus
Then watch as grace abounds

STONE TWELVE
Wounded Healer: Hope

*When we have found the anchor places for our lives
in our own center, we can be free to let others enter
into the space created for them and allow them
to dance their own dance, sing their own song,
and speak their own language without fear.*
– HENRI J. M. NOUWEN, FROM *THE WOUNDED HEALER*

L OOKING OUT INTO THE AUDIENCE, I
marveled at the beauty of the women—all over forty,
many dressed in colorful native garb. Their faces were
lifted in curiosity towards me, a fifty-five-year-old American
woman who had traveled across the ocean to Nairobi, Kenya
to minister, but even more so for this appointment with them.
Sitting in the crowd was a woman named Amara.[92] Amara's
profession up to this point in her life had been working in a
casino in another Kenyan town, trading her body for gifts
and money. Just a week earlier, she had shown up at her sister
Makena's door with a story to tell. One day, Amara had woken
up in a fancy hotel with no memory of the past twenty-four
hours. In her despair she cried out to God. Her prayer went
something like this, "I'm at the end, God. I've made a mess of
my life and I don't know how to find you." The answer came
swift and sure. *Give away every possession you own that you
received from prostitution.* Amara opened her suitcase and began

sorting its contents into two piles. Into one pile went fancy perfume, expensive clothing, lavish gifts for her son and pricey electronics. Into the other pile went whatever she owned that didn't come from trading sexual favors. She then took all the trappings of her shame and gave them to the poor. The rest she loaded in a suitcase for her journey to her sister Makena's house in Nairobi, ready to hear more about the God who saw her in that lonely hotel room.

Upon hearing Amara's story, Makena immediately thought of this workshop, but wasn't sure if Amara could come. First of all, Amara was thirty-seven, and the event was only for women over forty. She wasn't a believer yet, and the event was for members of the church. So Makena called the organizer... *please, may I bring Amara?*

I knew none of this. But standing up front to address this glorious gathering, I knew I was there as an ambassador of Jesus. Minutes before I walked to the front, I quickly glanced over a lesson on the Samaritan woman I hadn't looked at in seven years. The night before I had confessed to my daughter Bekah, who had traveled with Dave and me to Africa, that I didn't know what I would share. She remembered the lesson and insisted I teach it. I sensed the Spirit in her words.

You see, I came to Kenya weary, weak and wounded. In the three weeks before, I had suffered some fierce spiritual and physical attacks. First a rabid bat had shown up in my bathroom in Boise, Idaho, wings fully spread, hissing at me.

Although my quick actions prevented it from harming me, I felt terrorized. In fact, I read it as a personal attack from Satan. Just a week earlier, my book *Eve's Song* had just been released. In one scene of spiritual attack in the book, a bat bit Eve in the cheek.

Just a week after the bat's appearance in our bathroom, Dave and I were in a wilderness bed and breakfast. After getting out of a claw foot tub, a poisonous spider bit me on the top of my right foot, leaving a hive as large as the top of a coffee cup. It also imparted a neurotoxin that wouldn't be diagnosed until after I returned from Africa. This second attack came once again when I was unclothed, making me think of the talk I had given on the Garden of Eden in different locales around the world.

But the assaults were far from over. The week before I came to Kenya, I had been in Uganda helping build a school for orphans. On Ssese Island, I suffered from an intestinal bug that left me so dehydrated I had to be evacuated to Kampala, after which intense hallucinations ensued. My nervous system was failing. Dave was ready to evacuate me and call off our trip to Kenya, but I felt God's call to continue. I knew Dave could carry us through our joint presentations of a marriage workshop for 500 couples, as well as a singles workshop for over 700 unmarried men and women. In our advance conversation, no one had mentioned a breakfast workshop, so that event came as a complete surprise. It seems that God didn't want me to prepare in advance. He already knew his plans and needed me weak enough to execute them.

So here I was in Kenya, at this workshop for women over forty, teaching about the Samaritan woman because Bekah told me to, and because my frazzled brain couldn't formulate a new lesson or even remember one I'd taught elsewhere. As I began to speak, the Spirit blew through. Amara and Makena were stunned. It seemed that every word came from God for Amara. She immediately related to the Samaritan woman, whose self-esteem had also been tied up in men (five husbands to be exact).*
I also told my story of recovering from abandonment, addiction

303

* JOHN 4:4-26

and abuse. During a break in the lesson, I asked all the women to turn to someone and share. During those five minutes, Makena opened up to Amara about her own childhood sexual losses. Shame was lifted. At the end of the lesson, we saw how God used the Samaritan woman to be an ambassador to her city. History tells us a large church was born in Samaria. Scholars think it had its root in this Samaritan woman Jesus met at the well. Before she had met Jesus, she was so ashamed that she snuck to the well when no one else was around. After her encounter with Jesus, she was so empowered that she brought all the townspeople back to hear him speak. After the lesson, Amara sat there stunned. Was God not only seeking to heal her, but also calling her to become an ambassador?

Living out my call as a wounded healer meant ministering in Kenya despite personal hardship, trusting that God would provide the healing balm needed for a nation where sexual discussion is taboo and secrecy reigns. For Makena, being a wounded healer meant praying for her sister for long years, risking the relationship with occasional difficult talks, and then finding a way to get her the healing she needed. For Amara, it would mean first opening her own wounds for the healing balm to be applied and then using her past brokenness to offer healing to others. And for all three of us, it would mean walking in the footsteps of Jesus, the wounded healer who died for us...*by his wounds we are healed* (Isaiah 53:5).

Now you can see why this balm is so precious, that God would call Amara to give away her possessions, travel across the Kenyan countryside, and make her way into this seminar. Armed with a new hope, Amara began Bible studies and gave her life to God.

What does this mean to you? This journey of Stones is not for you alone. It is a call to your own ministry. Your Creator has embedded a healing balm within your wounds. You've experienced this balm as you've stepped from Stone to Stone. Now it's time to learn to share it with others who desperately need it. What is this healing balm? It requires many ingredients, but the result is a contagious hope.

Healing wounds

> I was so thankful you sent some healing balm with me, Mother. I knew what to do...with the wound that is... because of you. I washed it with the lye soap you sent and then bandaged it with the healing balm. I thought of you and how you ministered to me when I was hurt. Eve's Song, p. 198

In *The Hunger Games*, the blockbuster movie adapted from a book, the heroes Katnis and Peeta are swept along on a horrible journey that they didn't choose. As the story goes, to make up for a past rebellion, the seat of government (the Capitol) holds a war game in a virtual arena once a year. One teen boy and girl are selected randomly from each of the twelve districts to particpate in this fight to the death with only one winner. Katnis and Peeta are allies from the same district.

One of the most telling moments in the first movie features a cave where they have taken refuge from the other remaining contestants who seek to kill them. As Peeta and Katnis vulnerably reveal their wounds, they discover the seeds of love. The problem is that Peeta's wound is bone deep and infected. He is ravaged by fever and in danger of death. In this, the Capitol sees the opportunity to exploit Katnis.

305

To lure her out of the cave, the lead game-maker, Plutarch Heavensbee, makes a broadcast announcement to all the contestants in this virtual world asking them to converge at the clearing to receive "gifts." Katnis immediately knows her gift will be healing balm for Peeta. After all, earlier she was stuck in a tree with a gaping wound on her leg, and it was only balm from a sponsor that saved her. Before he drifts asleep, Peeta makes her promise not to go to the clearing. What the Capitol intends is for all-out war to commence. It is a death trap.

Katnis knows she can't keep this promise. She has received healing and now it is time for her to fight for Peeta. Sure enough, at the clearing Katnis narrowly escapes being killed, but returns with the balm in hand and a wound of her own. First she addresses Peeta's infected leg wound with the balm. Then he insists on ministering to the bloody wound on her forehead. In the morning, they both wake up whole. Then another shocking announcement is broadcast. The Capitol has decided that instead of one winner, there can be two winners as long as they are from the same district (we find out later that this is another manipulation of Katnis and Peeta). After the news Katnis says, "Peeta, we can actually survive this." In their great vulnerability has come a precious gift—the ability to convey hope to the other.

I relate to this scene on many levels, both as an individual and in my marriage. Dave and I each had to learn to fight for recovery alone, before we could learn to engage in spiritual warfare together. Before I began recovery, my wounds of abandonment, abuse and addiction were still pushed down by repression. With my own wounds barely addressed, I didn't yet have a reservoir of faith available for another person's wounds. Secretly, I feared that acknowledging the extent of Dave's wounds might give him an excuse to keep hurting me. Dave had a similar battle. Would I reject him if he admitted how much he had hurt me? Would I ever fully admit my own struggles?

Only God's unconditional love could give Dave the safety he needed to face the full extent of the wounds he caused. Likewise, only God's love could open my heart to how my present losses were magnified by my past ones. By first doing whatever it took to find individual healing, Dave and I were eventually able to become part of God's healing balm for each other.

This again reminds me of Katnis. In the movie, the healing balm sent for her drifted out of the sky in a small box attached to a parachute, softly dinging to alert her. To reach the balm, Katnis had to risk climbing further up the tree with a raw, gaping wound on her leg. She could have thought, "The Capital is tricking me. I can't trust using anything they send!" She was already so far up the tree that a fall would likely kill her. Yet without that balm, the hallucinations, paranoia and fever caused by the injury would have kept her far away from Peeta. They wouldn't have come together…and that unity was what they needed most. She had to press past risk in order to find hope.

Similarly, in order to minister to the wounds of someone else, we must first accept help with our own. Let's read that again, slowly.

To minister to the wounds of another,
I must first accept help with my own.

For me, this meant seeking a counselor and joining a recovery group. Every time I exposed my wounds, risk was present. Yet the risk brought hope. With the help of others, I began to glimpse that my trauma and thorns went far beyond Dave. They were infectious, capable of spreading into every fiber of me. As I turned to Jesus and allowed his people to minister to me with

307

his healing balm, my compassion grew and flourished. I became a powerful advocate for my husband, able to help him unwind emotionally charged moments (the very ones that triggered my own pain).

Likewise, as Dave pressed past risk to invite other strugglers into his battles, he gained perspective and hope. In a sense, we were learning to… "Love your neighbor [each other] as yourself." *As myself* is the foundation. I have to love myself enough to seek care for my own wounds first. Love your neighbor spills out of self-care…now that I'm finding perspective I will lend a helping hand to someone else.

Whether she knew it or not, Suzanne Collins, the author of *Hunger Games*, tapped into this idea, that care of self and neighbor can help to redeem the most impossible situations. Obviously, loving self means I can't lose me in the equation. My healing is important. Loving my neighbor could take many forms—friends, fellow recovery group members, husband, brother or sister in Christ. Let's look to Luke's account of the greatest commandment for insight.

> *On one occasion an expert in the law stood up to test Jesus. "Teacher," he asked, "what must I do to inherit eternal life?"*
>
> *"What is written in the Law?" he replied. "How do you read it?"*
>
> *He answered, "'Love the Lord your God with all your heart and with all your soul and with all your strength and with all your mind'; and, 'Love your neighbor as yourself.'"*
>
> *"You have answered correctly," Jesus replied. "Do this and you will live."* LUKE 10:25-28

Not willing to let good enough alone, and wanting to justify his question, the man asked, "And who is my neighbor?" Jesus answered by telling him a parable...:

"A man was going down from Jerusalem to Jericho, when he was attacked by robbers. They stripped him of his clothes, beat him and went away, leaving him half dead. A priest happened to be going down the same road, and when he saw the man, he passed by on the other side. So too, a Levite, when he came to the place and saw him, passed by on the other side. But a Samaritan, as he traveled, came where the man was; and when he saw him, he took pity on him. He went to him and bandaged his wounds, pouring on oil and wine. Then he put the man on his own donkey, brought him to an inn and took care of him. The next day he took out two denarii and gave them to the innkeeper. 'Look after him,' he said, 'and when I return, I will reimburse you for any extra expense you may have.'

"Which of these three do you think was a neighbor to the man who fell into the hands of robbers?"

The expert in the law replied, "The one who had mercy on him."

Jesus told him, "Go and do likewise." LUKE 10:30-37

It is telling that Jesus used a Samaritan (a race despised by their Jewish brothers for intermarrying with unbelievers) as the hero of this story. Perhaps Jesus was thinking of the generosity and openness he had found in Samaria. And why did the priest and Levite, two men schooled in the Old Testament

309

Law (including to love your neighbor as yourself*), both pass by? Although Jesus didn't reveal their motives, I'm guessing his audience had their own ideas. The priest might have thought, "Who knows who this man is? Surely God is punishing him for some sin." The Levite might have thought, "He is going to die and then if I touch him I'll be ceremonially unclean." Only the Samaritan got involved.

But here's where the story gets even more interesting. He poured wine and oil on the man's wounds and then bandaged them. Wine served as an antiseptic, disinfecting the wound. Oil moistened the wound and provided a layer of protection. Bandages would keep the wounds moist.

Jesus' description of wound care wouldn't be fully validated until 1962, when George Winter (now known as the Father of Moist Wound Healing) discovered that wounds that were covered healed better than those exposed to air. Physician Karl S. Kurzeinicki (Dr. Karl) sums up what history has taught us…

> The "perfect" dressing should be able to remove toxic chemicals and secretions, while keeping the wound humid. It should allow gases to enter and leave, but still provide thermal insulation. It should also protect the wound from infection and be easily removable. There is no single dressing that can do all of these.[93]

Why do I share all this? In Jesus' mind, wound care is at least part of what it means to love our neighbor. The word *wound*, in the Latin, comes from *vulnus*, which means vulnerability. Likewise, the word vulnerability, also rooting in *vulnus*, means able to be wounded.

310

* LEVITICUS 19:9-18

wound = vulnus = *vulnerability*
vulnerability = vulnus = *able to be wounded*

In wound care we minister to each other's most vulnerable places—the sites of injuries. This calls us to use great tenderness. In the chart below, take a look at how this fleshes out:

Medical science	Good Samaritan	Wounded healer
The wound needs to be sanitized.	Used wine as an antiseptic.	Isn't repulsed by another's wound. Instead looks for a way to remove the sting.
It is important to keep the wound moist.	Used olive oil in his healing tonic to provide a layer of protection.	Honors the vulnerability of others and treats their disclosures with care.
Wounds heal better when they are covered, but the bandages need to let the wound breathe.	Carefully bandaged the man's wounds. Clothed the man in his own clothing.	Protects another's dignity when wounds are tender. Generous with what they've learned.
The more serious the wounds, the more ongoing wound care needed.	Carried the man on his donkey, and paid for additional care.	Sacrifices to carry another to where there is help. Stays invested.

We can see from the chart that dressing someone else's wound takes thoughtful preparation. Going back to Jesus' parable, the stranger was prepared to intervene—he carried a healing balm with him. Helping his "neighbor" was so important to the Samaritan that he clothed him in his own garments, laid him on his own donkey, and then paid for further care with his own money.

311

How does this love of neighbor instruct us on this journey? As we've stepped from Stone to Stone, we have gained knowledge, wisdom and practical help. Now we have a new calling—to continue our own healing as we invest in the healing of others. To pain trading, forgiveness and empathy, we can add the calling to give others hope as a wounded healer.

From pain trader to wounded healer

> *In a futile attempt to erase our past, we deprive the community of our healing gift. If we conceal our wounds out of fear and shame, our inner darkness can neither be illuminated nor become a light for others.*[94]

> *This hope is like a firm and steady anchor for our souls. In fact, hope reaches behind the curtain and into the most holy place.* HEBREWS 6:19 (CEV)

Why is this looking outward from our own battles so crucial? Remember that before we started a journey of spiritual recovery, we were tempted to conceal our wounds. Even now, after seeking healing, it is human to want any sign of those wounds to disappear. *Glad that is in the past!* Becoming a wounded healer means refusing to start concealing once again. Instead, we offer what we've learned (and are continuing to learn) as a healing gift to others. In doing so, we become light and hope.

If this sounds familiar, it's because of our earlier Stone of pain trading. In Stone nine, we went to the parable of the gold bags (talents) and saw that it can be applied to our pain. Our human temptation is to bury the pain away, fearing that we serve a harsh master. As pain traders, we instead invest our pain by sharing with others, so that the comfort can be multiplied. To become a wounded healer is the next logical step. Now that

I've learned how to see a harvest of righteousness from my own pain, I am ready to help someone else along that journey.

Pain trader: One who refuses to bury their pain, but instead invests it by swapping pain (our stories of loss, sin and spiritual attack) with those who need it.

Wounded healer: One who draws from the wisdom found in their own wounds, to serve as a guide for others with similar wounds.

Participating in a recovery group is a crash course in pain trading. In our groups in Idaho, we start with each member sharing for two minutes. This discipline (*only* two minutes) has taught us to enter the depth of our stories quickly. We no longer have to chatter on and on, giving long-winded explanations because we are avoiding vulnerability. With time, miracles start unfolding. The women move beyond swapping stories to administering healing balm to each other. This isn't in the form of fixing each other (we all agree that we aren't there for that purpose). No, healing comes as we listen to others gaining wisdom from their own spiritual cuts, emotional bruises or relational amputations, and then we naturally apply it to ours. It also comes as we summon our courage and invite others to minister to our wounds. To accomplish this, we ask God's Spirit to lead. He specializes in bringing us into community for the purpose of transformation.*

313

---

* *From him the whole body, joined and held together by every supporting ligament, grows and builds itself up in love, as each part does its work.*
EPHESIANS 4:16

Where does this transformation come from? I believe it is in the redefining and embracing of hope. The primary ingredient of the healing balm that Jesus produces from our anguish is pure, unadulterated hope. And those of us who have hopped from Stone to Stone are uniquely gifted in the making of this elixir.

In the Biblical Greek, the word for hope, *elpis*, is full of confidence and joy. It means to anticipate, expect something that is sure. According to *Strong's Greek Concordance*, it includes the idea of anticipating with pleasure. Biblical hope moves us forward, compelling us to take step after step, knowing we are anchored firmly.[95] But there's a caveat. Hope is also full of waiting, and the waiting can be excruciating.

> *A delayed hope makes one sick at heart, but a fulfilled longing is a tree of life.* PROVERBS 13:12 (GW)

> *Yet when I hoped for good, evil came; when I looked for light, then came darkness.* JOB 30:26

Since Jesus instructed us to let each day take care of itself, I'm thinking he knew we could only process hope in bite-sized pieces.

> *See to it brothers and sisters that none of you has a sinful, unbelieving heart that turns away form the living God. Encourage one another daily, as long as it is called "Today," so that none of you may be hardened by the deceitfulness of sin.* HEBREWS 3:12–13

We encourage one another daily, because we need a fresh infusion of hope for each day. And here's where the actual word *hope* can be helpful. Notice that hope includes the word hop. Hope is a hop with an e at the end. Hope is a long journey full of many short hops.[96] And in like manner, healing a deep wound doesn't usually come in one big leap (like the ointment Peeta and Katnis used). Rather, it comes hop by hop. So perhaps our task in bringing hope to others is to teach them how to take one step at a time. *What is your task today? What can you hope in today?*

When we boil it down to its essence, the end benefit of this journey of Stones is a transformed hope. In the chart on the following pages, take a look at how each Stone (and the hopping from Stone to Stone) has transformed your hope. Do you see new resilience and strength sprouting up in your soul? Take a moment to look up each of the scriptures.

We encourage one another daily, because we need a fresh infusion of hope for each day.

Stones of darkness	Transformed hope
Trauma (one)	We no longer hide from our trauma, but trust God for deliverance. 2 Corinthians 1:10
Triggers (two)	We separate past and current pain, finding fresh perspective. Romans 15:4
Thorns (three)	We no longer fear accusation since God's power is shown through our weakness. 2 Corinthians 12:9
Stones of Re-Creation	
Tears (four)	We allow our wounds to speak. We picture God sitting with us as we mourn. 2 Corinthians 1:3-4
Warfare (five)	As Jesus mediates our relationships we find patience and perspective. 2 Timothy 2:24-25
Dignity (six)	By standing with God, we reclaim our dignity. 1 Timothy 1:13-14
Acceptance (seven)	We drain our well of abandonment and shame as we move towards others. Romans 5:3-5
Sanctuary (eight)	We honor the sanctuary of our bodies, and pursue true intimacy, however painful. Philippians 1:9-10
Stones of Rest	
Pain Trading (nine)	Prompted by love, faith and hope, we invest our pain. 1 Thessalonians 1:3
Forgiveness (ten)	We learn a deeper work of forgiveness and let go of self-judgment. 2 Corinthians 2:7
Empathy (eleven)	We look beneath the surface to find hope for those who hurt us. James 2:12-13
Hope (twelve)	Our hope overflows, providing a healing balm for others. Romans 15:13-14

Becoming a wounded healer is the highest calling of my life. I praise God for using my great weakness as a key ingredient in helping others heal. Even when I've felt completely inadequate, God's Spirit has brought hope in the most unexpected places, in the most unexpected ways.

Grace calls

Throughout this journey, we've looked to Jesus again and again. As we stand on the twelfth Stone, it's important to remember that Jesus understands our wounds. In every way we've been wounded, Jesus was wounded as well—with deep, fatal wounds to his hands, feet and side. Do you feel scarred by the hurts in your life? The wounds on his hands, feet and side left scars as well. Are you ashamed of your scars? Here's where Jesus can help. He was resurrected with his scars intact. Healed? Yes. But visible? Yes!

Actually, it was these scars that led Thomas to recognize Jesus and exclaim, "My Lord and my God." Grace whispers… *Now it's time for you to rejoice a little in the scars you still carry, knowing they mark you as a tested spiritual warrior.*

Are you ready to consider the possibility of being a wounded healer? Does your heart thrill at the thought of imparting hope to others? Being a wounded healer isn't a call to be someone you aren't. Rather it's God's reminder that even in your weakness, you are a chosen vessel he can use you to bring hope and healing to others. Once more, it is a call to follow your Guide, Jesus.

Your spiritual journey

You've probably noticed that throughout this journey of Stones, we've gone back to Jesus for perspective often. I'm absolutely convinced that bringing Jesus into our healing changes everything. After crafting this journey of Stones, I

317

discovered Immanuel Therapy, a spiritual approach to moving through trauma developed by Karl Lehman, M.D. and Charlotte Lehman, M.Div. The basic premise is that when people healing from bewildering traumas intentionally invite Jesus to accompany them, they can heal more quickly. In particular, this therapy has been very effective in helping survivors of violent religious persecution (for instance, those who have witnessed rape, beatings and killings of loved ones) move through trauma without developing long-term symptoms of post traumatic stress disorder.[97] Reading their materials, I had to marvel a little that God had brought us to similar conclusions…that a journey this vulnerable needs Jesus as a guide.

Going forward, there are many ways to continue this journey. If you did not collect twelve stones the first time through, it might be time to take a deeper plunge into the recovery work contained within these pages. Likewise, you might want to go back through the journaling after each Stone, and after "A Word from Dave," and complete the additional exercises. If you went through this book by yourself, perhaps it's time for a second journey through, this time with other women. Gathering a couple of friends with similar battles can be a great start. If you don't have a spiritual recovery group readily available, perhaps it's time to consider starting one. Regardless, I hope you find *Grace Calls* a friend you can go back to again and again for perspective.

As we finish this journey of Stones, it seems only appropriate to offer thanksgiving to our guide Jesus. If it weren't for the crazy risk he took for our sakes, where would we be? Jesus truly blazes a path ahead of us as we seek to become true wounded healers.

318

He himself bore our sins in his body on the cross, so that we might die to sins and live for righteousness; by his wounds *you have been* healed. I PETER 2:24 (EMPHASIS ADDED)

Circle of stones: hope

Are you ready to find your fourth stone of rest? On this twelfth and final stone you will write the word **hope**. Your stone of hope will join your other stones. Your stones of darkness: trauma, thorns and triggers. Your stones of re-creation: tears, warfare, dignity, acceptance and sanctuary. Your stones of rest: pain trading, forgiveness and empathy.

When you are ready, have a worshipful time of remembrance. Put your stones in a circle in front of you. Take each of the twelve stones in hand, one at a time, and thank the stone for its part in your re-creation and rest. For instance:

- *Trauma*, thank you for reminding me of my deep need for God.
- *Thorns*, thank you for the redemption within your bite. Thank you for reminding me that God's power is more than enough.
- *Tears*, thank you for releasing me from the deep anxiety I carried for years. Thank you for reminding me of the God of all comfort.
- *Warfare*, you were a difficult stone to embrace. Yet you have given some of the richest gifts as I've learned to see other people through Jesus.
- *Forgiveness*, thank you for hanging around after so long, nudging me to look deeper. Thank you for teaching me how to let the Master Potter do his work.
- *Hope*, thank you for all the deferred desires I've had and the spiritual discipline you've given me through waiting. Most of all thank you that I get to participate in God's care for other's wounds.

319

Journaling: Hope

On this Stone, we looked to Jesus' story of the Good Samaritan to discover how loving your neighbor includes caring about their wounds. Go back and read the gospel account in Luke 10:25-37.

How has this journey uniquely prepared you to love your neighbor? What wounds of yours have been healed? What have you learned that you can offer to others?

Now, review the chart on page 311, contrasting Medical Science, the Good Samaritan and the Wounded Healer. In the Wounded Healer column, pick one skill that you see as your strength and one you'd like to grow in. Write about both in your journal.

A word from Dave — Hope

And hope does not put us to shame, because God's love has been poured out into our hearts through the Holy Spirit, who has been given to us. ROMANS 5:5

Having traveled the world with Robin and watched how women of every culture connect with her and stand in line to share with her their sacred journeys of pain, I have seen this beautiful God-created paradox play out over and over again. There is something so disarming about someone showing you their wounds or openly confessing their sin. As you have read *Grace Calls*, I am sure you have been drawn into the wake of healing that comes as Robin shows you her scars. She is, indeed, a wounded healer.

I have had the privilege of being acquainted with other wounded healers as well. I am reminded of Kim, a co-worker of mine when I was working as a pharmaceutical representative. After Kim and I were put together as co-promotion partners, we quickly became good friends. Being the same age and having children the same ages, there was always plenty to talk about. She was the consummate image of a professional sales representative. She looked and dressed sharp, bubbling with personality and wit. She was a confident woman who took no guff from the doctors or even from our managers. Her boldness combined with her ability to laugh at herself made her easy to be around.

Since Kim was never a smoker, everyone in our company was shocked when her persistent cough was diagnosed as lung cancer. She was soon put on medical leave to allow for the ravages of chemotherapy and radiation. We still talked regularly over the phone and I saw her a couple of times during her treatment, sporting a well coiffed wig. You would hardly know that she had been ill. As time passed, our relationship changed from being just co-workers to me becoming her big brother and spiritual advisor. After her treatments for lung cancer, another challenge came. She was diagnosed with brain cancer, and other related problems that would require more radiation and surgery.

I will never forget walking into Kim's room and seeing her for the first time without her wig, her face swollen from steroid treatment. I barely recognized her, but then her unmistakable deep raspy voice rang out, "What do you think of my new look?" Deeply moved, I walked over to her bed, kissed her on the head and told her how much I liked it!

I came to encourage her, but the opposite happened. Kim told me how she had begun praying and seeking God with all her heart. With time, she began studying the Bible with Robin, and her heartfelt decision to surrender her life to Jesus was medicine to my wife's soul.

Up to the very end, Kim's greatest concern was not for herself, but for her family. Outward appearances now meant nothing to her or me. Her wounds brought healing to me every time I visited her. Her confident hope in God became a rich source of comfort and healing to all who had the privilege of knowing her. As her body was wasting away, her hope was being renewed.* And that was glorious!

What is it about wounds allow them to bring the deepest healing? What is it about weakness and trials that give them power to change despair into a living hope? In I Corinthians 1, the apostle Paul writes concerning the Cross of Christ:

---

* *Therefore we do not lose heart. Though outwardly we are wasting away, yet inwardly we are being renewed day by day. For our light and momentary troubles are achieving for us an eternal glory that far outweighs them all. So we fix our eyes not on what is seen, but on what is unseen, since what is seen is temporary, but what is unseen is eternal.* 2 CORINTHIANS 4:16-18

*But God chose the foolish things of the world to
shame the wise; God chose the weak things of the
world to shame the strong. God chose the lowly things
of this world and the despised things—and the
things that are not—to nullify the things that are,
so that no one may boast before him. vv. 27-29*

When we speak of our foolishness, our weakness and our
lowliness, people are drawn in. When we share our despicable
acts, people begin to trust us. When we share all the things
that we "are not," it impresses them more that telling them the
things we want them to think we are. When we tell them how
we came to the very edge of hopelessness and then found hope,
they begin to think they can find hope as well. Wounded healers
are effective because they align themselves with the power of the
cross of Jesus and the hope of the resurrection.

You see, appearances are all for nothing if we are not taking
our value from the cross of Jesus—*he suffered for me in my very
worst moments, so I can serve him with confidence.* However, if
the cross becomes our glory, we can stop wearing our masks
and covering up our flaws and say like Kim, "What do you
think of my new look?" I can't think of anything more satisfying
than being a part of God's redemptive plan of healing. Yet the
healing power can only flow through us as we share our wounds.
I suspect that this is why Paul "delighted in his weakness,"
because he knew that his human frailty and even his deeply felt
sinfulness, could bring healing and hope to the harassed and
brokenhearted.

So Robin and I will keep on telling the stories of our most
pathetic failures, knowing they are rich with the potential of
igniting hope. We will repeat often the tales of our darkest

323

moments. And we will keep on watching with amazement the healing of lives and marriages through the power of God!

> *May the God of hope fill you with all joy and peace as you trust in him, so that you may overflow with hope by the power of the Holy Spirit.* ROMANS 15:13

Back to your journal

In this heart-moving story, Dave challenges us to stop wearing masks and covering the very wounds that could be helpful to others. As he says, "the healing power can only flow through us as we share our wounds."

Think of a time you shared a wound with another person in an effort to help or encourage them. What was the result? How did you feel afterwards? How does the sharing of wounds increase hope?

Now make a list of some of the most hurtful wounds that have come to you through abandonment, addiction or abuse. Circle the ones you've been most hesitant about sharing with others. When you are ready, write a prayer of surrender to God, giving him those wounds to use for the good of others.

Afterword

*For while the Law was given through Moses,
grace (unearned, undeserved favor and spiritual
blessing) and truth came through Jesus Christ.*

JOHN 1:17 (AMPC)

I N T H E T W O C R E A T I O N A C C O U N T S I N G E N E S I S,
two different names for God are used—*Elohim* in chapter 1
and *Adonai Elohim* in chapter 2. It is interesting to note that
Elohim is often associated with justice, while *Adonai* is linked to
mercy. And so some Jewish scholars talk about how these two
names flesh out the essence of creation—God's quest to embed
a perfect balance of justice and mercy. Some Jewish teachers
even propose that God had to create at least one practice world
and destroy it, before he finally perfected Earth. The story goes
that he looked at the first world and realized that if he ruled it
from his justice alone it would undermine all he intended. So,
to arrive at the final product, he added mercy as the perfect
counterbalance.[98]

Although I can't find theological support for the notion that
God created and destroyed at least one world before ours came
to be, I do relate as an author who has wrestled through almost
three years and multiple drafts of *Grace Calls* to find that sweet
spot of truth (justice) and grace (mercy) that underlies spiritual
recovery. It comforts me that God's creation, underpinned by
his perfect wisdom, found the balance that we as human beings
find so evasive. Perhaps this counterbalance of truth and grace is
best shown through God's first children, Adam and Eve. After
sadly informing them of the consequences of their fall in the
garden (God's justice), God, in love, covered them with skins

reaped by killing another part of his creation (God's mercy). Ultimately, my second book, *Eve's Song*, hinges around upon one redemptive action of God that pointed all the way to the cross.

This needed balance also explains another reason why *spiritual* recovery is so essential. The more Jesus transforms us into his image, the better we can balance justice (truth) and mercy (grace) in our relationships, especially after abandonment, addiction and abuse. We need the wisdom of our maker to face our wounds, let them teach us, and then harvest a healing balm that transforms the lives of others.

Speaking of balance, just as I finished a second draft, the Spirit nudged me to invite my husband Dave to come on board. It seemed my telling of our stories from my limited perspective needed a counterbalance. I think you'll agree that Dave's words flesh out a more coherent picture. Even more so, Dave has awed me with the raw vulnerability that has come tumbling out in his responses. I don't know if you appreciate the great risk Dave has taken to let you into these tender places. His words have moved me to tears again and again. This process has been largely redemptive for Dave and me. Figuring out how to seamlessly incorporate his voice has meant us sitting together long hours in the writing cabin he lovingly fashioned for me out of a shed, talking at length about some of our most vulnerable moments. But instead of anxiety, we could only find laughter. In fact, we laughed ourselves silly at the lunacy of some of our struggles. As usual, we are better for the working together.

A book like this couldn't happen without many hearts. I especially want to thank Jennifer Konzen, Ph.D., who has carefully combed through this from a counselor's perspective. Her specialties of marriage recovery, addiction, and sexual healing have made her the perfect advocate. I've sought to reflect every bit of wisdom she has offered. I'm also grateful for my other partners in recovery who have participated. A special thank you to Dr. Charles Rix, who generously agreed his story being told in the introduction to Stones 4 to 8. I am also indebted to the recovery group of women from two cities that sat with me (via Skype) throughout the writing and final editing of *Grace Calls*. You threw your hearts at me and at each other. Theresa Clark and Michelle Sutton, thank you for bringing all your knowledge of recovery leadership to bear on these words. Thank you to my layout artist Tara Price, whose design made the words sing. A very talented family has made this a family affair. My niece Shari Robertshaw designed the gorgeous cover, and my nephew's wife Gina Poirier contributed her editorial skills. And a good friend of the family Stephen Haberkorn added proofreading. Most of all, I'd like to thank the numerous audiences who've received these concepts with joy. Your responses have given me courage to offer the needed vulnerability. On the days I've woken up anxious over the releasing of such intimate stories, I've remembered you—your heartfelt questions, your tears, the long lines you've stood in to respond, and most of all your words… *thank you for letting me know I'm not alone.*

To take this journey deeper, consider the accompanying study guide to *Grace Calls*. Inside you'll find journal exercises, sections for those who want to help others, direction for groups, and a deeper dive into spiritual recovery.

As I close, my heart is full of anticipation at your responses. I would love to hear your stories, your most pressing questions or even receive a photo of your altar of stones at rwcopywriting@comcast.net. Know that as you continue to step from Stone to Stone, there are numerous like-minded individuals beside you.

— Robin Weidner, April 19, 2016

Book List

HERE IS A PARTIAL LIST OF SPIRITUAL BOOKS whose truths are somehow reflected in the pages of *Grace Calls: Spiritual Recovery after Abandonment, Addiction or Abuse.*

*Acedia and Me: A Marriage, Monks, and
A Writer's Life* by Kathleen Norris
Addiction and Grace by Gerald G. May
Disclosing Secrets by M. Deborah Corley
and Jennifer Schneider
Finding Your Path to Forgiveness by Linda Brumley
False Intimacy by Harry W. Schamburg
Learning to Walk in the Dark by Barbara Brown Taylor
Mindful Recovery by Thomas and Beverly Bien
Redeeming Love by Francine Rivers
Secrets in the Dark by Frederick Buechner
The Cup of Our Life by Joyce Rupp
The Dark Night of the Soul by Gerald May
The Desert Pilgrim by Mary Swander
The Grace of Catastrophe by Jan Winebrenner
The Lord is My Shepherd by Robert J. Morgan
The Journey from Abandonment to Healing by Susan Anderson
The Murmuring Deep by Avivah Gottlieb Zornberg
The Singer, The Song and *The Finale* by Calvin Miller
The Wounded Healer by Henri J. M. Nouwen
Transcending Post-Infidelity Stress Disorder by Dennis Ortman

About the Authors

ROBIN WEIDNER IS ALSO THE AUTHOR OF *Secure in Heart* and *Eve's Song*, both healing journeys of the soul. As the principal of Robin Weidner Copywriting & Consulting, Robin writes for health organizations and other businesses. Robin earned her BA from Western Illinois University's Board of Governors program (concentrating in English) and has four years of study in Social Work. She is a popular speaker for women's days, retreats and business events. You can read more about Robin at robinweidner. com and secureinheart.com.

David Weidner is the author of *Pure in Heart*, an audio recovery series used by men and groups around the world to find freedom. David has a BA in Biblical Languages and a MS in Organizational Psychology. Dave and Robin also authored an audio/video series for couples, *Building a Pure Marriage in an Impure World*. They have spoken in the United States and abroad about marriage and sexual integrity.

Together, Dave and Robin established Purity Restored, a ministry devoted to sexual purity. They co-lead the annual Pure and Simple Conference that launches and supports journeys of recovery for individuals and marriages. They also have written articles on sexual purity and marriage for the Focus on the Family website.

You can reach Robin at rwcopywriting@comcast.net and David at purityrestored@gmail.com.

Also from Robin Weidner

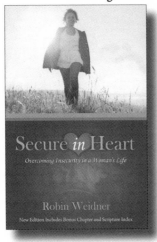

Secure in Heart—
Overcoming Insecurity
in a Woman's Life

"*Secure in Heart* charts a path to security that women across the world are finding life-changing. By taking us into her own struggles, and deep into the hearts of other women, Robin demonstrates how to translate the knowledge of God into a battle-tested security. It addresses an issue that continues to be a huge need in our culture today. You'll want to read this book and recommend it to others."

—Mitch Temple, Marriage Expert
and author of *The Marriage Turnaround*

Eve's Song—within one woman's story lies every woman's journey

"Every woman who has experienced grief, regret or confusion will find hope and relief in this poetic portrayal of Eve's journey with God. I predict *Eve's Song* will become a classic."

—Linda Brumley, Author,
Finding Your Path to Forgiveness

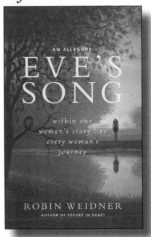

From David and Robin Weidner

Pure the Journey
Forty Days of Seeing God

"Blessed are the pure in heart for they will see God." This daily devotional focusing on purity as every disciple's legacy, introduces you to concepts, tools and an affirming vision of living pure. Each day for 40 days, you receive a 3 page pdf, with a 8 minute lesson to read morning and night, practical exercises and media fast. "My wife and I have no words to describe the impact of *Pure the Journey.* I have been sharing with all my friends that it is the best things I have done in the last 10 years."

Email purityrestored@gmail.com to sign up.

Also from David Weidner

Pure in Heart: Biblical Principles for
Restoring Purity (audio series)
With clarity and candor about his own battle, David brings fresh
hope to men who long to restore their personal purity.

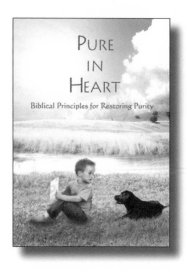

All of David and Robin's Weidner's publications are available
from Illumination Publishers.

www.ipibooks.com

Footnotes

PREPARING THE GROUND

1. *The legend says the Phoenix lives for 1,000 years and then throws itself on the fire. Through death, it is reborn and then rises from the ashes for another 1,000 years of life. Some think this legend was inspired by certain birds that will sit on the dying embers of a fire to warm themselves or get rid of feather mites. Retrieved 2/24/16 from http://www.shades-of-night.com/aviary/phoenix.html.*

2. *Ken Russell, "The Spiral of Growth," the way of seeing (blog), Retrieved February 2016 from http://thewayofseeing.com/article_spiral-growth.html.*

3. *Some of the Biblical twelves include the 12 patriarchs (sons of Jacob) in the Old Testament who became the 12 tribes of Israel, and the 12 apostles in the New Testament. Jesus was found in the temple impressing the priests with his knowledge at age 12. Biblically, 12 represents perfection and/or completion.*

PART ONE: DARKNESS OVER THE DEEP

4. Eve's Song *p. 179*

5. *Gerald G. May, M.D.* The Dark Night of the Soul: A psychiatrist explores the connection between darkness and spiritual growth. *(Harper Collins, 2004). pp. 33-36.*

6. *David Wilkerson,* You Cannot Carry Your Own Cross, *World Challenge Pulpit, sermon presented May 1, 1979, http://sermons.worldchallenge.org/en/node/1349.*

STONE ONE: TRAUMA

7. *An electrocardiogram (EKG) is a test that checks for problems with the electrical activity of your heart. www.webmd.com/heart-disease/electrocardiogram.*

8. *Jennifer Scheneider and Deborah Corley,* Surviving Disclosure: A Partner's Guide for Healing the Betrayal of Intimate Trust. *(Recovery Resources Press, 2012). See pages 52 to 53, "Prepare to Manage Emotions."*

9. *The American Heritage Dictionary of the English Language, Fourth Edition published by Houghton Mifflin Harcourt Publishing Company.*

10. *WebMD calls PTSD "a lasting consequence of traumatic ordeals that cause intense fear, helplessness, or horror."*

11. *Susan Anderson,* Journey from Abandonment to Healing. *Retrieved from www.abandonment.net on March 24, 2016.*

12. *Randi Kreger, "High Conflict Relationships can Lead to Stress Disorder,"* Psychology Today, *December 12, 2010. Retrieved online on March 24, 2016.*

13. *Similarly in God's church, by labeling pornography and masturbation as a man's struggle that that wives should stay out of since they couldn't possibly relate, we made it difficult for women to process these losses.*

14. *Barbara A. Steffens and Robyn L. Rennie, "The Traumatic Nature of Disclosure for Wives of Sexual Addicts.* Sexual Addiction & Compulsivity, *13:247-267, 2006, p. 260. Retrieved online on December 23, 2015.*

15. *For a thorough discussion of the impact of staggered disclosure see the two well-written and practical books by Jennifer P. Schneider, M.D., Ph.D, and M. Deborah Corley, Ph.D:* Disclosing Secrets *and* Surviving Disclosure.

STONE TWO: THORNS

16. *David Catchpoole, "A thorny issue." From the website of Creation Ministries International, creation.com. Retrieved on May 15, 2015.*

17. *Brene Brown,* Daring Greatly: How the courage to be vulnerable transforms the way we live, love, parent and lead. *(Avery Publishing Group, 2012). pp. 69 - 71.*

18. *Ralph Radford, "Nature on Trail: Devil's Club," Washington Trails Association, retrieved from http://www.wta.org/hiking-info/nature-on-trail/devils-club.*

19. *Radford, ibid.*

20. *"Devil's Club" Wikipedia, retrieved from http://en.wikipedia.org/wiki/Devil's_Club.*

21. *Gerald May defines mind tricks as "the mind's battle to deceive itself, with all its insidious tricks and strategies…for the single purpose: to keep the addictive behavior going."* Addiction and Grace, *p. 43.*

STONE THREE: TRIGGERS

22. *J.R. Miller, "The Work of the Plough," retrieved on June 25, 2015 from http://www.gracegems.org/Miller/work_of_the_plough.htm.*

23. *Harry Schaumburg,* False Intimacy. *(NavPress, 1993).*

24. *From the Spurgeon Archive, "The Parable of the Sower. Retrieved from http://www.spurgeon.org/misc/sower.htm*

25. *Dr. Siegfried Mense, "Muscle Pain: Mechanisms and Clinical Significance," in Disch Arzteblatt Int. Published online March 21, 2008. Retrieved from http://www.ncbi.nlm.nih.gov/pmc/articles/PMC2696782/*

26. *Travell & Simons.* Myofascial Pain and Disfunction: The trigger point manual, *(Lippencott Williams & Wilkens, 1999). Volume 1, p. 12.*

27. *Clair, Davis,* The Trigger Point Therapy Workbook: Your self-treatment guide for pain relief, *(New Harbinger, 2013). p. 21.*

Stone Four: Tears

28. *"Hard Belly Fat vs. Soft Belly Fact." The Tesh Media Group, 2015 at www.tesh.com.*

29. *"Soft addictions are those seemingly harmless habits like over-shopping, overeating, watching too much TV, endlessly surfing the internet, procrastinating—that actually keep us from the life we want. They cost us money, rob us of time, numb us from our feelings, mute our consciousness, and drain our energy." Judith Wright, Wright Leadership Institute, www. softaddictions.com*

30. *Dr. Joe Dispenza,* Breaking the Habit of Being Yourself: How to lose your mind and create a new one, *(Hay House, 2012). p. 45.*

31. *Ibid. p. 45*

32. *List modified from Castro, Jill "Exploring Body Dissociation," CoSozo, March 1, 2013, http://www.cosozo.com/article/exploring-body-dissociation.*

33. *For an explanation of presence and its role in re-creating intimacy see* Don't Call it Love: Recovery from Sexual Addiction by Patrick Carnes, Ph.D., p. 264.

34. *Matthew Henry, "Psalm CXXVI," Christian Classics Ethereal Library, retrieved online July 24, 2014 from http://www.ccel.org/ccel/henry/mhc3. Ps.cxxvii.html.*

35. *Matthew Henry, ibid.*

36. *Shani Gelstein, Yaara Yeshurun, Liron Rozenkrantz, Sagit Shushan, Idan Frumin, Yehudah Roth, and Noam Sobel, "Human Tears Contain a Chemosignal," Science, 6 January 2011 DOI: 10.1126/science.1198331.*

37. *Mark van Vugt, Ph.D., "Why only humans weep: the science behind our tears" Psychology* Today, *May 12, 2013, http://www.psychologytoday.com/ blog/naturally-selected/201305/why-only-humans-weep-the-science-behind-our-tears.*

38. *Judith Orloff, M.D., "The Health Benefits of Tears." Psychology* Today, *July 27, 2010, http://www.psychologytoday.com/blog/emotional-freedom/201007/the-health-benefits-tears.*

STONE FIVE: SPIRITUAL WARFARE

39. *A war room is "a room at military headquarters in which strategy is planned and current battle situations are monitored." Retrieved from dictionary.com.*

40. *Eric Simmons, "I Hate Porn,"* Desiring God, *October 15, 2103, http://www.desiringgod.org/articles/i-hate-porn.*

41. Bible Hub, *"ochuróma," http://biblehub.com/greek/3794.htm.*

42. *ibid.*

43. *"The Ghost Army," is a PBS documentary film, book and soon to be released movie. The documentary was written by Rick Beyer and produced by Plate of Peas Productions.*

44. *For an interesting take on the demons' possible ways of creating deception in the lives of humans, I recommend Tosca Lee's fictional saga,* Demon. *In her book, the demons found humans particularly unnerving who seemed to be looking right back at them.*

STONE SIX: DIGNITY

45. *Staggered disclosure is the way addicts progressively reveal bits of their addiction, making for multiple traumas for those who hear them. See the books* Disclosing Secrets *and* Surviving Disclosure *by Jennifer P. Schneider, M.D., Ph.D, and M. Deborah Corley, Ph.D.*

46. *Henry Cloud and John Townsend,* Boundaries: When to say yes, when to say no to take control of your life. *(New York: Zondervan, 1992). pp. 13-14.*

47. *Joel Lawrence,* Bonhoefer, A guide for the perplexed. *(Bloomsbury T&T Clark, 2010). p. 99.*

48. *Dietrich Bonhoeffer,* Discipleship. *(Fortress Press, 2003) p. 95.*

49. *Joel Lawrence, p. 99.*

50. *Pia Mellody,* Facing Love Addiction. *(HarperSanFrancisco, 2003.) p. 10.*

51. *"dignity". Dictionary.com Unabridged. Random House, Inc. 14 Apr. 2016. Dictionary.com http://www.dictionary.com*

52. *Dr. Frank Seekins,* Hebrew Word Pictures. *(Developed by Hebrew World).*

53. *See the discussion in Mark B. Kastleman's book,* The Drug of the New Millennium. *(PowerThink Publishing, 2007). p. 83 to 98.*

54. *Based on brain scans by Dr. Daniel Amen, M.D.* Change Your Brain, Change Your Life. *(Harmony, 2015).*

55. *Confess in the Greek is exomologeo: to fully agree and to acknowledge that agreement openly (whole-hearted) without reservation. Strong's New Testament Concordance online.*

56. *A mind trick is the way an addicted person unconsciously avoids any moment of real presence in at attempt from keeping from facing realities that are too painful. Mind tricks include denial, repression, rationalization, hiding and delaying tactics. For more, see* Addiction and Grace *by Gerald May, pp. 40-52.*

STONE SEVEN: ACCEPTANCE

57. *By chronic shame, I mean the persistent feeling that I am flawed and inferior to other people.*

58. *A fertilizer we've used over the years to speed and sustain growth of our gardens.*

59. *Cynthia Hand.* The Last Time We Say Goodbye. *(Harper Teen, 2015).*

60. *Jeffrey Young, Ph.D. "Early Maladaptive Schemas." Retrieved December 15, 2014 from schematherapy.com, 2012.*

61. *Jane Bolton, Psy.D., M.F.T., "What We Get Wrong About Shame." Retrieved on November 7, 2015 from psychologytoday.com.*

STONE EIGHT: SANCTUARY

62. *Drs. Bill & Ginger Bercaw,* The Couple's Guide to Intimacy: How sexual reintegration therapy can help your relationship heal. *(California Center for Healing, 2010). p. 10. [Note: Written especially for couples with sexual addiction issues].*

63. *Note that this covenant protected each part of loving God... body (do not commit adultery), emotions (love your neighbor), mind (do not envy) and spirit (you shall have no other Gods before me).*

64. *"How to Make Sense of Catholic Teachings on Sex," Second Spring, http://www.secondspring.co.uk/christianity/sex11.htm*

65. *I am happy to say that both my father and mother went through recovery—Dad in A.A. and my mother in ALANON. Yet without the spiritual component of recovery, my father couldn't quickly repair the damage, so for years he scooted around it. Eventually we repaired our relationship.*

66. *Bien, Thomas, Ph.D., and Beverly Bien, M.Ed.* Mindful Recovery, *(Wiley, 2002). pp. 14 and 29.*

67. *For an in-depth discussion of how to replace these with consecration, see* Addiction and Grace: Love and spirituality in the healing of addictions, *by Gerald G. May. (Harper Collins, 2009). pp. 161-181.*

68. *In some Jewish tradition, God enticed Adam to come into the garden, after he was created outside of the garden. See chapter 1, "Seduced into Eden,"* The Murmuring Deep: Reflections on the Biblical Unconscious, *by Avivah Gottlieb Zornberg. (Knopf Doubleday Publishing Group, 2009).*

69. *For an in-depth discussion of God's question to Adam, "Where are you?" see* The Murmuring Deep, *p.17.*

70. *For a discussion on the difference between men and women's brains, see* The Brain in Love: 12 lessons to enhance your love life, *Dr. Daniel Amen (Harmony, 2009).*

71. *Gardner, Tim Alan and Scott M. Stanley.* Sacred Sex: A spiritual celebration of oneness in marriage. *(Waterbrook, 2002).*

72. *www.powerthesaurus.org*

PART THREE: REST

73. *Strong's Hebrew Concordance, "rib or rub." Retrieved April 2016 from http://biblehub.com/hebrew/7378.htm.*

STONE NINE: PAIN TRADING

74. *Frederick Buechner,* Secrets in the Dark. *(Harper Collins, 2007). p 216.*

75. *Buechner, ibid, p. 217.*

76. *Shinzen Young, "Break Through Pain: Practical Steps for Transforming Physical Pain into Spiritual Growth," retrieved on November 3, 2015 from www.shinzen.org/Articles/artPain.htm.*

77. *Young, ibid*

78. *Young, ibid.*

STONE TEN: FORGIVENESS

79. *Easton's 1897 Bible Dictionary, s.v. "scapegoat," accessed September 3, 2015.*

80. *Easton's 1897 Bible Dictionary s.v. "scapegoat, ibid.*

81. *Shame based language might include, "What's wrong with you? Why do you always do this? You'll never change. Are you trying to destroy us? I can't believe you would go so low. I would never do that to you! You should think about someone other than yourself!"*

82. *V. Norskov Olsen. "The Usage of the Greek Words Translated Forgive and Forgiveness." Ministry: International Journal for Pastors (May 1963). Retrieved February 2016 from https://www.ministrymagazine.org.*

83. *For a deep exposition of the idea of "costly grace" see Dietrick Bonhoeffer's classic, The Cost of Discipleship. (Touchstone, 1995).*

84. *Desmond Tutu and Mpho Tutu, "Why We Forgive." Spirituality & Health Magazine, March & April 2014 issue, Retrieved online on March 11, 2016.*

85. *This is one of the more conservative estimates of the amount the servant owed. Some estimate that one talent of gold was worth 15 years of wages, thus 10,000 talents would be worth 150,000 years of wages. In other words, an inconceivable amount of money.*

STONE ELEVEN: EMPATHY

86. *Arthur and Judy Halliday,* Get Thin, Stay Thin: A Biblical Approach to Food, Eating, and Weight Management. *(Revnell, 2008). p. 41.*

87. *In the 1984 version of the NIV,* sumpathes *is translated sympathize. In the newer version, translators changed this to the more fitting empathize.*

88. *Strong's Greek Concordance, "astheneia," Retrieved April 2016 from http://biblehub.com/greek/769.htm.*

89. *Being easily flustered animals, sheep will only drink from water that is still. Likewise Jesus teaches us to slow our hearts and minds, and rest with him.*

90. *Gerald May, M.D.,* Addiction and Grace: Love and Spirituality in the Healing of Addictions. *(Harper Collins, 2009). p. 11.*

91. *For a deeper dive into this topic, I recommend reading* Addiction and Grace.

STONE TWELVE: HOPE

92. *Names of the two sisters changed for confidentiality.*

93. *Karl S. Kurzeinicki, "Wound healing and air." Dr. Karl's Great Moments in Science. ABC Science. 2006. www.abc.net.au/science.*

94. *Brennan Manning,* Abba's Child: The Cry of the Heart for Intimate Belonging. *(NavPress, 2015).*

95. *Strong's Greek Concordance, "elpis." Retrieved April 2016 from http://biblehub.com/greek/1680.htm.*

96. *Thanks to Kathleen Norris for her upbeat description of hope and hopping in* Acedia & Me: A Marriage, Monks, and a Writer's Life *(Riverhead Books, 2008).*

97. *For more on Immanuel Therapy, see the Lehman's website, www.immanuelapproach.com.*

98. *Carol K. Ingall, "The wisdom of creation from a Jewish perspective," The Way, accessed on April 2016 from http://www.theway.org.uk .*